POST HARVEST TECHNOLOGY
OF CEREALS, PULSES AND OILSEEDS

Post Harvest Technology of Cereals, Pulses and Oilseeds

Third Edition

Amalendu Chakraverty
Professor
Post Harvest and Food Engineering
Indian Institute of Technology
Kharagpur

Oxford & IBH Publishing Co. Pvt. Ltd.
New Delhi
(A Unit of CBS Publishers & Distributors Pvt Ltd **)**

CBSPD

CBS Publishers & Distributors Pvt Ltd

New Delhi • Bengaluru • Chennai • Kochi • Kolkata • Lucknow • Mumbai
Hyderabad • Jharkhand • Nagpur • Patna • Pune • Uttarakhand

Post Harvest Technology of Cereals, Pulses and Oilseeds
Third Edition

ISBN-13: 978-81-204-0969-9
ISBN-10: 81-204-0969-8

Published by Satish Kumar Jain and produced by Varun Jain for
CBS Publishers & Distributors Pvt Ltd
4819/XI Prahlad Street, 24 Ansari Road, Daryaganj, New Delhi 110 002, India
Ph: 011-23289259, 23266861, 23266867   Website: www.cbspd.com
Fax: 011-23243014   e-mail: delhi@cbspd.com;
                                         cbspubs@airtelmail.in.

Corporate Office: 204 FIE, Industrial Area, Patparganj, Delhi 110 092, India
Ph: 011-4934 4934   Fax: 011-4934 4935   e-mail: publishing@cbspd.com;
                                               publicity@cbspd.com

Branches

- **Bengaluru:** Seema House 2975, 17th Cross, KR Road, Banasankari 2nd Stage, Bengaluru 560 070, Karnataka, India
  Ph: +91-80-26771678/79   Fax: +91-80-26771680   e-mail: bangalore@cbspd.com
- **Chennai:** 7, Subbaraya Street, Shenoy Nagar, Chennai 600 030, Tamil Nadu, India
  Ph: +91-44-26680620, 26681266   Fax: +91-44-42032115   e-mail: chennai@cbspd.com
- **Kochi:** 42/1325, 1326, Power House Road, Opp KSEB, Power House, Ernakulam Kochi 682 018, Kerala, India
  Ph: +91-484-4059061-65,67   Fax: +91-484-4059065   e-mail: kochi@cbspd.com
- **Kolkata:** 147, Hind Ceramics Compound, 1st Floor, Nilgunj Road, Belghoria, Kolkata-700056, West Bengal, India
  Ph: +91-9096713055/7798394118, 9836841399   e-mail: kolkata@cbspd.com
- **Lucknow:** Basement, Khushnuma Complex, 7 Meerabai Marg (Behind Jawahar Bhawan), Lucknow-226001, UP, India
  Ph: +0522-4000032   e-mail: tiwari.lucknow@cbspd.com
- **Mumbai:** PWD Shed, Gala no 25/26, Ramchandra Bhatt Marg, Next to JJ Hospital Gate no. 2, Opp. Union
  Bank of India, Noorbaug, Mumbai-400009, Maharashtra, India
  Ph: 022-66661880/89   e-mail: mumbai@cbspd.com

Representatives

- Hyderabad   0-9885175004   • Jharkhand   0-9811541605   • Nagpur   0-9421945513
- Patna   0-9334159240   • Pune   0-9623451994   • Uttarakhand   0-9716462459

Printed at Chaman Enterprises, Daryaganj, New Delhi, India

Dedicated to

my mother

PREFACE TO THE THIRD EDITION

The book entered its second decade of use in 1991. Since then it was felt that a revision was needed with the addition of a new section on Food Grain Storage in order to make it more complete. Hence the above new section has been added to the third edition and necessary corrections have also been made.

The author wished to record his appreciation to Mrs. S. Chakravorty, M.Sc. for her special contribution to Rodent control in section- V. He also appreciates the assistance of Mr. Krishnendu Chakraborty and Mr. Soumendu Chakraborty in correcting printing Mistakes. Special thanks are due to Prof. S. Mukherjee and Prof. A.N. Bose for their continuous support and encouragement. The author pays homage to all the pioneering researchers in the field of post harvest technology.

October, 1994   A. CHAKRAVERTY
Indian Institute of Technology,
Kharagpur.

PREFACE TO THE REVISED EDITION

The second edition of this book has been revised and corrected as far as possible A chapter on processing of oil seeds is also incorporated. Though the book was out of print for some time, the book remained equally popular to the teachers, researchers and students. A special word of thanks is due to them.

The author is grateful to Professor A. N. Bose and Professor S. Mukherjee for their contribution on parboiling of paddy and to Professor D. S. De for his encouragement and to Mrs. S. Chakraverty for her painstaking effort to correct the printing mistakes.

August, 1987   A. CHAKRAVERTY
IIT, Kharagpur

PREFACE TO THE FIRST EDITION

The post harvest technology of cereals and pulses is under development. There are specialised books and monographs on grain drying, paddy parboiling, wheat milling, corn milling, husk utilisation etc. but a comprehensive book with a special reference to engineering principles, design calculations, testing procedures and other practical aspects of different grain dryers, grain milling machinery, husk fired furnaces and heat exchangers, is not available. In the present energy crisis modern furnaces fired with agricultural waste calls for immediate attention.

One object of this book is to organise the scattered information and to deal with the recent development of the processes, operations, designs and other engineering aspects of drying, parboiling, milling and by-products utilisation of some common cereal grains and pulses. Emphasis is also placed on generalised hydrothermal treatment, generalised grain milling systems and bibliography. Adoption of metric system is another feature of the present volume. The book in its own way endeavours to help in the development of post harvest technology in India.

The book has been mainly designed to serve as a text and reference book for the students and others engaged in Agricultural Engineering and Food Technology for specialisation in Processing of Cereals and Pulses.

The subject—post harvest technology is interdisciplinary and cannot be dealt with properly without any joint venture. Contributors to this volume are from the faculty of different disciplines specialised in their respective fields.

The senior author wishes to record his indebtedness to his teacher Professor Sunit Mukherjee and Professor A. N. Bose, Jadavpur University for their special contribution of the CHAPTERS 7 and 8 on PARBOILING OF PADDY and to his colleague and coauthor Dr. D. S. De for his contribution of the CHAPTERS 14 and 15 on FUELS AND FURNACES FOR

GRAIN PROCESSING. He is also indebted to Mrs. S. Chakraverty for her kind painstaking assistance in the preparation of the manuscript.

The authors wish to acknowledge the cooperations of the students of Post Harvest Technology Centre, Indian Institute of Technology, Kharagpur in checking some problems.

The authors pay their homage to the pioneers in research and development of post harvest technology of cereals and pulses.

A. CHAKRAVERTY

I.I.T., Kharagpur,
May 1981

D. S. DE

CONTENTS

Parboiling

Milling

Processing of Oilseeds and Rice Bran

Storage of Food Grain

SECTION I

GRAIN DRYING AND DRYERS

CHAPTER 1

Physico–Chemical Properties of Grains

A grain is a living biological product which germinates and respires also. The respiration process in the grain is externally manifested by the decrease in dry weight, utilisation of oxygen, evolution of carbon dioxide and release of heat. The rate of respiration is dependent upon moisture content and temperature of the grain. The rate of respiration of paddy increases sharply (at 25° C) at 14 to 15 per cent moisture content which is called the critical point. On the other hand the rate of respiration increases with the increase of temperature to 40° C. Above this temperature the viability of the grain as well as the rate of respiration decreases significantly.

Structure

Wheat and rye consist mainly of pericarp, seed coat, aleurone layer, germ and endosperm whereas oats, barley, paddy, pulses and some other crops consist not only of the above five parts but an outer husk cover also. The husk consists of strongly lignified floral integuments. The husk reduces the rate of drying significantly.

The embryo or germ is the principal part of the seed. All tissues of the germ consist of living cells which are very sensitive to heat. The endosperm, which fills the whole inner part of the seed consists of thin-walled cells, filled with protoplasm and starch granules and serves as a kind of receptacle for reserve foodstuff for the developing embryo. The structures of a few important grains are shown in Figs. 1.1 to 1.4.

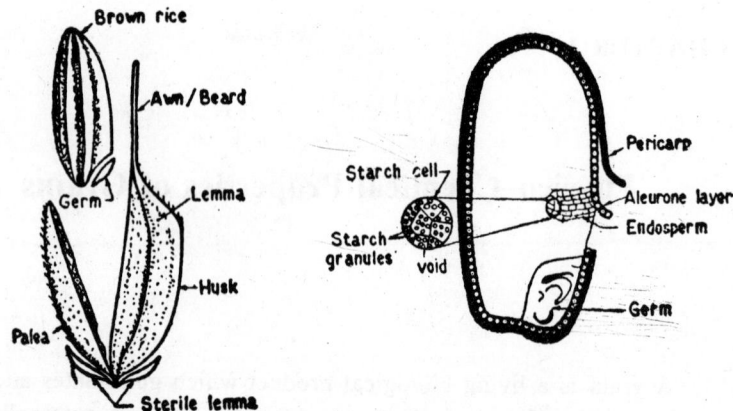

Fig. 1.1. Different Parts of Paddy.

Fig. 1.1a. Structure of Brown Rice Kernel (Longitudinal Section).

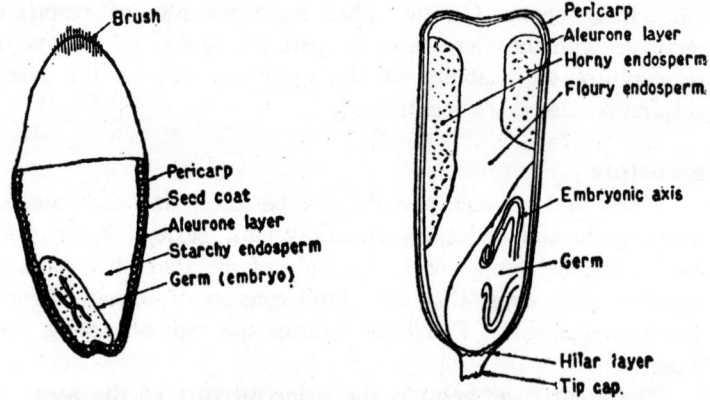

Fig. 1.2. Structure of wheat.

Fig. 1.3. Structure of shelled corn (Longitudinal section).

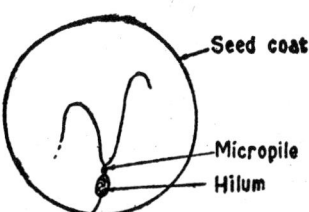

FIG. 1.4. Whole arhar pulses
(*Cajanus-Cajan*).

Chemical Composition

The grain is composed of both organic and inorganic substances, such as carbohydrates, proteins, vitamins, fats, ash, water, mineral salts and enzymes. Paddy, corn, wheat, buck wheat seeds are specially rich in carbohydrates whereas legumes are rich in proteins and oil seeds rich in oils.

Generally, pericarp (and floral integuments also) contains cellulose, pentosan and ash, the aleurone layer contains mainly albumin and fat. The endosperm contains the highest amount of carbohydrate in the form of starch, small amount of reserve protein and a very little amount of ash and cellulose whereas the germ contains the highest amount of fat, protein and a small amount of carbohydrate in the form of sugars and a large amount of enzyme. The chemical compositions of different grains are given in Table 7 (Appendix).

Effects of temperature on the quality of grain

Proteins

The proteins present in cereal grains and in flour are hydrophillic colloids. The capacity of flour proteins to swell plays an important role in the preparation of dough. At temperatures above 50° C denaturation and even coagulation of proteins take place. As a result, the water absorbing capacity of the proteins and their capacity for swelling decreases.

Starch

Starch is insoluble in cold water. It swells in hot water. Up to a temperature of 60° C, the quality of starch does not change appreciably. With a further increase in temperature, particularly above 70° C, and especially in the presence of high moisture in the grain, gelatinisation and partial conversion of starch to dextrin take place. In addition, a partial caramelisation of sugars with the formation of caramel may take place which causes deterioration in colour of the product. These effects have been discussed in detail in Section II on Parboiling.

Fats

Fats are insoluble in water. Compared to albumins and starch, fats are more heat resistant. But at temperatures above 70° C, fats may also undergo a partial decomposition resulting in an increase of acid numbers.

In the range of temperatures from 40 to 45° C, the rate of enzymatic activity on fats increases with the increase of moisture and temperature. With a further rise of temperature the enzymatic activity begins to decrease, and at temperatures between 80 and 100° C the enzymes are completely inactivated.

Vitamins

The heat sensitive B-vitamins present in the germ and aleurone layer are destroyed at high temperature.

Physical Properties

The knowledge of important physical properties such as shape, size, volume, surface area, density, porosity, colour, etc., of different grains is necessary for the design of various separating and handling, storing and drying systems. The density and specific gravity values are also used for the calculation of thermal diffusivity and Reynolds number. A few important physical properties have been discussed here.

Sphericity

Sphericity is defined as the ratio of surface area of sphere having same volume as that of the particle to the surface area of the particle. Sphericity is also defined as :

$$\text{sphericity} = \frac{d_i}{d_o}$$

where d_i = diameter of largest inscribed circle and d_c = diameter of smallest circumscribed circle of the particle. The sphericity of different grains vary widely.

Porosity

It is defined as the percentage of volume of inter-grain space to the total volume of grain bulk. The per cent void of different grains in bulk are often needed in drying, air flow, and heat flow studies of grains. Porosity depends on (a) shape, (b) dimensions, and (c) roughness of the grain surface. Porosity of some crops are tabulated as follows :

Grain	Porosity per cent
Corn	40—45
Wheat	50—55
Paddy	48—50
Oats	65—70

COEFFICIENT OF FRICTION AND ANGLE OF REPOSE

Angle of repose and frictional properties of grains play an important role in selection of design features of hoppers, chutes, dryers, storage bins and other equipment for grain flow.

Coefficient of friction

The coefficient of friction between granular materials is equal to the tangent of the angle of internal friction for the material. The frictional coefficient depends on (a) grain shape, (b) surface characteristics, and (c) moisture content.

Angle of repose

The flowing capacities of different grains are different. It is characterised by the angle of natural slope (angle of repose).

The angle of repose is the angle between the base and the slope of the cone formed on a free vertical fall of the grain mass to a horizontal plane.

The angle of repose for a few important grains are tabulated as follows :

Grain	Angle of repose (degrees)
Wheat	23—28
Corn	30—40
Millets	20—25
Rye	23—28
Oats	31—44
Barley	28—40
Paddy	30—45

Thermal Properties

The raw foods are subjected to various types of thermal treatment namely, heating, cooling, drying, freezing, etc., for processing. The change of temperature depends on the thermal properties of the product. Therefore knowledge of thermal properties, namely, specific heat, thermal conductivity, thermal diffusivity, is essential for the design of different thermal equipments and for solving various problems on heat transfer operation.

Specific heat

The specific heat of a substance is defined as the amount of heat required to raise the temperature of unit mass through 1° C. The specific heat of wet grain may be considered as the sum of specific heat of bone dry grain and of its moisture content. It can be expressed as follows :

$$c = \left(\frac{m}{100}\right) c_w + \left(\frac{100-m}{100}\right) cd_r$$

$$\text{or} \quad c = \left(\frac{m}{100}\right) + \left(\frac{100-m}{100}\right) cd_r \quad \text{kcal/(kg °C)}$$

where cdr = specific heat of the bone dry grain ; c_w = specific heat of water ; and m = moisture content of the grain, per cent (w.b).

The specific heat of bone dry grain varies from 0.35 to 0.45 kcals/kg° C.

The above linear relationship between C and m exists above $m = 8$ per cent moisture content only (Gerzhoi, A.P., 1958).

The thermal conductivity is defined as the amount of heat flow through unit thickness of material over an unit area per unit time for unit temperature difference. The thermal conductivity of the single grain varies from 0.3 to 0.6 kcal/(m.hr°C) whereas the thermal conductivity of grains in bulk is about 0.10 to 0.15 kcal/(m.hr°C) which is due to the presence of air space in it. The thermal conductivity of air is 0.02 kcal/(m. hr °C) only.

Thermal conductivity of the single grain is three to four times greater than that of the grain bulk. The thermal conductivity of the wheat bulk with moisture contents ranging from 10 to 20 per cent (d.b) can be expressed as follows (Gerzhoi, A. P., 1958).

$$K = 0.060 + 0.002\ M\ \text{kcal/(m. hr °C)}$$

where K = thermal conductivity
M = Moisture content (d.b).

Aerodynamic Properties

For designing air and water conveying and separating systems (i.e., pneumatic or hydrodynamic systems), the knowledge of aerodynamic and hydrodynamic properties of agricultural products is necessary. In this connection the knowledge of terminal velocities of different crops in a fluid is necessary.

The air velocity at which an object remains in a suspended state in a vertical pipe under the action of the air current is called terminal velocity of the object.

Thus in free fall, the object attains a constant terminal velocity, V_t, when the gravitational accelerating force, Fg becomes equal to the resisting upward drag force Fr.

Hence, $Fg = Fr$ when $V = V_t$

or $W\left[\dfrac{\rho_p - \rho_t}{\rho_p}\right] = \dfrac{1}{2}\ Ca_p \rho_t V_t^2$

$V_t = \left[\dfrac{2W(\rho_p - \rho_t)}{\rho_p \rho_t a_p C}\right]^{1/2}$

V_t = terminal velocity, m/sec
W = weight of the particle, kg

$\rho_p, \rho_t = $ mass density of the particles and fluids,
$(kg\text{-}sec^2)/m^4$

$a_p = $ projected area of the particle perpendicular to the direction of motion, m^2

$C = $ overall drag coefficient (dimensionless).

Grains	Terminal velocity, m/sec
Wheat	9 —11.5
Barley	8.5—10.5
Small oats	19.3
Corn	34.9
Soybeans	44.3
Rye	8.5—10.0
Oats	8.0— 9.0

RESISTANCE OF GRAIN BED TO AIR FLOW

In the design of blowers for grain dryers, it is necessary to know the resistance exerted by the grain bed to the air current blown through it. The resistance is dependent upon : (a) the bed thickness, (b) the air velocity, (c) orientation of the grains, and (d) type of grain.

Symbols

a_p Projected area, m^2

c Specific heat, kcal/(kg°C)

C Drag coefficient, dimension less

m Moisture content, per cent (w.b.)

M Moisture content, per cent (d.b.)

ρ_p, ρ_t Mass density of particle and fluid, $(kg-sec^2)/m^4$

V_t Terminal velocity, m/sec

W Weight of particle, kg

K Thermal conductivity, kcal/(m hr°C)

CHAPTER 2

Psychrometry

Introduction

Ambient air is a mixture of dry air and water vapour. In many unit operations moist air is necessary. To work out such problems it is essential to have a knowledge of the amount of water vapour present in air under various conditions, the thermal properties of such a mixture, and changes in the heat and moisture contents as it is brought in contact with water or wet solid. Particularly in grain drying, the natural or heated air is used as a drying medium. Although the proportion of water vapour in air is small, it has a profound effect on the drying process.

Problems in air-water vapour mixture which include heating, cooling, humidification, dehumidification, and mixing can be solved with the help of mathematical formulae. As these calculations are time consuming, special charts containing the most common physical and thermal properties of moist air have been prepared and are known as psychrometric charts. The psychrometric chart is, therefore, a graphical representation of the physical and thermal properties of atmospheric air.

The different terms used to express the physical and other thermodynamic properties of air-water vapour mixture are defined and discussed here.

Humidity

The absolute humidity, H is defined as kilogrammes of water vapour present in one kilogramme of dry air under a given set of conditions.

H depends upon partial pressure of water vapour, p_w in air and total pressure, P.

Therefore, H can be expressed mathematically as follows :

$$H = \frac{18\ p_w}{29(P - p_w)} \qquad (2.1)$$

when $P = 1$ atm (for psychrometry).

$$H = \frac{18\ p_w}{29(1 - p_w)}\ \text{kg/kg} \qquad (2.2)$$

As p_w is small,

$$H = \frac{18 p_w}{29} \qquad (2.3)$$

Again from equation (2.1)

$$H = \frac{p_w}{\frac{29}{18}(P - p_w)} = \frac{p_w}{1.611(P - p_w)} \qquad (2.4)$$

Rearranging, equation (2.4)

$$p_w = \left(\frac{1.611H}{1 + 1.611H}\right) P \qquad (2.5)$$

Saturated air is the air in which water vapour is in equilibrium with the liquid water at a given set of temperature and pressure.

Percentage humidity

It is the ratio of the weight of water present in 1 kg of dry air at any temperature and pressure and the weight of water present in 1 kg of dry air which is saturated with water vapour at the same temperature and pressure.

Percentage humidity $= (H/H_s) \times 100 \qquad (2.6)$

Relative humidity

Relative humidity RH is defined as the ratio of the partial pressure of water vapour in the air to the partial pressure of water vapour in saturated air at the same temperature :

$RH = (p_w/p_s) \times 100$

The relation between percentage humidity and RH :

$$\text{Percentage humidity} = RH\left(\frac{1 - p_s}{1 - p_w}\right) \qquad (2.7)$$

Humid heat

Humid heat is the number of kcal necessary to raise the

temperature of 1 kg dry air and its accompanying water vapour
through 1° C.

$$S = 0.24 + 0.45H, \text{ kcal/kg/° C} \tag{2.8}$$

Enthalpy

Enthalpy h' of an air and water vapour mixture is the total
heat content of 1 kg of dry air plus its accompanying water
vapour. If the datum temperature and pressure are 0° C and
1 atm respectively, then the enthalpy at $t°$ C for air and water
vapour mixture :

$$h' = 0.24 \ (t-0) + H \ [\ \lambda + 0.45 \ (t-0) \ ] \tag{2.9}$$
$$= (0.24 + 0.45H)t + \lambda H \text{ kcal/kg}$$

Humid volume

Humid volume, v is the total volume in cubic metre of 1 kg
dry air and its accompanying water vapour.

$$v = \frac{22.4}{29} \left(\frac{t+273}{273}\right) + \frac{22.4}{18} H \left(\frac{t+273}{273}\right)$$
$$= (22.4/273)(t+273)\left[\frac{1}{29} + \frac{H}{18}\right] \tag{2.10}$$
$$= (0.00283 + 0.00456 H)(t+273) \text{ m}^3/\text{kg}$$

Saturated volume

Saturated volume is the volume of 1 kg of dry air plus
that of the water vapour necessary to saturate it.

Dew point

Dew point is the temperature to which a mixture of air and
water vapour has to be cooled (at constant humidity) to make
it saturated.

Wet bulb temperature

Under adiabatic condition, if a stream of unsaturated air at
constant initial temperature and humidity, is passed over a wetted
surface (which is approximately at the same temperature as that
of air), then the evaporation of water from the wetted surface
tends to lower the temperature of the liquid water. When the
water becomes cooler than the air, sensible heat will be transferred from the air to the water. Ultimately a steady state

will be reached at such a temperature that the loss of heat from the water by evaporation is exactly balanced by the sensible heat passing from the air into the water. Under such conditions, the temperature of the water will remain constant and this constant temperature is called wet bulb temperature.

Wet bulb theory

By definition of wet bulb temperature:

q = sensible heat flowing from air to the wetted surface

= latent heat of water vapour diffusing from the wetted surface to the air, kcal/hr.

$$q = (h_G + h_r) A \ (t_G - t_w) = \lambda_w \ 18 \ K_G \ A \ (p_w - p_G) \qquad (2.11)$$

where h_G = heat-transfer coefficient by convection from the air to the wetted surface, kcal/(hr m^2 °C),

h_r = heat-transfer coefficient corresponding to radiation from the surroundings, kcal/(hr m^2 °C),

$t_G \ t_w$ = temperatures of air and interface, ° C,

$p_G \ p_w$ = partial pressure of water vapour in air and interface, atm,

A = area of the wetted surface, m^2,

K_G = mass transfer coefficient, kg mole/hr m^2 atm,

λ_w = latent heat of water at t_w, kcal/kg

Therefore,

$$p_w - p_G = \frac{h_G + h_r}{18 \ \lambda_w \ K_G} (t_G - t_w) \qquad (2.12)$$

If $h_r = 0$, $p_w = \frac{29 H_w}{18}$ and $p_G = 29 H_G / 18$

Then

$$H_w - H_G = \frac{h_G}{29 \ \lambda_w \ K_G} (t_G - t_w) \qquad (2.13)$$

The ratio h_G / K_G may be considered as constant. If the ratio h_G / K_G is constant, then the equation (2.13) can be used to determine the composition of the air-water vapour mixture from the observed values of t_G, the dry bulb temperature and t_w, the wet bulb temperature.

It is apparent from equation (2.13) that the wet bulb temperature depends only upon the temperature and humidity of the
air, provided h_r is negligible and h_G/K_G is constant.
It may be noted that the equation for the adiabatic cooling
line is (Fig. 2.2b) :

$$H_S - H_G = \frac{s}{\lambda_S}(t_G - t_S) \tag{2.14}$$

where t_S = temperature of water
  H_S = saturated humidity
  λ_S = latent heat of evaporation at t_S and
  s = humid heat

If $h_G/K_G\ 29 = s$, equations (2.13) and (2.14) become identical. Fortuitously for air-water vapour, $h_G/29\ K_G = s = 0.26$
at a humidity of 0.047. Therefore, under ordinary conditions
the adiabatic cooling line can be used for wet bulb problems.

Introduction of Psychrometric Chart

Usually a psychrometric chart is prepared for 1 atm pressure
In this chart humidities are plotted as ordinates against temperatures as abscissa. Any point on this chart represents the
humidity and temperature of a given sample of air. The psychrometric chart is bound by extreme left-hand curve representing
humidities of saturated air (100 per cent RH) and the horizontal
x-axis giving various dry bulb temperatures (0 per cent RH).
The family of curved lines below the 100 per cent RH line represents various per cent RH. These are shown in Fig. 2.1.
Values of H for the saturation curve can be calculated by putting
saturated pressure values from a steam table for different temperatures in equation (2.4). The vapour pressure of water in air
for different humidities is calculated by the equation (2.5) and
is added to the plot in the position shown in Fig. 2.1. The oblique
isovolume straight lines (humid volume lines) are plotted in the
chart with steeper slopes than those of wet bulb lines. They are
not exactly parallel. The humid volume at any temperature and
humidity can be found out from these lines. The humid volumes
corresponding to these lines can be computed by the equation
(2.10). The humid heat can be calculated by the equation (2.8)
and is sometimes plotted against humidity. The values of the

enthalpy lines are usually indicated on a scale on the upper left hand side of the chart. The wet bulb lines presented in the chart for different temperatures and humidities are actually adiabatic cooling lines. The straight wet bulb lines are inclined at angles of slightly unequal magnitudes.

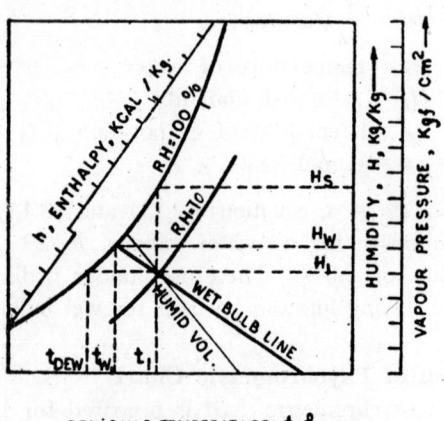

FIG. 2.1. Introduction of Psychrometric Chart (1 atm) pressure.

Use of psychrometric chart

The psychrometric chart can be used to find out the following :

    (*a*) dry bulb temperature,
    (*b*) wet bulb temperature,
    (*c*) dew point temperature,
    (*d*) absolute humidity,
    (*e*) relative humidity,
    (*f*) humid volume, and
    (*g*) enthalpy.

Any one of the above physical properties of air and water vapour mixture can be obtained from the psychrometric chart provided two other values are known. Figure 2.1 shows that the meeting point of any two property lines represent the state point from which all other values can be obtained.

The following points may be noted from the psychrometric chart :

(a) The t_G, t_w and dew point temperatures are equal when RH is 100 per cent.

(b) The pressure of water vapour nearly doubles for each 10° C rise in temperature.

(c) The rate of heat transfer from air to the water (grain moisture) is proportional to $(t_G - t_w)$.

Psychrometric representation of several operations, namely, heating & cooling, drying, mixing, cooling and dehumidification of moist air are given in Figs 2.2a to 2.2e.

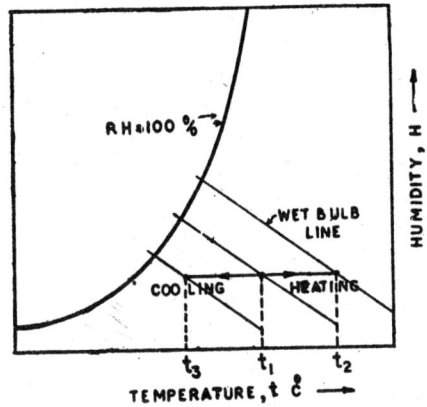

Fig. 2.2a. Heating and Cooling.

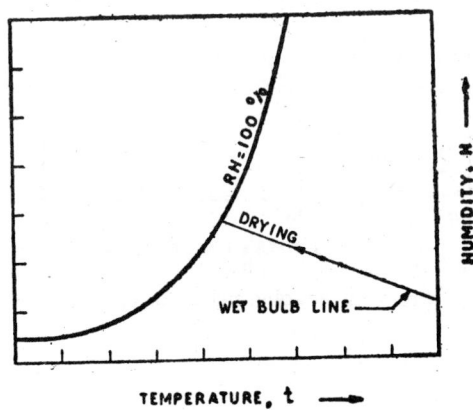

Fig. 2.2b. Adiabatic Cooling/Drying.

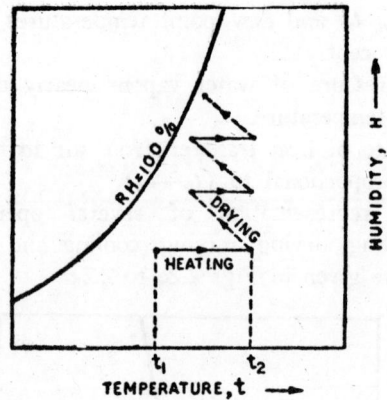

FIG. 2.2c. Heating, drying, reheating
and recycling.

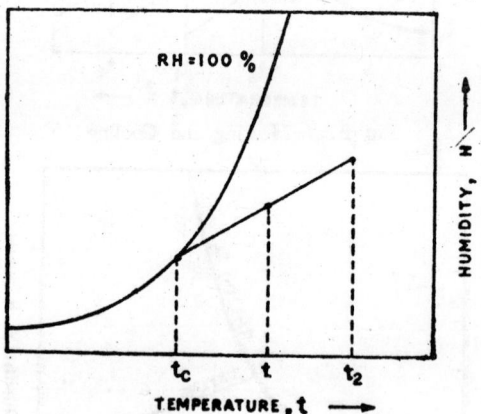

FIG. 2.2d. Cooling and dehumidifying.

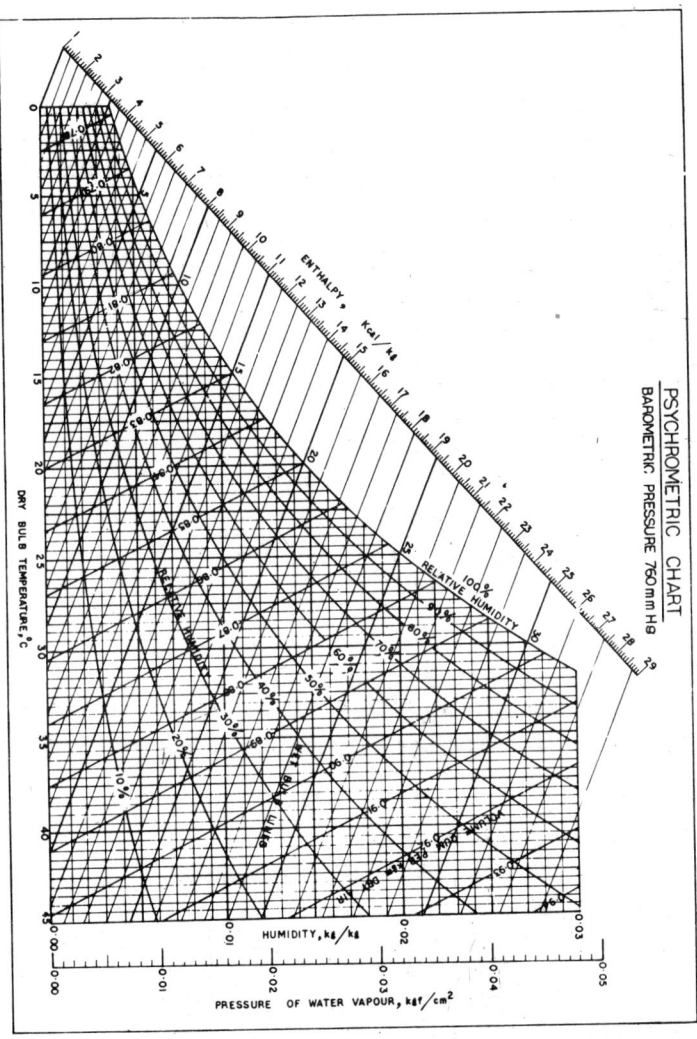

FIG. 2.3. Humidity—temperature diagram
(psychrometric chart).

Problems on Psychrometry

SOLVED PROBLEMS

(1) Moist air at 25° C dry bulb and 45 per cent relative humidity is heated to 80° C. Calculate the humid volume, percentage humidity, and humid heat at the initial condition and check the results from chart. Find also the final condition of the air.

Data given

     Initial condition : Dry bulb temperature = 25°C RH = 45%
     Final condition = 80° C

From psychrometric chart

     Humid heat = 0.244 kcal/kg° C
     Humid volume = 0.856 m³/kg
     Humidity = 0.009 kg/kg
     Saturated humidity = 0.02 kg/kg

     Per cent humidity $= \dfrac{0.009}{0.02} \times 100 = 45$ per cent

     Enthalpy = 11.5 kcal/kg

Final Condition

     Humid volume = 1.015 m³/kg
     Relative humidity = 3 per cent
     Enthalpy = 25.5 kcal/kg

By calculation

     Humid heat = $0.24 + 0.45\ H$
               $= 0.24 + 0.45 \times 0.009 = 0.24405$

     Humid Volume

$$= \frac{22.4}{273 \times 29}(t+273) + \frac{22.4\,H}{273 \times 18}(t+273)$$

$$= (0.00283 + 0.00455\ H)\ (t+273)$$

     When $t = 25°$ C and $H = 0.009$ kg/kg
     Humid volume $= (0.00283 + 0.00455 \times 0.009) \times 298$
                   $= (0.00283 + 0.000041) \times 298$
                   $= 0.856$ m³/kg
     Enthalpy $= (0.24 + 0.45H)t + \lambda H$
                  $= 0.24405 \times 25 + 580 \times 0.009$

$[\because \lambda = 580 \, kcal/kg]$

Therefore $h = 11.4 \, kcal/kg$

(2) In a grain dryer, one stream of air at $50 \, m^3/min$ at $25°$ C and $23°$ C W.B., is mixed with another air stream at $50 \, m^3/min$ at $60°$ C and $52°$ C W.B. temperatures.

Determine the D.B. and W.B. temperatures of the mixture.

Solution

Stream $= 1$

Rate of flow $= 50 \, m^3/min$

Dry bulb temperature $= 25°$ C

Wet bulb temperature $= 23°$ C

From the psychrometric chart

Enthalpy $= 16.5 \, kcal/kg$

Humid volume $= 0.866 \, m^3/kg$

Therefore, $m_1 = \dfrac{50}{0.866} = 57.7 \, kg/min.$

Stream $= 2$

Rate of flow $= 50 \, m^3/min$

D.B. temperature $= 60°$ C

W.B. temperature $= 52°$ C

From the chart

Enthalpy $= 72.5 \, kcal/kg$

Humid volume $= 1.084 \, m^3/kg$

Therefore, $m_2 = \dfrac{50}{1.084} = 46.12 \, kg/min$

We know that

$$\frac{m_1}{m_2} = \frac{h_2 - h_3}{h_3 - h_1}$$

$$\frac{57.7}{46.12} = \frac{72.5 - h_3}{h_3 - 16.5}$$

Therefore, enthalpy of the final mixture state :

$h_3 = 41.38 \, kcal/kg.$

From the psychrometric chart

Dry bulb temperature $= 41°$ C

Wet oulb temperature $= 40.75°$ C

(3) The air to be used in a dryer at a dry bulb temperature of 26.66° C and wet bulb temperature 21.1° C is heated to 71.1° C and blown into the dryer. In the dryer it cools along an adiabatic cooling line and leaves the dryer fully saturated. Find the dew point temperature at the initial condition, absolute humidity of initial air, percentage humidity of initial air, amount of heat needed to heat 2.8 m³/min of entering air and temperature of the air leaving the dryer.

Solution

Data supplied·

Dry bulb temperature = 26.66° C
Wet bulb temperature = 21.10° C
Heated to   = 71.10° C
Volume of air entering = 2.8 m³/min

From Psychrometric chart

(1) Dew point temperature = 18° C
(2) Humidity Ratio, $H = 0.0132$ kg/kg
(3) Saturated humidity, $H_s = 0.022$ kg/kg
(4) Percent $H = \dfrac{H}{H_s} \times 100 = \dfrac{0.0132}{0.022} \times 100 = 60$ per cent
(5) Relative humidity at initial condition = $RH = 64\%$
(6) Initial humid volume, $v = 0.867$ m³/kg dry air (at $H = 0.0132$)
(7) Temperature of air leaving dryer = 31.8° C
(8) Amount of heat needed to heat = 2.8 m³/min

$$\frac{\text{Volume of air}}{\text{Humid volume}} \times \Delta t \times \text{ humid heat}$$

Humid heat

$s = 0.24 + 0.45\ H$
  $= 0.24 + 0.45 \times 0.0132$
  $= 0.24 + 0.0058$
  $= 0.246$ kcals/kg° C

Hence, heat required $= \dfrac{2.8}{0.867} \times (71.11 - 26.66) \times 0.246$

$$= 35.3 \text{ kcal/min}$$

Exercises

(1) The air supply for a dryer has a dry bulb temperature of 27° C and wet bulb temperature of 21° C. It is heated to 94° C and blown it through the dryer and in the dryer it cools along adiabatic line and leaves the dryer saturated. Find the following :

> Dew point temperature of the initial air
> Absolute humidity of the initial air
> Percentage humidity.
> Amount of heat needed to heat 100 m³/min entering air.
> Temperature of the air leaving the dryer.

(2) Temperature and dew point of the air entering a dryer are 70° C and 26° C. What additional data can be obtained from the psychrometric chart ?

(3) Air is heated by a heating system from 30° C, 80 per cent RH to 60° C. Find out the relative humidity wet bulb temperature, dew point temperature of the heated air. Determine the quantity of heat added per kg. of dry air.

(4) The dry bulb and wet bulb temperatures of an air supply are 60° C and 40° C respectively. Calculate the Relative humidity, Humid volume, dew point temperature, and enthalpy at 60° C and check the answers by psychrometric chart.

(5) A grain dryer requires 300 m³/min of heated air at 45° C. The atmospheric air is at 24° C and 80 per cent relative humidity. Calculate the amount of heat required per hour to raise the air temperature from 24° C to 45° C. Check the answer with the help of the psychrometric chart.

SYMBOLS

A	Area, m^2
H, H_G, H_W, H_S	Humidity, humidity at dry bulb temperature, humidity at wet bulb temperature, and saturation humidity respectively, kg/kg
h_G	Heat transfer coefficient, $kcal/(hr\ m^2\ °C)$
h_r	Heat transfer coefficient equivalent to radiation, $kcal/(hr\ m^2\ °C)$
h_I	Enthalpy, kcal/kg
K_G	Mass transfer coeff. kg mole/(hr m^2 atm)

P	Total pressure, atm
p_a	Partial pressure of water vapour in air, atm
p_w	Partial pressure of water vapour in air at the interface, atm
q	Rate of heat transfer, kcal/hr
s	Humid heat, kcal/(kg °C)
RH	Relative humidity, per cent
t_a, t_w, t_d	Dry bulb, wet bulb and dew point temperatures respectively, °C
t_s	Temperature of water, °C
v	Humid volume, m³/kg.
λ	Latent heat of evaporation of water, kcal/kg.

CHAPTER 3

Theory of Grain Drying

Generally the term drying refers to the removal of relatively small amount of moisture from a solid or nearly solid material by evaporation. Therefore, drying involves both heat and mass transfer operations simultaneously. In convective drying the heat required for evaporating moisture from the drying product is supplied by the external drying medium, usually air. Because of the basic differences in drying characteristics of grains in thin layer and deep bed, the whole grain drying process is divided into thin layer drying and deep bed drying.

THIN LAYER DRYING

Thin layer drying refers to the grain drying process in which all grains are fully exposed to the drying air under constant drying conditions, i.e., at constant air temperature, and humidity. Generally, up to 20 cm thickness of grain bed (with a recommended air-grain ratio) is taken as thin layer. All commercial flow dryers are designed on thin layer drying principles.

The process of drying should be approached from two points of view : the equilibrium relationship and the drying rate relationship.

For convenience, a few terms used in describing the drying process are defined and discussed.

Moisture content

Usually the moisture content of a substance is expressed in percentage by weight on wet basis. But the moisture conten: on dry basis is more simple to use in calculation as the quantity of moisture present at any time is directly proportional to the moisture content on dry basis.

The moisture content, m, per cent, wet basis is :

$$m = \frac{W_m}{W_m + W_a} \times 100 \qquad (3.1)$$

where W_m = weight of moisture and W_a = weight of bone dry material.

The moisture content, M, dry basis, per cent is :

$$M = \frac{W_m}{W_a} \times 100 = \frac{m}{100 - m} \times 100 \qquad (3.2)$$

The moisture content, X, dry basis is sometimes expressed in decimal also :

$$X = \frac{M}{100} \qquad (3.3)$$

Two additional useful equations for moisture content are given below for the calculation of the following :

$$\frac{W'_m}{W_1} = \frac{m_1 - m_2}{100 - m_2} = \frac{M_1 - M_2}{100 + M_1} \qquad (3.3a)$$

$$\frac{W'_m}{W_2} = \frac{m_1 - m_2}{100 - m_1} = \frac{M_1 - M_2}{100 + M_2} \qquad (3.3b)$$

Where W_1 = Initial weight of wet material = $(W_m + W_a)$ kg

        W_2 = Final weight of dried product, kg

        W'_m = Weight of moisture evaporated, kg

    m_1, m_2 = Initial and final moisture contents respectively, per cent, wet basis

    M_1, M_2 = Initial and final moisture contents respectively, per cent, dry basis.

Moisture measurement

Moisture content can be determined by direct and indirect methods. Direct method includes air-oven drying method ($130° \pm 2°$ C) and distillation method. Direct methods are simple and accurate but time consuming whereas indirect methods are convenient and quick but less accurate.

DIRECT METHODS

The air-oven drying method can be accomplished in a single stage or double stage in accordance with the grain samples containing less than 13 per cent or more than 13 per cent moisture content (Hall, 1957).

Single stage method
Single stage method consists of the following steps :
(a) Grind 2-3 gm sample.
(b) Keep the sample in the oven for about 1 hour at 130°±2° C.
(c) Place the sample in a dessicator and then weigh. The samples should check within 0.1 per cent.

Double stage method
(a) In this method keep 25-30 gm whole grain sample in the air oven at 130°±2°C for 14-16 hours so that its moisture content is reduced to about 13 per cent.
(b) Then follow the same procedure as in single stage method.

Other methods
Place the whole grain sample in the air-oven at 100° ± 2° C for 24 to 36 hours depending on the type of grain and then weigh.
The vacuum oven drying method is also used for the determination of moisture content.
However, moisture determination should be made according to the standard procedure for each grain which is laid down by the Government or by the Association of Agricultural Chemists.

Brown-Duvel distillation method
The distillation method directly measures the volume of moisture, in cc condensed in a measuring cylinder by heating a mixture of 100 gm grain and 150 cc oil in a flask at 200° C for 30 to 40 minutes.
Moisture content can be measured by the toluene distillation mehod also.

INDIRECT METHODS
Indirect methods are based on the measurement of a property of the grain that depends upon moisture content.
Two indirect methods are described as follows :

Electrical resistance method

Resistance type moisture meter measures the electrical resistance of a measured amount of grain sample at a given compaction (bulk density) and temperature. The electrical resistance varies with moisture, temperature and degree of compaction.

The universal moisture meter (U.S.A.), Tag-Happenstall moisture meter (U.S.A) and Kett moisture meter (Japan) are some of the resistance type moisture meters. They take only 30 seconds for the moisture measurement.

Dielectric method

The dielectric properties of grain depend on its moisture content. In this type of moisture meter, 200 gm grain sample is placed between the condenser plates and the capacitance is measured. The measured capacitance varies with moisture, temperature and degree of compaction.

The Motomco moisture meter (U.S.A) and Burrows moisture recorder (U.S.A.) are some of the capacitance type of moisture meters. They take about 1 minute for the measurement of moisture. These are also known as safe crop moisture testers as they do not damage the grain sample.

Equilibrium moisture content

When a solid is exposed to a continual supply of air at constant temperature and humidity, having a fixed partial pressure of the vapour, p the solid will either lose moisture by evaporation or gain moisture from the air until the vapour pressure of the moisture of the solid equals p. The solid and the gas are then in equilibrium, and the moisture content of the solid in equilibrium with the surrounding conditions is known as equilibrium moisture content E.M.C. (Fig. 3.1). The E.M.C. is useful to determine whether a product will gain or lose moisture under a given set of temperature and relative humidity conditions. Thus E.M.C. is directly related to drying and storage. Different materials have different equilibrium moisture contents. The E.M.C. is dependent upon the temperature and relative humidity of the environment and on the variety and maturity of the grain. The E.M.C. of different grains at different temperatures and humiditics are given in Table I (Appendix). A plot of the equilibrium relative humidity and moisture content of a particular material

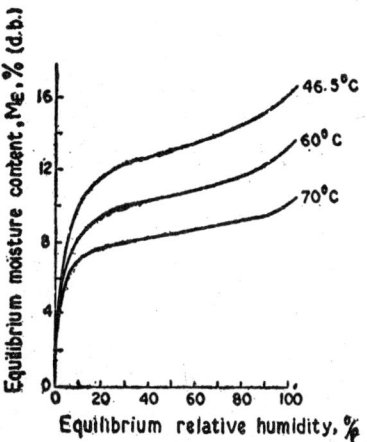

FIG. 3.1. Desorption isotherms for
Patnai-23 variety of paddy.
(Kachrew, R. P. *et al.*, 1971)

at a particular temperature (usually 25° C) is known as equilibrium moisture curve or isotherm. Grain isotherms are generally S-shaped and attributed to multi-molecular adsorption.

DETERMINATION OF EQUILIBRIUM MOISTURE CONTENT

Generally E.M.C. is determined by two methods : (a) the static method, and (b) the dynamic method. In the static method, the grain is allowed to come to equilibrium with the surrounding still air without any agitation, whereas in the dynamic method, the air is generally mechanically moved. As the static method is time consuming, at high relative humidities mould growth in the grain may take place before equilibrium is reached. The dynamic method is faster and is thus preferred. The E.M.C. is to be determined under constant relative humidity and temperature conditions of air. Generally a thermostat is used to control the temperature and aqueous acid or salt solutions of different concentrations are used to control the relative humidity of air.

E.M.C. Models

A number of E.M.C. equations namely BET equation (1938), Harkin and Jura equation (1944), Smith equation (1947), Henderson equation (1952), Chung and Fost equation (1967), etc., have been developed for different ranges of relative humidities. A few purely empirical E.M.C. equations namely Haynes equation (1961), Baker and Arkema equation (1974), etc., have also been proposed for different ranges of relative humidities for different cereal grains. Of them Henderson's equation is well known and discussed here :

Using Gibb's adsorption equation, Henderson (1952) developed the following equation to express the equilibrium moisture curve mathematically :

$$1-RH = \exp[-cTM_e^n] \qquad (3.4)$$

Where RH = equilibrium relative humidity, decimal
M_e = E.M.C., dry basis, per cent
T = temperature, °K and
c and n = product constants, varying with materials.
Values of c and n for some grains are given in Table II (Appendix).

But Henderson's equation has been found to be inadequate for many cereal grains. A few useful empirical modified forms of Henderson equation for different cereal grains are given as follows :

Day and Nelson (1965) proposed the following equation for wheat :

$$1-(p_o'/p_s') = \exp[-J'M_e^{k'}] \qquad (3.5)$$

where $J' = 4.1606 \times 10^{-9}(t+17.78)^{3.3718}$
$K' = 11.6300(t+17.78)^{-0.41733}$

Thompson (1965) proposed the following E.M.C. equation for corn :

$$1-(p_o'/p_s') = \exp[-3.8195 \times 10^{-5}(1.8t+82)M^2] \qquad (3.6)$$
$$= \exp[-6.875 \times 10^{-5}(t+45.55)M^2]$$

Hysteresis

Many solid materials including cereal grains exhibit different equilibrium moisture characteristics depending upon whether the equilibrium is reached by adsorption/sorption or desorption of the moisture. This phenomenon is known as hysteresis which is shown in Fig. 3.2.

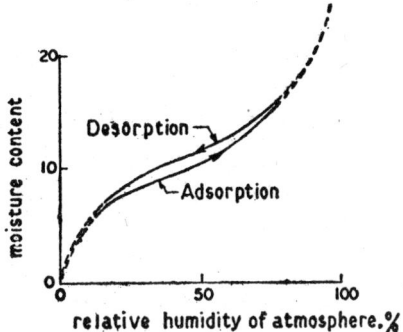

FIG. 3.2. Relation between equilibrium moisture content of paddy and relative humidity showing hysteresis.

Bound moisture

This refers to the moisture contained by a substance which exerts equilibrium vapour pressure, less than that of the pure liquid at the same temperature (Fig. 3.3). The bound moisture may be contained inside the cell walls of the plant structure, moisture in loose chemical combination with the cellulosic material, moisture held in small capillaries and crevasses throughout the solid.

Unbound moisture

This refers to the moisture contained by a substance which exerts equilibrium vapour pressure equal to that of the pure liquid at the same temperature (Fig. 3.3).

Free moisture

Free moisture is the moisture contained by a substance in excess of the equilibrium moisture, $X - X_E$ (Fig. 3.3). Only free moisture can be evaporated and the free water content of a solid depends upon the vapour concentration in the air.

The above relations are shown in Fig. 3.3 for a solid of moisture content X exposed to air of relative humidity RH.

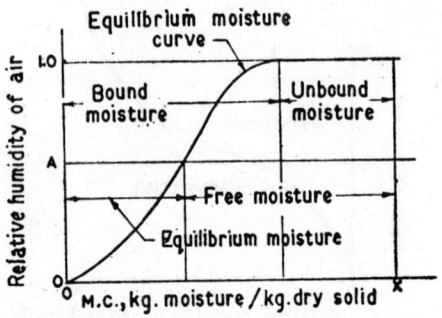

FIG. 3.3. Types of moisture.

A typical drying curve is shown in Fig. 3.4. The figure clearly shows that there are two major periods of drying, namely, the constant-rate period and the falling-rate period.

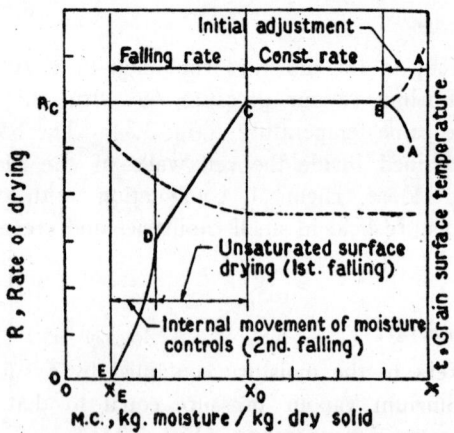

FIG. 3.4. Typical drying rate curve,
constant drying condition.

The plots of moisture content versus drying time or drying rate versus drying time or drying rate versus moisture content are known as drying curves (Figs. 3.4 to 3.8)

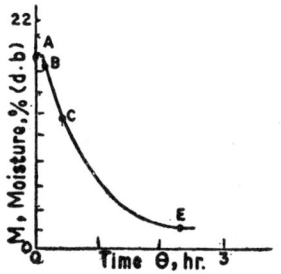

FIG. 3.5. Moisture content versus drying time.

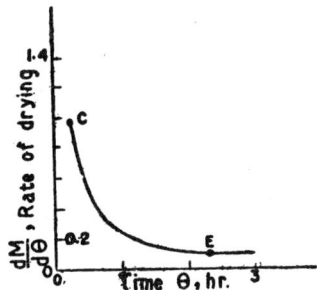

FIG. 3.6. Drying rate versus drying time.

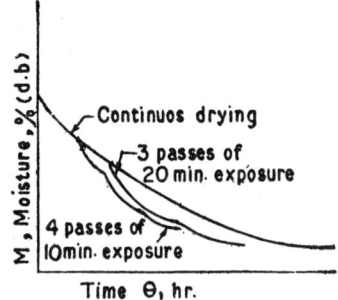

FIG. 3.7. Effects of tempering on intermittent drying.

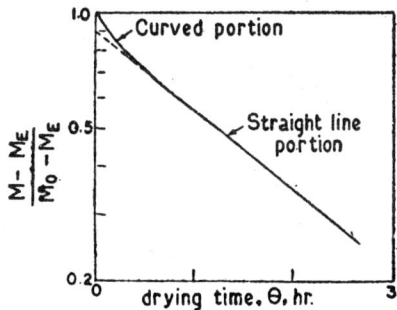

FIG. 3.8. Relation between moisture ratio and drying time.

3

Constant-rate period

Some crops including cereal grains at high moisture content are dried under constant-rate period at the initial period ot drying. Falling-rate period follows subsequently. As for example, wheat is dried under constant-rate period when its moisture content exceeds 72%.

In the constant-rate period the rate of evaporation under any given set of air conditions is independent of the solid and is essentially the same as the rate of evaporation from a free liquid surface under the same condition. The rate of drying during this period is dependent upon : (a) difference between the temperature of air and temperature of the wetted surface at constant air velocity and relative humidity, (b) difference in humidity between air stream and wet surface at constant air velocity and temperature, and (c) air velocity at constant air temperature and humidity.

Under adiabatic and controlled drying air conditions, the temperature of the wetted surface attains the wet bulb temperature. In the constant-rate period drying takes place by surface evaporation and moisture moves by vapour pressure difference. The moisture content at which the drying rate ceases to be constant is known as the critical moisture content of the solid. The average critical moisture content, X_c for a given type of material depends upon the surface moisture concentration, bed thickness of the material and rate of drying. The critical moisture content of a product also depends upon the characteristics of the solid such as shape, size and the drying conditions.

If the drying takes place entirely within the constant-rate period so that X_1, $X_2 > X_c$.

Then by definition, $R = -\dfrac{W_d}{A}\dfrac{dX}{d\theta}.$

Separating the variables and integrating the equation within proper limits, we get :

$$\text{time of drying, } \theta_c = \frac{W_d}{A}\left(\frac{X_1 - X_2}{R_c}\right), \tag{3.7}$$

where W_d = Weight of dry solid kg,
      A = Wet surface, m^2

X_1 = Initial moisture content, kg moisture/kg dry solid

X_2 = Final moisture content, kg/kg

X_c = Critical moisture content, kg/kg

R_c = Rate of drying in the constant rate period, kg moisture evaporated/(hr m^2)

θ_c = drying time, hr.

The constant drying rate of a crop can also be expressed as follows by use of wet bulb temperature theory :

$$\frac{dw}{d\theta} = 18 \, kA\,(p_s - p_a) = h_{fa}A\,(t_a - t_s)/\lambda_s \tag{3.8}$$

where

$\frac{dw}{d\theta}$ = constant rate of drying, kg/hr,

p_a, p_s = Water vapour pressures at t_a and t_s respectively, atm

t_a, t_s = air and water temperature respectively, ° C,

h_{fa} = film heat transfer coefficient of air at air-water interface, kcals/hr m^2 ° C,

λ_s = latent heat of water at t_s, kcals/kg,

A = water surface area, m^2

k = water vapour transfer coefficient at the water-air interface, kgmole(hr m^2 atm)

Falling-rate period

Cereal grains are usually dried entirely under falling-rate period.

The falling-rate period enters after the constant drying rate period and corresponds to the drying cycle where all surface is no longer wetted and the wetted surface continually decreases, until at the end of this period the surface is dry. The cause of falling off in the rate of drying is due to the inability of the moisture to be conveyed from the centre of the body to the surface at a rate comparable with the moisture evaporation from its surface to the surroundings.

The falling-rate period is characterised by increasing temperatures both at the surface and within the solid. Furthermore, changes in air velocity have a much smaller effect than during the constant-rate period. The falling-rate period of drying is controlled largely by the product and is dependent upon the movement of moisture within the material from the centre to the surface by liquid diffusion and the removal of moisture from the surface of the product.

The falling-rate period of drying often can be divided into two stages : (a) unsaturated surface drying, and (b) drying where the rate of water diffusion within the product is slow and is the controlling factor. Practically all cereal grains are dried under falling-rate period if their moisture contents are not very high.

Many theories have been proposed to describe the moisture movement phenomena in cereal grains. Of them, the following are most popular :

(1) Liquid movement due to moisture concentration differences (liquid diffusion surface) ;

(2) Liquid movement due to surface forces (capillary flow) ;

(3) Liquid movement due to moisture diffusion in the pores (surface diffusion) ;

(4) Vapour movement due to differences in vapour pressures (vapour diffusion) ;

(5) Vapour movement due to temperature differences (thermal diffusion) ; and

(6) Liquid and vapour movement due to total pressure differences (hydrodynamic flow).

DRYING EQUATIONS

(A) On the basis of the above mechanisms Luikov et al. (1966) developed mathematical models to describe the drying of capillary porous products as follows :

$$\frac{\delta M}{\delta \theta} = \nabla^2 K_{11} M + \nabla^2 K_{12} t + \nabla^2 K_{13} P \qquad (3.9)$$

$$\frac{\delta t}{\delta \theta} = \nabla^2 K_{21} M + \nabla^2 K_{22} t + \nabla^2 K_{23} P \qquad (3.10)$$

$$\frac{\delta P}{\delta \theta} = \nabla^2 K_{31} M + \nabla^2 K_{32} t + \nabla^2 K_{33} P \qquad (3.11)$$

where K_{11}, K_{22}, K_{33} are the phenomenological coefficients and the other K terms are the coupling coefficients which resulted from the combined effects of moisture, temperature and pressure.

In grain drying analyses the effects of total pressure and temperature gradients need not be considered. Therefore, the final simplified Luikov's equation will be of the form :

$$\frac{\delta M}{\delta \theta} = \nabla^2 K_{11} M \tag{3.12}$$

If it is accepted that the movement of moisture takes place by liquid or vapour diffusion, then the transfer coefficient K_{11} may be replaced by the diffusion coefficient D_V.

If D_V is taken as constant, then the equation (3.12) can be written as :

$$\frac{\delta M}{\delta \theta} = D_V \left[\frac{\delta^2 M}{\delta r'^2} + \frac{c'}{r'} \frac{\delta M}{\delta r'} \right] \tag{3.13}$$

where $c' = 0$ for planar symmetry, $c' = 1$ for cylindrical body and $c' = 2$ for sphere.

Under the following boundary conditions :

$M(r', 0) = M_0$ (IMC), and $M(r_0', \theta) = M_e$ (EMC),

the solutions of equation (3.13) are as follows :

$$\frac{M - M_e}{M_0 - M_e} = \frac{8}{\pi^2} \sum_{n'=0}^{\infty} \frac{1}{(2n'+1)^2} \exp\left[-\frac{(2n'+1)^2 \pi^2}{4} X'^2 \right]$$

for infinite plane (3.14)

$$\frac{M - M_e}{M_0 - M_e} = \frac{6}{\pi^2} \sum_{n'=1}^{\infty} \frac{1}{n'^2} \exp\left[-\frac{n'^2 \pi^2}{9} X'^2 \right]$$

for sphere (3.15)

$$\frac{M - M_e}{M_0 - M_e} = \sum_{n'=1}^{\infty} \frac{4}{\lambda^2_{n'}} \exp\left[-\frac{\lambda_{n'}'}{4} X'^2 \right]$$

for infinite cylinder (3.16)

where $\lambda_{n'}'$ are the roots of the Bessel function of zero order,

$X' = \frac{A}{V} (D_V \theta)^{1/2}$,

A = surface area,

V = Volume of the body,

$\frac{A}{V} = \frac{1}{\text{half thickness}}$ for plane,

$\frac{A}{V} = \frac{3}{\text{radius}}$ for sphere and

$\frac{A}{V} = \frac{2}{\text{radius}}$ for cylinder.

(B) If the moisture contents X_1 and X_2 are both less than $\bar{X}_c$ so that drying occurs under conditions changing R, (i.e., under falling-rate period) the drying time in this period may be expressed as follows :

The rate of drying is by definition :

$$R = -\frac{W_a}{A} \int \frac{dx}{d\theta}$$

Rearranging and integrating over the time interval while the moisture content changes from its initial value X_1 to its final value X_2 :

$$\theta_f = \int_0^{\theta_f} d\theta = \frac{W_a}{A} \int_{X_2}^{X_1} \frac{dx}{R} \qquad (3.17)$$

General case : For any shape of falling-rate curve equation (3.17) may be integrated graphically by determining the area under a curve of $1/R$ as ordinate, X as abscissa, the data for which may be obtained from the rate of drying curve.

(C) Based on Newton's equation for heating or cooling of solids, a simple drying equation can be derived as follows :

The Newton's equation is $\frac{dt}{d\theta} = -K\,(t-t_e)$.

If the temperature term t is replaced by the moisture term M, then

$$\frac{dM}{d\theta} = -K\,(M - M_e) \qquad (3.18)$$

where M = Moisture content (d.b), %
        θ = time, hr,
        M_e = EMC, (d.b.), %
        K = drying constant, 1/hr.

Rearranging the equation (3.18) :

$$\frac{dM}{M - M_e} = -K d\theta$$

Integrating the above equation within proper limits, we get :

$$\frac{M - M_e}{M_0 - M_e} = \exp\,[-K\theta] \qquad (3.19)$$

or $\qquad \theta = \frac{1}{K} \ln \frac{M_0 - M_e}{M - M_e} \qquad (3.20)$

$\dfrac{M - M_e}{M_0 - M_e}$ is known as the moisture ratio, M.R.

(D) The similar form of the equations (3.14) and (3.15) can be derived assuming concentration difference as the driving force in diffusion of liquid through solid :

$$\frac{\delta C}{\delta \theta} = D_V \frac{\delta^2 C}{\delta x^2} \qquad (3.21)$$

where D_V = Diffusivity, m^2/hr

C = Concentration, θ = time, hr

x = Distance from the Centre of the material, m

If the concentration term be replaced by the moisture content term, M, the above equation will be of the form :

$$\frac{\delta M}{\delta \theta} = D_V \frac{\delta^2 M}{\delta x^2} \qquad (3.22)$$

The solutions of the equation are as follows :

$$\frac{M-M_e}{M_0-M_e} = \frac{8}{\pi^2}\left[\exp\left(-D_V\theta\,\frac{\pi^2}{4a^2}\right)+\frac{1}{9}\exp\left(-9D_V\theta\,\frac{\pi^2}{4a^2}\right)\right.$$
$$\left.+\frac{1}{25}\exp\left(-25\,D_V\theta\,\frac{\pi^2}{4a^2}\right)+\cdots\right] \qquad (3.23)$$

for a slab of infinite length.

where a = half of the thickness of the slab.

$$\frac{M-M_e}{M_0-M_e} = \frac{6}{\pi^2}\left[\exp\left(-D_V\theta\,\frac{\pi^2}{r^2}\right)\right.$$
$$\left.+\frac{1}{4}\exp\left(-4D_V\theta\,\frac{\pi^2}{r^2}\right)+\cdots\right] \qquad (3.24)$$

for a sphere.

where r = radius of the sphere

If MR is plotted against θ on a semilog graph paper, a curve of the type shown in Fig. 3.8 is obtained. The curvature portion of the Fig. 3.8 results from the effects of second, third and following terms in the series.

The equation of the straight line portion of the curve can be expressed as follows :

As θ increases, the terms other than first approach zero.

Neglecting higher terms of the equation,

$$\frac{M-M_e}{M_0-M_e} = \frac{6}{\pi^2}\left[\exp\left(-D_V\theta\,\frac{\pi^2}{r^2}\right)\right]=\frac{6}{\pi^2}\,e^{-K\theta}$$

i.e., $\qquad \dfrac{M-M_e}{M_0-M_e} = B \exp\left[-K\theta\right] \qquad (3.25)$

where $K = D_v \dfrac{\pi^2}{r^2}$ for a sphere

and $B = 6/\pi^2$, B is the shape factor.

Determination of Drying Constant

(1) *Graphical method*

    For straight portion of the curve shown in Fig. 3.8, the drying constant, K can be worked out easily by finding out the slope of the straight line. This method is illustrated in example 2 (page 59).

(2) *Half-life period method*

    If the time of one-half response in a drying process be defined as the number of hours necessary to obtain a moisture content ratio of one-half, then the drying equation

$$\frac{M - M_e}{M_0 - M_e} = \exp\,[-K\theta] \text{ can be written as}$$

$$\tfrac{1}{2} = \exp\,[-K\theta_{1/2}] \text{ or } \theta_{1/2} = \frac{\ln 2}{K}$$

and $\tfrac{1}{4} = \exp\,[-K\theta_{1/4}]$ or $\theta_{1/4} = \dfrac{\ln 4}{K}$.

    Therefore, by knowing the values of $\theta_{1/2}$ or $\theta_{1/4}$ K can be found out.

Remarks on thin layer drying equations

    None of the theoretical equations presented in this chapter represents the drying characteristics of grains accurately over a wide range of moisture and temperature, on account of the following limitations :

    (1) The theoretical drying equations are based on the concept that all grains in thin layer are fully exposed to the drying air under constant drying conditions (at constant drying air temperature and humidity) and dried uniformly. Therefore, there is no gradient in thin layer of grain which is not true for finite mass depths.

    (2) The grain drying equations developed from diffusion equation are based on the incorrect assumptions that D_v and K are independent of moisture and temperature.

(3) It is not possible to choose accurate boundary condition and shape factors for drying of biological materials.

(4) Drying equation developed from Newton's equation for heating or cooling does not take into account of the shape of the material.

Therefore, the uses of the theoretical drying equations are limited. However, if accurate results are not desired and the values of D_v and K are known then the theoretical drying equations can be used and give fairly good results within a limited range of moisture.

Many empirical drying equations for different cereal grains are found to be useful and frequently used as they give more accurate results in predicting drying characteristics of a particular grain for a certain range of moisture, temperature, air flow rate and relative humidity. A few empirical drying equations are presented below.

Becker (1959) proposed the following equations for wheat :

$$MR = 1 - 8.78 \, (D_r\theta)^{\frac{1}{2}} + 13.22 \, (D_r\theta) \qquad (3.26)$$

$$\text{for } (D_r\theta)^{\frac{1}{2}} < 0.0104$$

$$MR = 0.509 \times \exp\,[-58.4 \, D_r\theta] \qquad (3.27)$$

$$\text{for } (D_r\theta)^{\frac{1}{2}} \geqslant 0.0104$$

where $D_r = 7.135e^{-19944/T}$, $\qquad (3.28)$

$D_r = m^2/hr$, $\theta = hr$ and $T = {}^\circ K$.

Based on drying equation for planar symmetry Pabis and Henderson (1961) developed the following expression for diffusivity for thin layer drying of corn :

$$D_{r \, \text{corn}} = 5.853 \times 10^{-10} \, \exp\,[-12502/T] \qquad (3.29)$$

On the basis of drying equation for sphere the following expression for drying constant, K corn has been developed :

$$K_{\text{corn}} = 5.4 \times 10^{-1} \, \exp\,[-9041/T] \qquad (3.30)$$

where $K = 1/\text{sec}$, $T = {}^\circ K$.

Effects of different factors on the drying process

The drying rate is dependent upon many factors, namely air temperature, air flow rate, relative humidity, exposure time, types, variety and size of the grain, initial moisture content, grain depth,

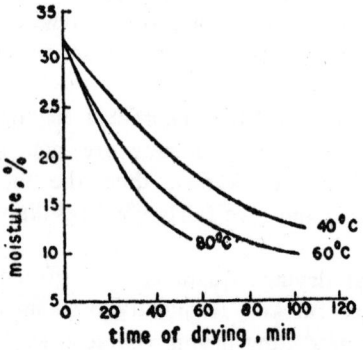

FIG. 3.9. Effects of air temperatures on drying characteristics of parboiled paddy (Bhattacharya et al, 1967).

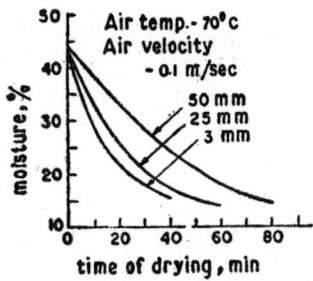

FIG. 3.10. Effects of grain thickness on thin layer drying of wheat (Gerzhoi, 1958).

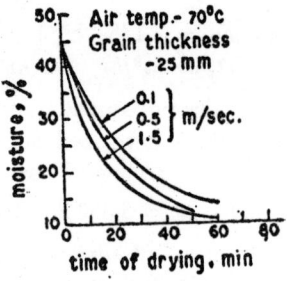

FIG. 3.11. Effects of Air velocity on thin layer of drying of wet corn (Gerzhoi, 1958).

THEORY OF GRAIN DRYING

etc. Of them first four factors are important drying process variables which have been discussed below. The effects of some of the factors are shown in Figs. 3.9 through 3.11.'

EFFECT OF AIR TEMPERATURE

Simmonds et al. (1953a) showed that the rate of drying of wheat was sharply dependent upon the temperature of air varying from 21 to 77° C. The rate of drying increases with the rise of air temperature. But the equilibrium moisture content falls as air temperature increases. These observations are true for other cereal grains also.

The effects of air temperature on the quality of grains have been discussed in Chapter 1.

EFFECT OF AIR VELOCITY

It is generally assumed that the internal resistance to moisture movement of agricultural materials is so great when compared to the surface mass transfer resistance that the air rate past the particles has no significant effect on the time of drying or on the drying coefficient. Henderson and Pabis found that air rate had no observable effect on thin layer drying of wheat when air flow was turbulent. According to them air flow rate varying from 10 cm³/sec/cm² to 68 cm³/sec/cm² had no significant effect on the drying rate of wheat. But in cases of paddy and corn it has been found that air rate has some effect on rate of drying.

However, the recommended air flow rates per unit mass of different grains are given in Table 8.

EFFECT OF AIR HUMIDITY

When the humidity of the air increases the rate of drying decreases slightly. The effect, however, is much smaller in comparison to the effect of temperature changes.

EFFECT OF AIR EXPOSURE TIME

In the case of intermittent drying, drying rate of grain depends on its exposure time to the drying air in each pass. Total drying· time which is the sum of all exposure times, is dependent upon exposure time. Total drying time reduces as exposure time decreases (Chakraverty, 1975).

DEEP BED DRYING

In deep bed drying all the grains in the dryer are not fully exposed to the same condition of drying air. The condition of drying air at any point in the grain mass changes with time and at any times it also changes with the depth of the grain bed. Over and above the rate of air flow per unit mass of grain is small compared to the thin layer drying of grain. All onfarm static bed batch dryers are designed on deep bed drying principle. The condition of drying in deep bed is shown in Fig. 3.12.

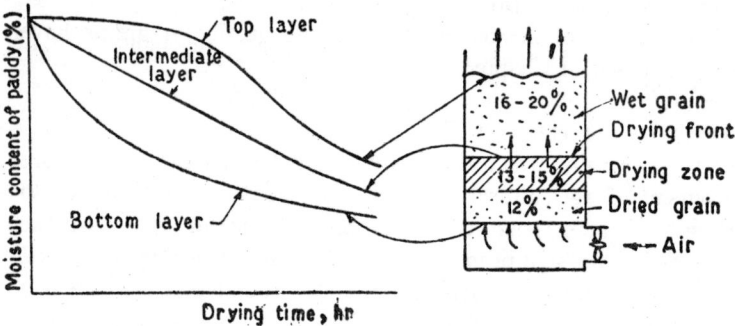

FIG. 3.12. Deep bed drying characteristics at different depths.

The drying of grain in a deep bin can be taken as the sum of several thin layers. The humidity and temperature of air entering and leaving each layer vary with time depending upon the stage of drying, moisture removed from the dry layer until the equilibrium moisture content is reached. Little moisture is removed, rather a small amount may be added to the wet zone until the drying zone reaches it. The volume of drying zone varies with the temperature and humidity of entering air, the moisture content of grain and velocity of air movement. Drying will cease as soon as the product comes in equilibrium with the air.

Time of advance of drying front

The time period taken by the drying front to reach the top of the bin is called the maximum drying rate period.

The time taken by the drying front to reach the top of the bed can be calculated by the following equation :

$$\frac{W_d (M_1 - M_x)}{100} = AG(H_s - H_1)\theta_1$$

or $$\theta_1 = \frac{W_d (M_1 - M_x)}{AG (H_s - H_1) \times 100}$$ (3.31)

where

$M_1 =$ initial moisture content of grain (d.b.), %

$M_x =$ average moisture content, (d.b.), % at the end of drying front advance at the top.

$\theta_1 =$ time of advance, hr

$A =$ cross-sectional area of the dryer, through which air passes, m²

$G =$ mass flow rate of dry air, kg/hr m²

$H_s =$ humidity of the saturated air leaving the dryer kg/kg

$H_1 =$ humidity of the air entering into the dryer, kg/kg

$W_d =$ weight of dry grain in the bin, kg

Decreasing rate period

As soon as the drying front reaches the top of the bin, the rate of drying starts decreasing and is termed as decreasing rate period. The time of drying for this decreasing rate period can be expressed by the following equation :

$$\theta_2 = (1/K)\ln \left(\frac{M_x - M_e}{M - M_e}\right)$$ (3.32)

where

$\theta_2 =$ time of drying during decreasing rate period, hr

$M_e =$ equilibrium moisture content of the grain (d.b.)

$K =$ drying constant, 1/hr

$M =$ average moisture content (d.b.) at the end of decreasing rate period.

$M_x =$ average initial moisture content (d.b.), at the beginning of decreasing period.

The total drying time for grains in the bin is the sum of the time required for the maximum drying rate and decreasing rate periods.

Total drying time, $\theta = \theta_1 + \theta_2$

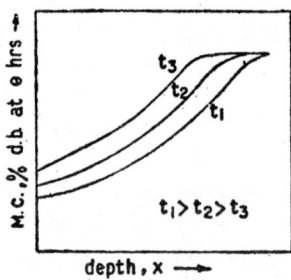

FIG. 3.13. Effect of drying air temperature 't' on the moisture content distribution within a fixed bed of grain after a drying period θ.

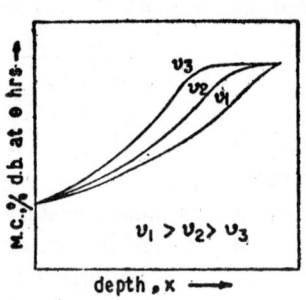

FIG. 3.14. Effects of air flow rate 'v' on the moisture content distribution within a fixed bed of grain after a drying period θ.

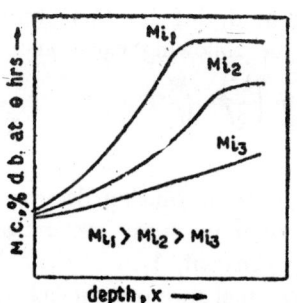

FIG. 3.15. Effect of initial moisture content. Mi on the moisture content distribution within a fixed bed of grain after a drying period θ.

Deep bed drying problems can be solved by Hukill's analysis also (Hukill, 1947). The effects of air temperature, air velocity, bed depth and initial moisture content of grain on deep bed drying characteristics of grain are shown in Figs. 3.14 through 3.18.

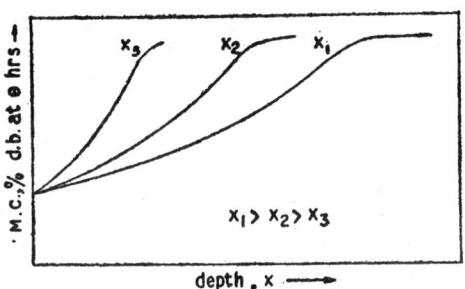

FIG. 3.16. Effect of bed depth X on the moisture content distribution within a fixed bed of grain after a drying period θ.

From these figures, the following general observations can be made in regard to deep bed drying :

(1) The rate of drying of a grain bed increases with an increase in drying air temperature (Fig. 3.13).

(2) The bottom layer of a static grain bed is dried more than the top layer. The moisture gradient across the grain bed increases as the inlet drying air temperature increases (Fig. 3.13).

(3) The rate of drying of a grain bed is increased with an increase in air flow rate (Fig. 3.14).

(4) The drying zone passes more quickly through a grain bed if the initial moisture content of grain is low (Fig. 3.15).

(5) Moisture gradient across the grain bed increases with an increase in bed depth (Fig. 3.16).

Remarks on deep bed drying

(1) If drying air at high relative humidity and relatively low temperature is used, then the total drying time will be very long due to slow rate of drying which may cause spoilage of grains.

(2) The correct choice of air flow rate is very important.

(3) Drying air at high temperature cannot be used due to development of moisture gradients within the grain bed. It leads to non-uniform drying of grain. In general an air temperature of 40° C (15° C rise) is recommended for deep bed drying.

MASS AND HEAT BALANCE IN GRAIN DRYING

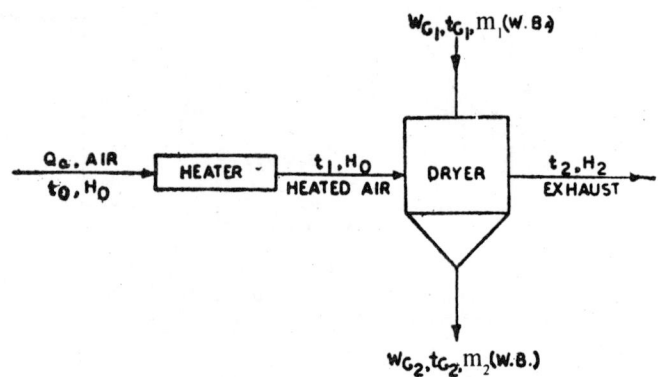

Mass balance

$$\text{Let} \quad W = W_{G_1} - W_{G_2} \tag{3.33}$$
$$\text{or} \quad W_{G_1} = W_{G_2} + W$$

Amount of dry material entering into the dryer

$$= \frac{100 - m_1}{100} W_{G_1} \text{ kg/hr.}$$

Amount of dry material leaving the dryer $= \dfrac{100 - m_2}{100} W_{G_2}$ kg/hr

But $\dfrac{100 - m_1}{100} W_{G_1} = \dfrac{100 - m_2}{100} \times W_{G_2}$

$$W_{G_2} = W_{G_1} \frac{100 - m_1}{100 - m_2} \tag{3.34}$$

Put the equation (34) in equation (33)

$$W = W_{G_1} - W_{G_1} \frac{100 - m_1}{100 - m_2} = W_{G_1} \left(\frac{m_1 - m_2}{100 - m_2}\right)$$

Similarly,

$$W = W_{G_2} \frac{m_1 - m_2}{100 - m_1}, \quad W_{G_1}\left(\frac{m_1 - m_2}{100 - m_2}\right) = W_{G_2} \frac{m_1 - m_2}{100 - m_1} \tag{3.35}$$

If f_d, the dryer factor be defined as follows :

$$f_d = \frac{W}{W_{G_1}} \times 100 = \frac{W_{G_1} - W_{G_2}}{W_{G_1}} \times 100 = \left(\frac{m_1 - m_2}{100 - m_2}\right) \times 100$$
(3.36)

Heat Balance

$$W_d \times Cp_g \times (t_{G_2} - t_{G_1}) + W_d \times (X_1) \times Cp_w (t_{G_2} - t_{G_1}) + W_d(X_1 - X_2)\lambda$$

$$\qquad\qquad \text{Sensible heat} \qquad\qquad\qquad \text{Latent heat}$$

$$\qquad\qquad = Q_a \times (0.24 + 0.45 H_0) \times (t_1 - t_2) \times \theta \qquad (3.37)$$

where, W_d = B.D. mat., kg ; Q_a = air rate kg/hr ;

θ = time, hr ;

X_1, X_2 = moisture content, (d.b), decimal

Dryer performance

Dryer performance can be expressed in terms of various efficiency factors which are given below :

Thermal efficiency

Thermal efficiency can be defined as the ratio of the latent heat of evaporation credited to the heat energy of the fuel charged. Thermal efficiency can be expressed mathematically as follows :

$$\frac{\left(\frac{dM}{d\theta}\right) W_d \lambda}{q}$$
(3.38)

where $\quad q = \dfrac{60\, VA}{v} (h_1 - h_0)$ (3.39)

$\dfrac{dM}{d\theta}$ = drying rate, kg/(hr kg)

W_d = weight of dry material, kg.

λ = latent heat of evaporation, kcal/kg.

q = rate of heat flow, kcal/hr

V = air rate, $m^3/(\min m^2)$

A = area, m^2

v = humid volume of air (at the point of rate measurement) m^3/kg

h_1 and h_0 = enthalpy of drying and ambient air, kcals/kg.

Heat Utilisation Factor

H.U.F. may be defined as the ratio of temperature decrease due to cooling of the air during drying and the temperature increase due to heating of air.

Heat utilisation factor

$$= \frac{\text{Air temperature decrease during drying}}{\text{Air temperature increase during heating}}$$

$$\text{H.U.F} = \frac{\text{Heat utilised}}{\text{Heat supplied}} = \frac{t_1 - t_2}{t_1 - t_0} \qquad (3.40)$$

H.U.F. may be more than unity under certain drying conditions.

The Coefficient of Performance

The coefficient of performance (C.O.P.) of a grain dryer is expressed mathematically as follows :

$$\text{C.O.P} = \frac{t_2 - t_0}{t_1 - t_0} \qquad (3.41)$$

where t_2 = dry bulb temperature of exhaust air, $^\circ$ C

t_0 = dry bulb temperature of ambient air, $^\circ$ C

t_1 = dry bulb temperature of drying air, $^\circ$ C

The relationship between H.U.F. and C.O.P.

$$\text{H.U.F} = 1 - \text{C.O.P.} \qquad (3.42)$$

The Effective Heat Efficiency (E.H.E.)

The E.H.E. is mathematically defined as follows :

$$\text{E.H.E} = \frac{t_1 - t_2}{t_1 - t_{w_1}} \qquad (3.43)$$

where t_{w_1} = wet bulb temperature of drying air, $^\circ$ C.

Effective heat efficiency considers the sensible heat in drying air as being the effective heat for drying.

PROBLEMS ON MOISTURE CONTENT, HENDERSON'S EQUATION AND DRYING

Solved problems on Moisture Content

(1) Two tonnes of paddy with 22 per cent moisture content on wet basis are to be dried to 13 per cent moisture content on dry basis. Calculate the weight of bone dry products and water evaporated.

Solution

Weight of bone dried sample

$$= 2000 - \frac{2000 \times 22}{100}$$

$$= 1560 \text{ kg.}$$

Moisture content on dry basis for 22 per cent moisture on wet basis :

$$= \frac{22}{100 - 22} \times 100$$

$$= 28.2 \text{ per cent (d.b.)}$$

Therefore, water evaporated

$$= 1560 \times (0.282 - 0.13)$$

$$= 237.2 \text{ kg.}$$

Amount of dried product

$$= 2000 - 237.2$$

$$= 1762.8 \text{ kg.}$$

(2) Determine the quantity of parboiled paddy with 40 per cent moisture content on wet basis required to produce 1 tonne of product with 12 per cent moisture content on wet basis. Work out the problem on wet basis and check the answer using dry basis.

Solution

On wet basis : Weight of paddy with 12 per cent moisture on wet basis = 1 tonne.

Weight of bone dry paddy

$$= 1 - \frac{12 \times 1}{100}$$

$$= 0.88 \text{ tonne}$$

Let x be the amount of water present in the paddy with 40 per cent moisture content.
Therefore,

$$\frac{x}{0.88+x} \times 100 = 40$$

$$x = \frac{40 \times 0.88}{60} = 0.587 \text{ tonne}$$

Therefore, quantity of paddy with 40 per cent moisture content on wet basis :

$$= 0.587 + 0.88$$
$$= 1.467 \text{ tonne}$$

On dry basis :
40 per cent m.c. (w.b) = 66.66 per cent (d.b.)
Similarly 12 per cent m.c. (w.b) = 13.65 per cent (d.b.)
Amount of moisture evaporated

$$= 0.88 \left(\frac{66.66 - 13.65}{100} \right)$$

$$= 0.467 \text{ tonne}$$

Total weight of paddy should be $1 + 0.467 = 1.467$ tonne

(3) Determine the values of c and n from the Henderson's equation for the following data obtained from thin layer paddy drying studies :

$RH = 30$ per cent, $t = 50°$ C, $M_e = 10.5$ per cent   (i)
$RH = 55$ per cent, $t = 50°$ C, $M_e = 15.5$ per cent   (ii)

Solution

Henderson's equation is expressed as,

$$1 - RH = \exp[-cTM_e^n]$$

Putting condition (i) in Henderson's equation we get
$$1 - 0.3 = \exp[-c(50+273)(10.5)^n]$$
$$0.7 = \exp[-c \times 323 \times (10.5)^n]$$
$$e^{-0.357} = \exp[-c \times 323 \times 10.5)^n]$$
$$0.357 = c \times 323 \times (10.5)^n \qquad (1)$$

Substituting condition (ii) in Henderson's equation we get
$$1 - 0.55 = \exp[-c(50+273) \times (15.5)^n]$$
or $\quad 0.45 = \exp[-c \times 323 \times (15.5)^n]$
or $\quad e^{-0.796} = \exp[-c \times 323 \times (15.5)^n]$
or $\quad 0.796 = c \times 323 \ (15.5)^n \qquad (2)$

Dividing equation (2) by equation (1),

$$\frac{0.796}{0.357} = \frac{c \times 323 \times (15.5)^n}{c \times 323 \times (10.5)^n}$$

or $\quad 2.23 = \left(\frac{15.5}{10.5}\right)^n$

or $\quad (1.475)^n = 2.23$

Therefore $n = 2.07$.

Substituting the value of n in equation (1),

$$0.357 = c \times 323 \,(10.5)^{2.07}$$

or $\quad c = \dfrac{0.357}{323 \times 130}$

Therefore $c = 8.5 \times 10^{-6}$

EXERCISES

(1) Calculate the amount of moisture evaporated from 100 kg of grain for drying it from an initial moisture content of 25 per cent to a final moisture content of 13 per cent on wet basis.

(2) Draw a graph showing moisture content of grain on wet basis versus moisture content on dry basis. Take moisture content of grain on wet basis from 10 to 60 per cent at equal intervals of 5 per cent.

(3) 1000 kg of parboiled paddy is to be dried from 32 to 13 per cent moisture content (w.b.). Calculate the amount of moisture to be evaporated.

(4) Determine the equilibrium moisture content of Sorghum at $RH = 10$ per cent and $t = 60°$ C using Henderson's equation, where $c = 6.12 \times 10^{-6}$ and $n = 2.31$.

(5) Determine the values of c and n from Henderson's equation for the following data :

(a) $RH = 40$ per cent, $t = 60°$ C, $M_e = 8.65$ per cent.
(b) $RH = 80$ per cent, $t = 60°$ C, $M_e = 14.62$ per cent.

Solved problems on Drying

(1) In an experiment on drying of raw paddy at an air temperature of 55° C, the following data were obtained. Initial weight of the sample = 1000 gm.

Initial moisture content = 30.8 per cent (d.b.)

Sl. No	Drying time in min	Moisture removed in gm
1	0	0.0
2	10	22.9
3	20	38.2
4	40	57.4
5	60	68.8
6	80	78.0
7	100	84.0
8	140	101.0
9	180	112.5
10	220	121.0
11	260	128.4
12	300	131.8

Prepare a drying rate curve for the experiment.

Solution

I.M.C. = 30.8 per cent (d.b.)

Therefore, the amount of bone dry material in the sample

$$= \frac{100}{130.8} \times 1000 = 764.5 \text{ gm.}$$

The amount of moisture present in the sample
= 235.5 gm.

After 10 minutes, 22.9 gm of water was removed.

Therefore, moisture content of the sample after 10 min.

$$= \frac{235.5 - 22.9}{764.5} \times 100$$

= 27.8 per cent (d.b.)

Drying rate, R in gm of water per minute per 100 gm of bone dry material is expressed as follows :

$$R = \frac{\text{Amount of moisture removed}}{\text{Time taken} \times \left(\dfrac{\text{Total bone dry weight of sample in gm}}{100}\right)}$$

For example, for the second reading,

$$R = \frac{22.9}{10 \times \left(\frac{764.5}{100}\right)}$$

$$= 0.300 \frac{\text{gm of water}}{\text{min } 100 \text{ gm. of b.d. material}}$$

Similar calculations are made for all readings and the following table is prepared.

S. No.	Drying time min	Moisture removed gm	Moisture present in the sample gm	Moisture content (d.b) per cent	Average moisture content (d.b) per cent	Drying rate, R (gm of water/min 100 gm. of b.d materials)
1	0	0.0	235.5	30.8		
					29.30	0.299
2	10	22.9	212.6	27.8		
					26.80	0.249
3	20	38.2	197.3	25.80		
					24.545	0.189
4	40	57.8	178.10	23.29		
					22.545	0.150
5	60	68.8	166.70	21.80		
					11.20	0.128
6	80	78.0	157.5	20.60		
					20.205	0.110
7	100	84.0	151.5	19.81		
					18.70	0.944
8	140	101.0	134.5	17.59		
					16.835	0.081
9	180	112.5	123.0	16.08		
					15.525	0.072
10	220	121.0	114.5	14.97		
					14.485	0.065
11	260	128.4	107.1	14.0		
					13.79	0.054
12	300	131.8	103.7	13.58		

The drying rate curve is obtained by plotting the rate of drying against the average moisture content.

(2) The drying curve for a batch of solid dried from 25 to 6 per cent moisture (w.b.) is shown in Fig. 3.17. The initial weight of sol:d is 159 kg and drying surface is 1 m²/39 kg dry material. Determine the time for drying.

Solution

The time required for drying upto 'C' or time for constant-rate period :

$$\theta_o = \frac{W_d}{A}\left(\frac{X_1 - X_c}{R_o}\right)$$

$$\frac{W_d}{A} = \frac{1}{1/39} \text{ kg/m}^2$$

$$= 39 \text{ kg/m}^2$$

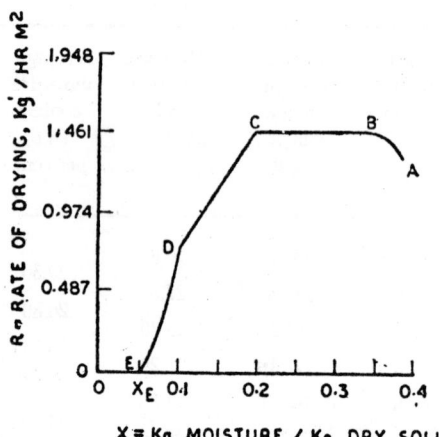

Fig. 3.17 Drying curve (for Problem 2).

$$X_1 = \frac{25}{100-25} = \frac{25}{75} = 0.333 \text{ kg/kg dry material}$$

$X_o = 0.2$ (from fig. 3.17)

$R_o = 1.461 \text{ kg/(m}^2\text{)(hr)}$ (from fig. 3.17)

$$\theta_o = 39 \times \frac{0.333-0.2}{1.461} = 3.55 \text{ hrs}$$

$\therefore \quad \theta_o = 3.55 \text{ hours}$ (1)

For falling-rate period

Time required for drying can be calculated by two methods :

(a) approximate method by assuming straight line, and
(b) graphical method.

(a) By assuming straight line

$$\theta_f = \frac{W_d}{A} \cdot \frac{X_c - X_2}{R_m}$$

where $R_m = \dfrac{R_o - R_2}{\ln(R_o/R_2)}$,

$R_o = 1.461 \text{ kg}/(m^2) \text{ (hr)} \quad \text{(from fig. 3.17)}$

$X_2 = \dfrac{6}{94} = 0.0637 \text{ kg/kg of dry material}$

$R_2 = 0.075 \text{ kg/m}^2 \text{ hr} \quad \text{(from fig. 3.17)}$

$$R_m = \frac{1.461 - 0.075}{2.3 \log \dfrac{1.461}{0.075}} = \frac{1.386}{2.3 \log 19.5} = \frac{1.386}{2.3 \times 1.29}$$

$$= 0.466 \text{ kg/hr m}^2$$

$$\theta_f = 39 \frac{0.200 - 0.0637}{0.466}$$

$$= 39 \times \frac{0.1363}{0.466} = 11.4 \text{ hours}$$

$\theta_f = 11.4 \text{ hr.}$

(b) In graphical solution divide the falling-rate curve in two parts :

(i) Unsaturated surface drying and

(ii) Drying under control of internal movement of moisture.

In unsaturated surface drying the falling-rate curve is a straight line, therefore, above method can be used up to the point 'D'

$$\theta_{f_1} = \frac{W_d}{A} \frac{X_c - X_d}{R_{md}}$$

where $R_{md} = \dfrac{R_c - R_d}{\ln \dfrac{R_c}{R_d}}$

From the curve :

$X_d = 0.1 \text{ kg/kg}$

$X_c = 0.2 \text{ kg/kg}$

$R_c = 1.461 \text{ kg/hr m}^2$

$R_d = 0.73 \text{ kg/hr m}^2$

$$R_{md} = \frac{1.461-0.73}{2.3 \log_{10} \frac{1.461}{0.73}} = \frac{0.731}{2.3 \log_{10} 2} = \frac{0.731}{2.3 \times 0.3010}$$

$$= 1.056 \text{ kg/hr m}^2$$

$$\theta_{f_1} = 39 \times \frac{0.2-0.1}{1.056} = 3.693 \text{ hrs.}$$

θ_{f_1}, time for falling rate period for unsaturated surface drying = 3.69 hours.

For the second part in which internal movement of moisture controls, a curve is plotted relating $1/R$ and X.

The area under that curve $= \int \frac{dX}{R}$.

X	0.1000	0.0950	0.0870	0.0785	0.0700	0.0637
R	0.73	0.568	0.460	0.290	0.180	0.075
$1/R$	1.37	1.76	2.195	3.450	5.55	13.35

Area under the curve $= 1 \times 60 + \frac{1}{100} \times 1371$

$$= 73.71$$

Area of each square = 0.001667 m^2 hr/kg

Total area, $\int \frac{dX}{R} = 0.001667 \times 73.71$

$$= 0.1228 \text{ m}^2 \text{ hr/kg}$$

Therefore, time required for drying for the second part

$$\theta_{f_2} = \frac{W_d}{A} \int \frac{dX}{R} = 39 \times 0.1228$$

$$= 4.78 \text{ hours.}$$

Total time required for drying in the falling rate period

$$\theta_f = \theta_{f_1} + \theta_{f_2} = 3.69 + 4.78 = 8.47 \text{ hrs.}$$

Therefore, total time required for the entire period of drying = time for constant rate period + time for falling rate period

$$\theta = \theta_c + \theta_f = 3.55 + 8.47$$

$$= 12.02 \text{ hours.}$$

(3) In an experiment on thin layer drying of parboiled wheat at

a drying air temperature of 75° C, the following drying data were obtained :

Drying time, min	0	10	20	80	40	50	70	90	110	180	150	180	210
M. C.(d,b.)	88.0	59.66	45.02	33.59	23.85	19.86	12.54	8.42	6.59	5.45	4.996	4.99	4.86

The EMC of parboiled wheat at 75° C was found to be 4.75 per cent (d.b.). Find out drying constant, K by graphical method.

Solution

Using above drying data the following table is prepared :

Drying time, min	0	10	20	80	40	50	70	90	110	180	150	180	210
$(M-M_e)/(M_o-M_e)$	1.0	0.702	0.515	0.869	0.263	0.193	0.0996	0.046	0.024	.00895	.00575	.00807	.0014

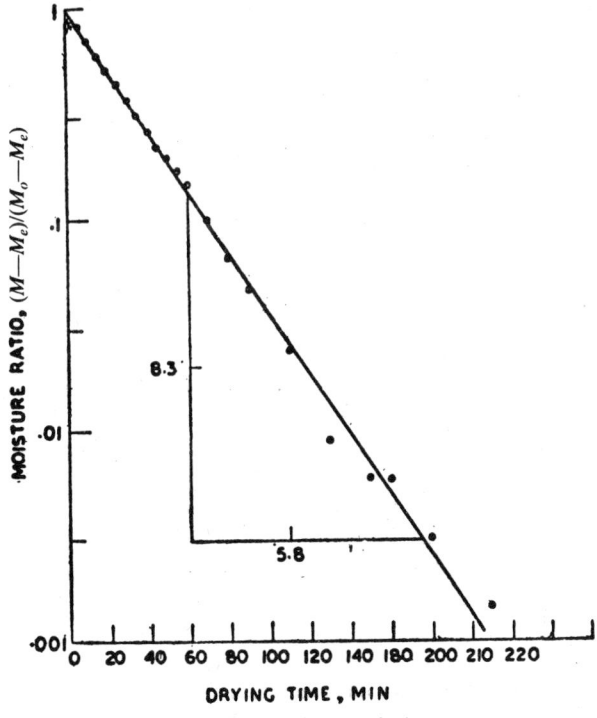

FIG. 3.18 Graph to calculate drying constant.

The moisture ratio, $(M-M_e)/(M_o-M_e)$ is plotted against drying time on a semilog graph paper (Fig. 3.18). From the graph, the slope of straight line, K is calculated below.

$$K = -\left(\frac{8.3}{5.8}\times\frac{1}{0.432\times100}\right) = -0.03313 \text{ (min)}^{-1}$$

EXERCISES

(1) The following data were obtained on the tray drying of sand. Obtain the drying rate curve for the test :

    (1) Area of the tray = 0.20 m²
    (2) Thickness of bed = 2.54 cm
    (3) Weight of dry sand = 10.0 kg

S. No.	Drying time hr	Total moisture present in the sample, kg
1	0 00	0.050
2	0.50	1.835
3	1.50	1.410
4	2.00	1.215
5	2.50	1.015
6	3.00	0.811
7	4.00	0.430
8	4.50	0.272
9	5.00	0.163
10	7.00	0.009
11	7.50	0.000

(2) In an experiment on thin layer drying of parboiled wheat with drying air at 85°C, the following data were obtained :

The initial and equilibrium moisture contents were found to be 83 per cent (d.b.) and 4.50 per cent (d.b.) respectively :

Time, min	Weight of the sample during drying, gm
0	200.0
15	159.0
30	138.0
45	128.0
60	122.0
90	117.0
130	114.5
210	114.25

Determine the drying constant, K by graphical method.

SYMBOLS

A	= area, m^2
a	= half of the thickness of the slab, cm
B	= shape factor, dimensionless
C	= concentration
c	= a constant, dimensionless
c'	= 0 or 1 or 2
Cp_g	= specific heat of grain, kcal/kg ° C
Cp_w	= specific heat of water, kcal/kg ° C
$D.B$	= dry bulb temperature, ° C
D_V	= diffusivity, m^2/hr
d.b.	= dry basis
d_c	= diameter, mm
G	= mass flow rate of base dry air, kg/hr m^2
H	= humidity, kg/kg
H_0	= humidity of atmospheric air, kg/kg
H_1	= humidity of drying air, kg/kg
H_2	= humidity of exhaust air, kg/kg
H_s	= humidity of saturated air, kg/kg
H_a	= humidity at t_a ° C
h_{f_a}	= film heat transfer coefficient kcal/(m^2 hr ° C)
h	= enthalpy, kcal/kg
h_0	= enthalpy of atmospheric air, kcal/kg
h_1	= enthalpy of drying air, kcal/kg
J'	= a constant in modified Henderson's equation
K	= drying constant, 1/hr
K'	= a constant in modified Henderson's equation
k	= water vapour transfer coefficient, kg/hr m^2 atm
k_{11}, k_{22}, k_{33}	= phenomenological coefficients in Luikov's equation
$k_{12}, k_{13}, k_{21},$	
k_{23}, k_{31}, k_{32}	= coupling coefficients in Luikov's equation
M	= moisture content, dry basis, per cent
M_E	= equilibrium moisture content, EMC, dry basis, per cent
M_1	= initial moisture content of grain, I.M.C., dry basis, per cent
M_2	= final moisture content of grain, F.M.C., dry basis, per cent
MR	= moisture ratio, $(M-M_c)/(M_o-M_c)$

M_x	= average moisture content at the end of maximum period of drying
n	= a constant, dimensionless
n'	= whole numbers
p_a	= partial pressure of water vapour at t_a, atm.
p_s	= partial pressure of water vapour at t_s, atm
p'_g	= water vapour pressure of the grain, kg/cm^2
p'_s	= saturated water vapour pressure at equilibrium temperature of the system, kg/cm^2
Q_a	= rate of air supply, kg/hr
q	= heat flow rate, kcal/hr
R	= rate of drying $kg/(hr\ m^2)$
R_c	= constant rate period drying, $kg/(hr\ m^2)$
r	= radius of the sphere, m
r'_o	= radius of a body, m
r'	= coordinate of a body, m
RH	= relative humidity, decimal
T	= temperature, $^\circ$ K
t_0	= temperature of the inlet or ambient air, $^\circ$ C
t_1	= temperature of the drying air (heated air), $^\circ$ C
t_2	= temperature of the exhaust air $^\circ$ C
t_a	= temperature of the air, $^\circ$ C
t_s	= temperature of the saturated air, $^\circ$ C
t_{w_0}	= wet bulb temperature of the ambient air, $^\circ$ C
t_{w_1}	= wet bulb temperature of drying air, $^\circ$ C
V	= Volumetric air flow rate, $m^3/(min\ m^2)$
v	= humid volume, m^3/kg
W_d	= weight of bone dry material, kg
W_m	= weight of moisture, kg
W	= grain flow rate at the inlet condition, kg/hr
W_{G_2}	= grain flow rate at the outlet condition, kg/hr
w	= moisture removed, kg
$W.B.$	= wet bulb temperature, $^\circ$ C
X	= moisture content, dry basis, decimal
X_1	= initial moisture content, dry basis, decimal
X_2	= final moisture content, dry basis, decimal
X_C	= critical moisture content, dry basis, decimal
X_E	= equilibrium moisture content, dry basis, decimal
X'	= dimensionless quantity

x	= distance from the centre, mm
θ	= time, hr
θ_1	= drying time for maximum rate period in deep bed drying, hr
θ_2	= drying time for decreasing rate period in deep bed drying, hr
θ_c	= drying time for constant-rate period, hr
θ_f	= drying time for falling-rate period, hr
λ	= latent heat of vaporisation, kcal/kg
λ_n'	= roots of Bessel function
λ_s	= latent heat at t_s, kcal/kg

CHAPTER 4

Methods of Grain Drying

So far, drying systems have not been classified systematically. However, drying methods can be broadly classified on the basis of either the mode of heat transfer to the wet solid or the handling characteristics and physical properties of the wet material. The first method of classification reveals differences in dryer design and operation, while the second method is most useful in the selection of a group of dryers for preliminary consideration in a given drying problem.

According to the mode of heat transfer, drying methods can be divided into : (a) conduction drying, (b) convection drying, and (c) radiation drying. There are other methods of drying also, namely, dielectric drying, chemical or sorption drying, vacuum drying, freeze drying, etc.

Of them, convection drying is commonly used for drying of all types of grain and conduction drying can be employed for drying of parboiled grain.

Conduction drying
When the heat for drying is transferred to the wet solid mainly by conduction through a solid surface (usually metallic) the phenomenon is known as conduction or contact drying. In this method, conduction is the principal mode of heat transfer and the vaporised moisture is removed independently of the heating media. Conduction drying is characterised by :

(a) Heat transfer to the wet solid takes place by conduction through a solid surface, usually metallic. The source of heat may be hot water, steam, flue gases, hot oil, etc. ;

(b) Surface temperatures may vary widely ;

(c) Contact dryers can be operated under low pressure and in inert atmosphere ;

(d) Dust and dusty materials can be removed very effectively ; and

(e) When agitation is done, more uniform dried product and increased drying rate are achieved by using conduction drying. Conduction drying can be carried out either continuously or batchwise. Cylinder dryers, drum dryers, steam tube rotary dryers are some of the continuous conduction dryers. Vacuum tray dryers, freeze dryers, agitated pan dryers are the examples of batch conduction dryers.

Convection drying

In convection drying, the drying agent (hot gases) in contact with the wet solid is used to supply heat and carry away the vaporised moisture and the heat is transferred to the wet solid mainly by convection. The characteristics of convection drying are :

(a) Drying is dependent upon the heat transfer from the drying agent to the wet material, the former being the carrier of vaporised moisture ;

(b) Steam heated air, direct flue gases of agricultural waste, etc., can be used as drying agents ;

(c) Drying temperature varies widely ;

(d) At gas temperatures below the boiling point, the vapour content of the gas affects the drying rate and the final moisture content of the solid ;

(e) If the atmospheric humidities are high, natural air drying needs dehumidification ; and

(f) Fuel consumption per kg of moisture evaporated is always higher than that of conduction drying.

Convection drying is most popular in grain drying. It can be carried out either continuously or batch-wise. Continuous tray dryers, continuous sheeting dryers, pneumatic conveying dryers, rotary dryers, tunnel dryers come under the continuous system, whereas tray and compartment dryers, batch through circulation dryers are the batch dryers.

Convection drying can be further classified as follows :

5

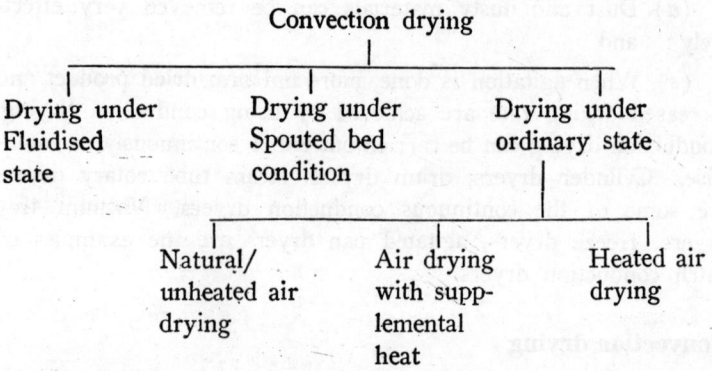

Pneumatic or fluidised bed drying : When the hot gas (drying agent) is supplied at a velocity higher than the terminal velocity of the wet solid, the drying of the wet solid occurs in a suspended or fluidised state. This phenomenon is known as *fluidised bed drying.*

Drying may be carried out in a semi-suspended state or *spouted bed condition* also.

Generally, the convection drying is conducted under ordinary state, i.e., drying agent is supplied at a velocity much lower than the terminal velocity of the wet material.

In *natural air drying,* the unheated air as supplied by the nature is utilised. In *drying with supplemental heat* just sufficient amount of heat (temperature rise within 5 to 10° C) only, is supplied to the drying air to reduce its relative humidity so that drying can take place.

In *heated air drying,* the drying air is heated to a considerable extent.

The natural air drying and drying with supplemental heat methods which may require one to four weeks or even more to reduce the grain moisture content to safe levels, are generally used to dry grain for short term storage in the farm. Heated air drying is most useful when large quantity of grain is to be dried within a short time and marketed at once. It is used for both short and long term storage.

Comparative advantages and disadvantages of the three convective drying methods are given as follows :

Natural Air Drying

Advantages

(1) Lowest initial investment and maintenance cost.
(2) No fuel cost.
(3) No fire hazard.
(4) Least supervision.
(5) Least mould growth compared to supplemental heat.

Disadvantages

(1) Very slow drying rate, drying period may be extended to several weeks.
(2) Weather dependent.
(3) More drying space necessary in comparison to heated air drying.
(4) Useful particularly for short-term storage in the farm.
(5) Not useful for humid tropics.

Supplimental Heat Drying

Advantages

(1) Lower cost of equipment and maintenance.
(2) Independent of weather.
(3) Requires less supervision.
(4) Most efficient use of bin capacity.

Disadvantages

(1) Fire hazard to a certain extent.
(2) Danger of accelerated mould growth.
(3) Rate of drying is still low.
(4) Useful particularly for short-term storage in the farm.

Heated Air Drying

Advantages

(1) Independent of weather.
(2) Fast drying.

(3) High drying capacity per fan horse-power.

(4) Used for both long and short-term storage of grains.

Disadvantages

(1) Higher initial investment and maintenance cost.

(2) Considerable fuel expenditure.

(3) Danger of fire hazard.

(4) Requires skilled manpower for control of drying condition.

(5) By direct firing with liquid fuel, the products may be contaminated with the flue gases.

Radiation drying

Radiation drying is based on the absorption of radiant energy of the sun and its transformation into heat energy by the grain. Sun drying is an example of radiation drying. Radiation drying can also be accomplished with the aid of special infra-red radiation generators, namely, infra-red lamps. Moisture movement and evaporation is caused by the difference in temperature and partial pressure of water vapour between grain and surrounding air. The effectiveness of sun drying depends upon temperature and relative humidity of the atmospheric air, speed of the wind, type and condition of the grain, etc.

Sun Drying

Sun drying is the most popular traditional method of drying. A major quantity of grain is still dried by the sun in most of the developing countries.

Advantages

(1) No fuel or mechanical energy is required.

(2) Operation is very simple.

(3) Viability, germination, baking qualities are fully preserved.

(4) Microbial activity and insect/pest infestation are reduced.

(5) Labour oriented.

(6) No pollution.

Disadvantages

(1) Completely dependent on weather.

(2) Not possible round the clock and round the year.

(3) Excessive losses occur due to shattering, birds, rodents, etc.

(4) Requires specially constructed large floor area, restricting the capacity of mill to a certain limit.

(5) The entire process is unhygienic.

(6) Unsuitable for handling of large quantity of grain within a short period of harvest.

INFRA-RED DRYING

Infra-red rays can penetrate into the irradiated body to a certain depth and transformed into heat energy. Special infrared lamps, or metallic and ceramic surfaces heated to a specified temperature by an open flame, may be used as generators of infra-red radiation.

Advantages

(1) Small thermal inertia.

(2) Simplicity and safety in operation of lamp radiation dryers.

Disadvantages

(1) High expenditure of electric power.

(2) Low utilisation factor.

Radiation dryers have been used in many countries for drying the painted surfaces of machinery, and in the timber processing, textile industry and cereal grain and other food industries.

Dielectric drying

In dielectric drying, heat is generated within the solid by placing it in a fixed high frequency current. In this method, the substance is heated at the expense of the dielectric loss factor. The molecules of the substance, placed in a field of high frequency current are polarised and begin to oscillate in accordance with the frequency. The oscillations are accompanied by friction, and thus a part of the electrical energy is transformed into heat. The main advantage of this method is that the substance is heated with extraordinary rapidity.

The dielectric drying has now been in use in different industries such as timber, plastics and cereal grain processing.

Chemical drying

Various chemicals such as sodium chloride, calcium propionate, copper sulphate, ferrous sulphate, urea, etc., have been tried for the preservation of wet paddy. Of these, common salt has been proved to be effective and convenient for arresting deteriorative changes during storage. When wet paddy is treated with common salt, water is removed from the rice kernel by osmosis. The common salt absorbs moisture from paddy but it cannot penetrate into the endosperm through the husk layer. This is an unique property of the paddy which has rendered the application of common salt preservation possible.

Advantages

(1) It not only dries paddy but also reduces the damage due to fungal, microbial and enzymatic activities and heat of respiration.

(2) It does not affect the viability of the grain.

(3) The milling quality of paddy is satisfactory.

(4) Loss of dry matter is negligible.

(5) It does not affect the quality of rice bran.

Disadvantages

(1) The moisture may be retained on the husk due to the presence of sodium chloride.

(2) The useful life of gunny will be shortened.

(3) The colour of husk changes to dark yellow.

(4) The common salt treated paddy requires an additional drying subsequently.

(5) Economy of the process has yet to be established.

Sack drying

This method is particularly suitable for drying of small quantity of seed to prevent mixing of varieties and conserve strain purity and viability.

The grain bags are laid flat over holes cut on the floor of a tunnel system so that heated air can be forced up through the grain from an air chamber underneath. Usually an air temperature of 45° C with an air flow rate of 4 m³/min at 3-4 cm static pressure per bag of 60 kg is used for fastest drying rate. The sacks are turned once during the drying operation. The sack drying process involves higher labour cost.

CHAPTER 5

Grain Dryers

Grain dryers can be divided into two broad categories, unheated air dryers and heated air dryers. Different types of grain dryers of both groups have been discussed in this chapter.

UNHEATED AIR DRYERS

Unheated or natural air drying is usually performed in the grain storage bin. That is why unheated air drying is also known as in-bin or in-storage drying.

Natural air drying is commonly used for on-farm drying for a relatively small volume of grains. Either full bin or layer-drying system is employed in natural air drying. The period of drying for either system may be as long as several weeks depending on the weather. In layer drying, the bin is filled with a layer of grain at a time and drying, is begun. After the layer is partially dried, other layers of grain are added periodically, perhaps daily with the continuation of drying until the bin is full and the whole grain mass is dried. In full-bin drying, a full bin of grain is dried as a single batch. Then the drying bin is used for storage purposes. The air flow rate provided is relatively low. Though natural air is supposed to be used, an air heating system should be kept so that supplemental heat may be supplied to the natural air during rainy seasons and during periods of high humidity weather and for highly moist grains. Natural air drying cannot be used if the ambient relative humidity exceeds 70 per cent. So also grains containing moisture higher than 20 per cent should not be dried with natural air.

Various types of unheated air dryers with different constructions, shapes, grain feeding and discharging mechanisms and aeration systems are available. . Some of the common types of dryers are described here.

As in natural air drying the grain is aerated (for drying) and stored in the same unit, the complete installation simply consists of a storage unit equipped with ducts for air distribution and devices for air exhaustion and a blower.

Storage unit

Any shape of grain holding bin such as semi-circular, circular, square or rectangular and of any material like metal, wood, concrete, asbestos or mineral agglomeration can be used provided the bin is made moisture proof. Different types of units are shown in Figs. 5.1 to 5.7.

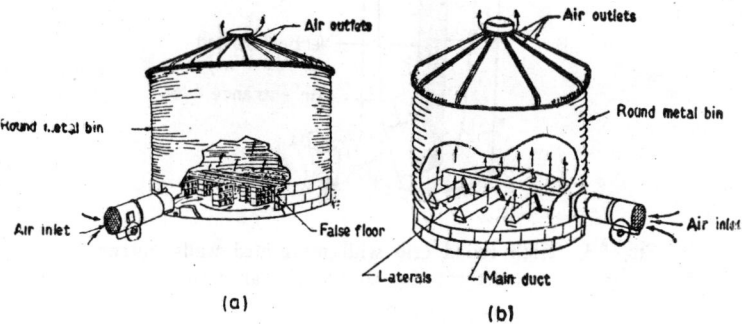

FIG. 5.1. Types of air distribution systems used in bin drying

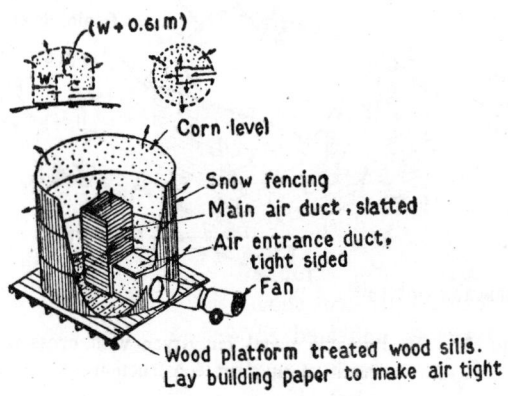

FIG. 5.2. An inexpensive, easily built crib for the mechanical drying of ear corn.

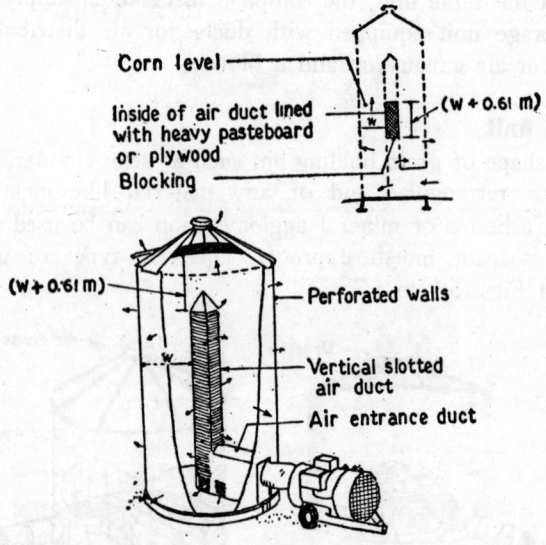

FIG. 5.3. High round crib with perforated walls (permanent
structure) for drying of ear corn.

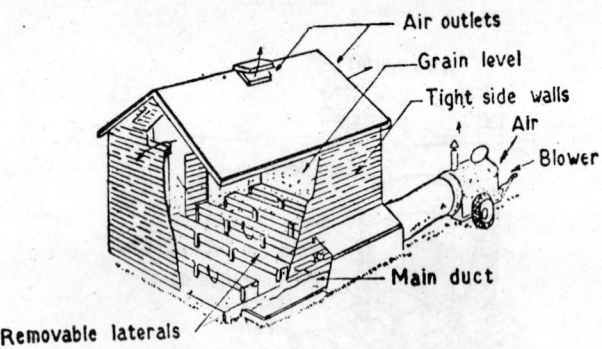

FIG. 5.4. Rectangular metal bin dryer with cross-wise air
ducts—permanent construction.

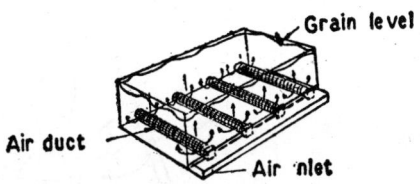

FIG. 5.5a. Rectangular metal bin dryer with cross-wise
air ducts—Temporary construction.

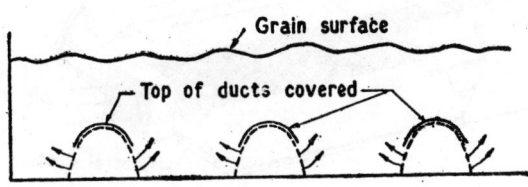

FIG. 5.5b. Most desirable ducting system.

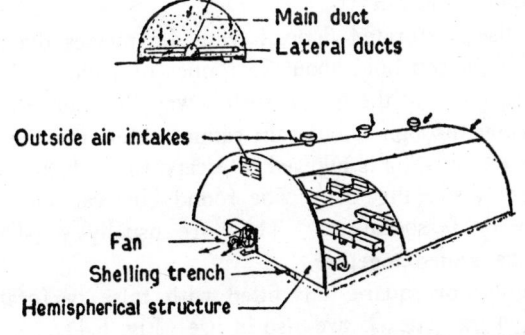

FIG. 5.6. General purpose building for drying and storing
of grain (Permanent structure).

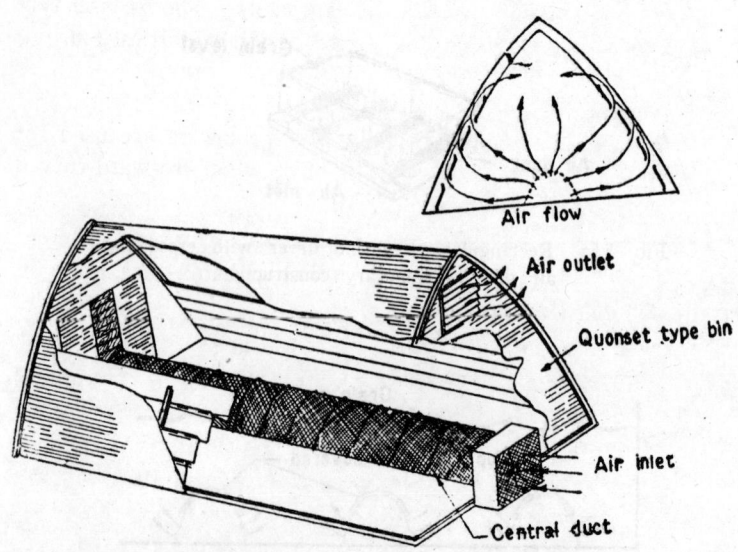

Air flow

Air outlet

Quonset type bin

Air inlet

Central duct

FIG. 5.7. Types of air distribution systems used in bin drying.

Of the many types of bins used in grain drying some of the common types are described as follows :

(a) A round metal bin

With false perforated floor, having 4.5 metres diameter and 3 metres height can hold about 25 tonnes of paddy. The bin is fitted with a cover at the top in such a way that only the exhaust air can escape through it but rain cannot enter into the bin. In some cases exhaust air is allowed to escape through the side walls of the dryer also (Fig. 5.3). The round bins can also be made of concrete or ferrocement. They are usually constructed of several rings sealed together.

Rectangular or square bins fitted with false perforated floor or main duct and laterals are also in use (Fig. 5.4).

(b) A screen tunnel quonset type storage unit

The unit is fitted with a central horizontal screen type duct and a special air outlet system near the top of each vertical wall (Fig. 5.7).

The bins are generally made circular to ensure uniform distribution of air and avoid stagnant pockets. The quonset type has the same advantages in this respect as the cylindrical bin.

Aeration system

Both propeller and centrifugal types of blowers are used for aeration. Centrifugal blowers may have either forward-curved or backward-curved blades.

The air flow and static pressure requirements for different types of grains and for different depths of grains are given in Table VIII (Appendix).

Air distribution system

Sufficient care should be taken in selecting and designing the air distribution system so that air is uniformly distributed throughout the grain bulk and void pockets are avoided. There are f.ve major systems of air distribution :

(a) Perforated floor,
(b) Central horizontal duct,
(c) Main duct and laterals, and
(d) Vertical slatted duct.

(a) *Perforated floor*

The circular storage bin (Fig. 5.1 can be fitted with the perforated false floor through which unheated air is blown. Though the system is suitable for small and medium sized round bins and for small depths of grain, it is used for large rectangular bins and for higher grain depths as well.

(b) *Central horizontal duct*

This system is used in the quonset type units (Fig. 5.7). This type of duct with openings in the wall can distribute air more uniformly through the grain bulk.

(c) *Main duct and laterals*

The system of main duct and laterals is most commonly used and is adopted in round, square and even rectangular bins (Figs. 5.1b, 5.4 and 5.6). The laterals are open at the bottom and raised off the floor of the bin so that the air can flow through the mass. The laterals are inverted V or U or rectangular in shape and are made of wood or steel or concrete or ferro-cement. The laterals are spaced in accordance with the size of the storage unit, quantity of grain to be aerated or dried and depth of the grain (Figs. 5.8 to 5.10).

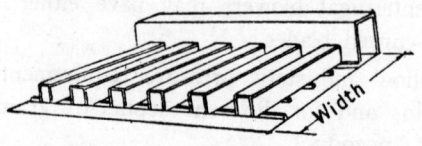

FIG. 5.8. Main side duct and laterals.

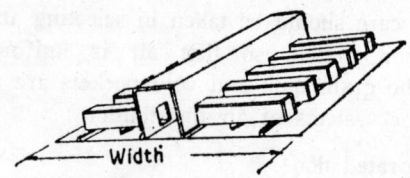

FIG. 5.9. Main central duct and laterals.

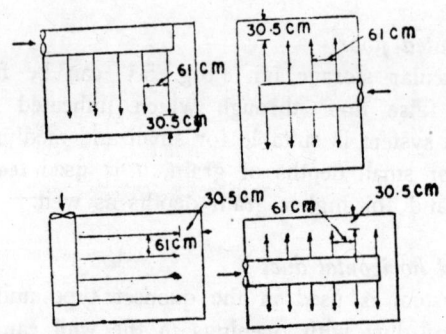

FIG. 5.10. Four common floor layouts for the main duct and laterals in bins.

In round bins the ducts can also be placed in the form of a ring on the bin floor.

(d) *Vertical ducts*

This system consists of either a vertical slatted duct (Figs.5.2 and 5.3) or a central vertical perforated tube (Fig. 5.11a). The air is blown through the slots or perforations and is spread laterally through the grain mass.

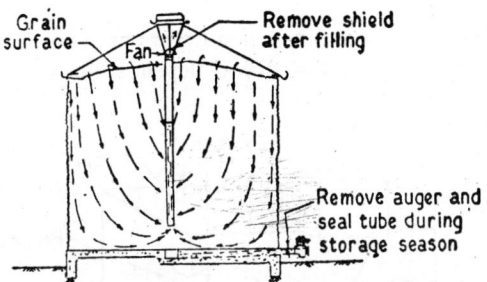

FIG. 5.11a.   Vertical duct aeration system for round bins.

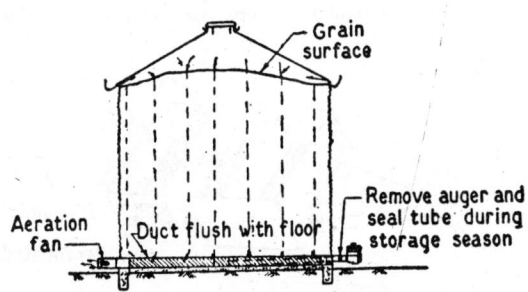

FIG. 5.11b.   Horizontal duct aeration system for round bins.

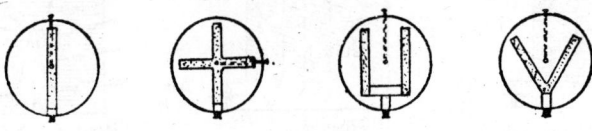

FIG. 5.11c.   Different duct patterns for aeration.

HEATED AIR DRYERS

Flat Bed Type Batch Dryer

This is a static, deep bed, batch dryer. This type of batch dryer is very simple in design and is most popular for on-farm drying in many countries.

Construction

The rectangular box type batch dryers are shown in Figs. 5.12 to 5.14. The size of the dryer depends on the area of the

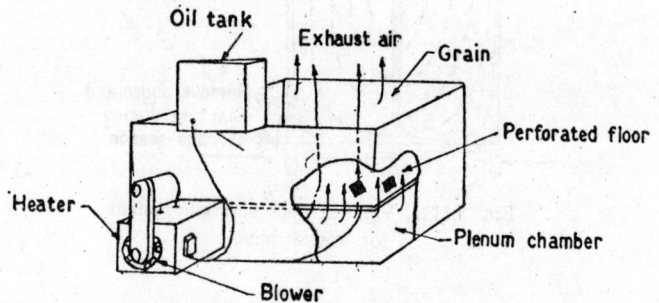

FIG. 5.12. Rectangular flat bed type batch dryer (Japan).

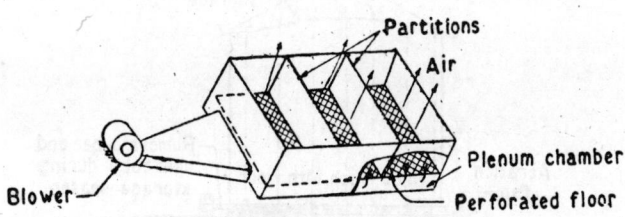

FIG. 5.13. Rectangular flat bed type batch dryer with partitions.

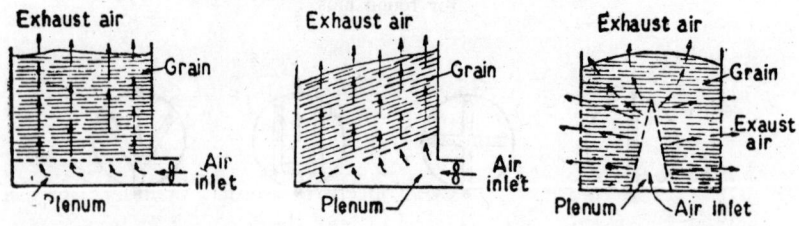

FIG. 5.14. Some aeration systems for deep bed batch dryers.

supporting perforated screen on which the grain is placed. The holding capacity of these dryers ranges from 0.25 to 1 tonne/batch only. The horsepower of the motor for the blower ranges from 1/4 to 1. For convenience an oil burner can be used but for economy a husk fired furnace should be used for the supply of heat.

Operation

The grain is placed on the supporting screen and the heated air is forced through the deep bed of grain. After drying of grains to the desired moisture level, they are discharged manually.

The temperature of the heated air should be limited to 45°C. The drying rate varies with the drying temperature.

Air flow rate varies from 20 to 40 m³/min per 1000 kg of raw paddy depending on the initial moisture content.

Advantages

(1) Fairly reasonable price.
(2) Intermittent drying can also be used.
(3) Operation is very simple.
(4) It can be manufactured locally using various types of materials like steel sheet, wood piece, etc.
(5) It can be used for seed drying and for storage purpose also after drying.

Disadvantages

(1) Rate of drying is slow.
(2) Uneven drying which results in higher percentage of brokens in grains.
(3) Holding capacity is small compared to flow dryers.

Recirculatory Batch Dryer (PHTC type)

This is a continuous flow non mixing type of grain dryer.

Construction

The dryer consists of two concentric circular cylinders made of perforated (2 mm dia) mild steel sheet of 20 gaug. The

6

two cylinders are set 15 to 20 cm apart. These two cylinders are supported on four channel sections. The whole frame can be supported by a suitable foundation or may be bolted to a frame made of channel section. A bucket elevator of suitable capacity is used to feed and recirculate the grain into the dryer. A centrifugal blower blows the hot air into the inner cylinder which acts as a plenum. The hot air from the plenum passes through the grain moving downward by gravity and comes out of the outer perforated cylinder. A torch burner is employed to supply the necessary heat with kerosene oil as fuel. The designs of PHTC dryer for 1/2, 1 and 2 tonnes holding capacity are available. The PHTC dryer of 2 tonnes holding capacity developed at PHTC, IIT, Kharagpur, India is shown in Fig. 5.15.

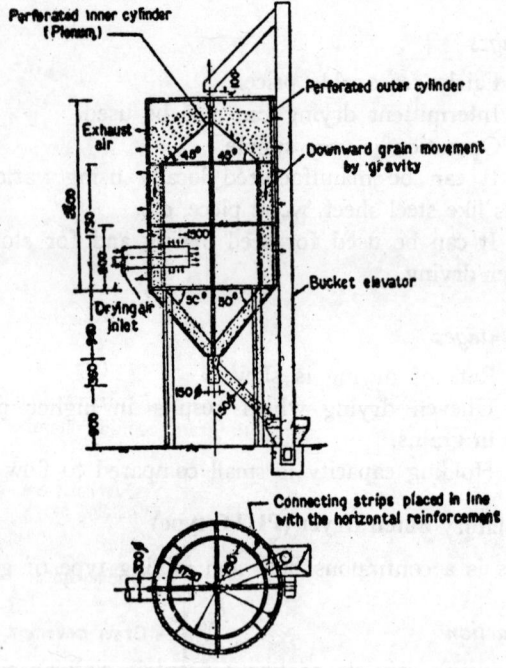

FIG. 5.15. PHTC Recirculating batch dryer (Holding capacity—2 tonnes).

Some Columnar Dryers (Non-Mixing)

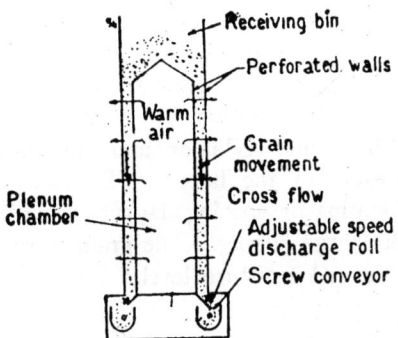

FIG. 5.16. Continuous flow type non-mixing double columnar dryer.

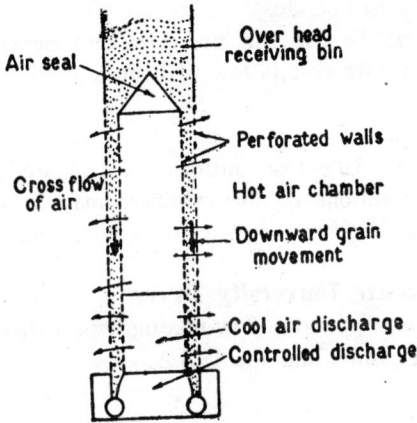

FIG. 5.17. Continuous flow type non-mixing double screen columnar dryer with grain cooling chamber.

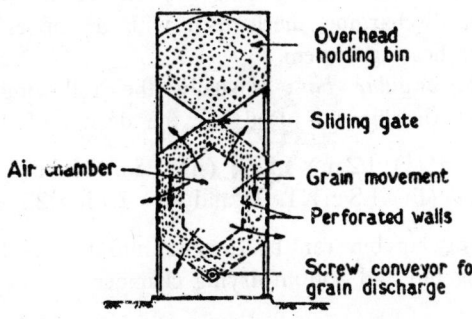

FIG. 5.18. Columnar dryer with overhead tempering bin.

Operation

The grain is fed to the top of the inside cylinder. While descending through the annular space from the feed end to the discharge end by gravity, the grain comes in contact with a cross flow of hot air. The exhaust air comes out through the perforations of the outer cylinder and the grain is discharged through the outlet of the hopper. The feed rate of grain is controlled by closing or opening the gate provided with the outlet pipe of the discharge hopper. The grain is recirculated till it is dried to the desired moisture level.

Advantages

(1) Price is reasonable.
(2) Simplest design amongst all flow type dryers.
(3) Easy to operate.
(4) It can be used on the farm and rice mill as well.
(5) Operating cost is low with husk fired furnace.

Disadvantages

(1) Drying is not so uniform as compared to mixing type.
(2) Perforations of the cylinders may be clogged with the parboiled paddy after using it for a long time.

Louisiana State University Dryer

This is a continuous flow-mixing type of grain dryer which is popular in India and the U.S.A.

Construction

It consists of : (1) a rectangular drying chamber fitted with air ports and the holding bin, (2) an air blower with duct, (3) grain discharging mechanism with a hopper bottom, and (4) an air heating system.

(1) *Rectangular bin* : Usually the following top square sections of the bin are used for the design of LSU dryers :

(i) 1.2 m×1.2 m, (ii) 1.5 m×1.5 m,
(iii) 1.8 m×1.8 m and (iv) 2.1 m×2.1 m.

The rectangular bin can be divided into two sections, namely, top holding bin and bottom drying chamber.

(2) *Air distribution system* : Layers of inverted V-shaped channels (called inverted V-ports) are installed in the drying chamber. Heated air is introduced at many points through the descend-

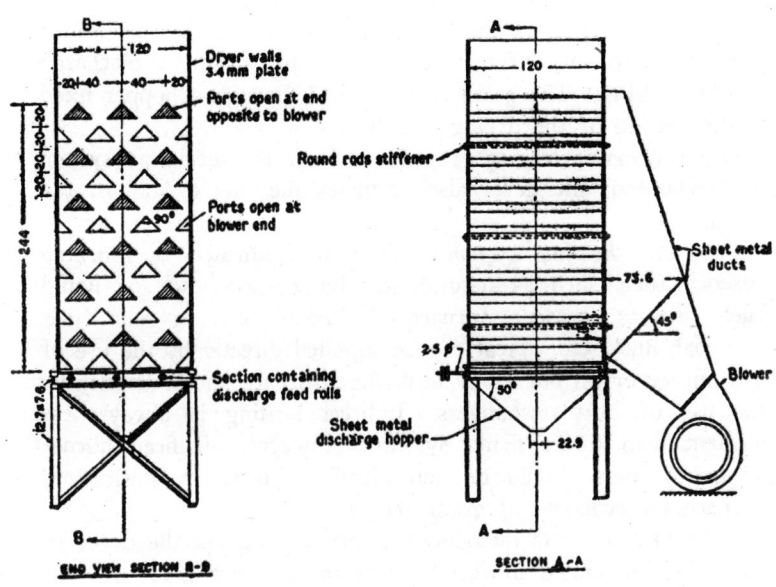

FIG. 5.19. LSU Type dryer details.

ing grain bulk through these channels. One end of each air channel has an opening and the other end is sealed. Alternate layers are air inlet and air outlet channels. In the inlet layers, the channel openings face the air inlet plenum chamber but they are sealed at the opposite wall, where as in the outlet layers, the channel openings face the exhaust but are sealed other side. The inlet and outlet ports are arranged one below the other in an offset pattern." Thus air is forced through the descending grain while moving from the feed end to the discharge end. The inlet ports consist of a few full size ports and two half size ports at two sides. All these ports of same size are arranged in equal spacing between them. The number of ports containing a dryer varies widely depending on the size of the dryer.

Each layer is offset so that the top of the inverted V ports helps in splitting the stream of grain and flowing the grains between these ports taking a zigzag path.

In most models, the heated air is supplied by a blower.

(3) *Grain discharging mechanism* : Three or more ribbed rollers are provided at the bottom of the drying chamber which can be rotated at different low speeds for different discharge rates of grains. The grain is discharged through a hopper fixed at the bottom of the drying chamber.

Causing some mixing of grain and air the discharge system at the base of the dryer also regulates the rate of fall of the grain.

(4) *Air heating system* : The air is heated by burning gaseous fuels such as natural gas, butane gas, etc., or liquid fuels such as kerosene, furnace oil, fuel oil, etc., or solid fuels like coal, husk, etc. Heat can be supplied directly by the use of gas burner or oil burner or husk fired furnace and indirectly by the use of heat exchangers. Indirect heating is always less efficient than direct firing system. However, oil fired burner or gas burners should be immediately replaced by husk fired furnace for economy of grain drying.

The heated air is introduced at many points in the dryer so as to be distributed uniformly through the inlet ports and the descending grain bulk. It escapes through the outlet ports.

This type of dryer is sometimes equipped with a special fan to blow ambient air from the bottom cooling section in which the dried or partially dried warm grain comes in contact with the ambient air.

In general, the capacity of the dryer **varies** from 2 to 12 tonnes of grain, but sometimes dryers of higher capacities are also installed. Accordingly power requirement varies widely.

Recommended air flow rate is 60—70 m^3/min/tonne of parboiled paddy and optimum air temperatures are 60° C and 85° C for raw and parboiled paddy respectively. A series of dryers can also be installed.

Advantages

(1) Uniformly dried product can be obtained if the dryer is designed properly.

(2) The dryer can be used for different types of grains.

Disadvantages

  (1) High capital investment.

  (2) Cost of drying is very high if oil is used as fuel.

Baffle Dryer

  This is a continuous flow mixing type of grain dryer (Figs. 5.20 and 5.21).

Construction

  The baffle dryer consists of : (1) grain receiving bin, (2) drying chamber fitted with baffles, (3) plenum fitted with hot air inlet, (4) grain discharge control device, and (5) hopper bottom. A number of baffles are fitted with the drying chamber to divert the flow and effect certain degree of mixing of grain. The two baffle plates with the outer and inner sides are set 20 cm apart for the passage of the grain in the drying chamber. The dryer is made of mild steel sheet.

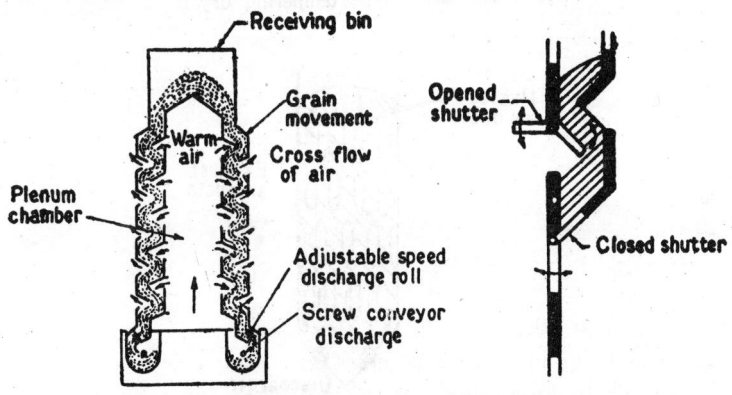

FIG. 5.20. Mixing type baffle dryer.

Operation

  Grain is fed at the top of the receiving bin and allowed to move downward in a zigzag path through the drying chamber where it encounters a cross flow of hot air. On account of zigzag movement, a certain degree of mixing of grain takes place. The partially dried grain discharged from the hopper bottom is recirculated by a bucket elevator until it is dried to the desired moisture level.

Some of the dryers are fitted with a large overhead bin at the top which acts as an overhead tempering bin. This type of tempering dryer is shown in Fig. 5.21.

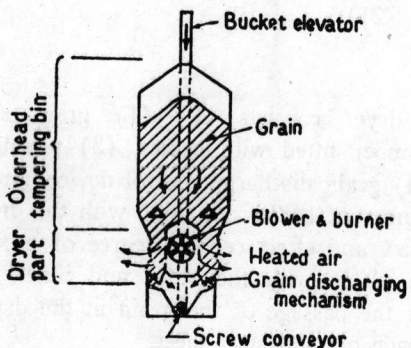

FIG. 5.21. Baffle type tempering dryer.

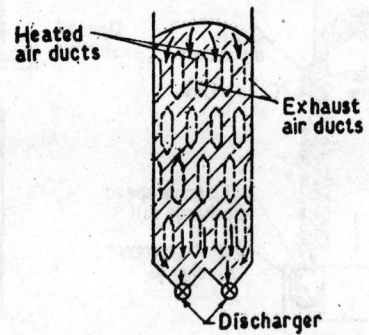

FIG. 5.22. Multiple air ducts type dryer.

Advantages

(1) Uniformly dried product is obtained.

Disadvantages

(1) Ratio of the volume of plenum to the total volume of the dryer is relatively high.

(2) Grains on the baffle plates move slowly than that of other sections. Other advantages and disadvantages are same as described in LSU dryer.

Rotary Dryer

This is a continuous dryer (Fig. 5.23) as it produces the final dried product continuously. Horizontal rotary dryers of various designs have been developed by different countries for the drying of parboiled paddy. Some of them are fitted with external steam jacket and internal steam tubes as well. As parboiled paddy can stand high temperature without significant increase of cracks in grains, these dryers can be employed for rapid drying of parboiled paddy using temperatures as high as 100 to 110° C. In India, the Jadavpur University, Calcutta introduced a rotary dryer of 1 tonne/hr capacity for the drying of parboiled paddy. The construction and operation of the same dryer are described as follows.

Construction

It consists of a cylindrical shell 9.15 m long and 1.22 m in diameter, with 48 pairs of 5 cm and 3.75 cm size steam pipes

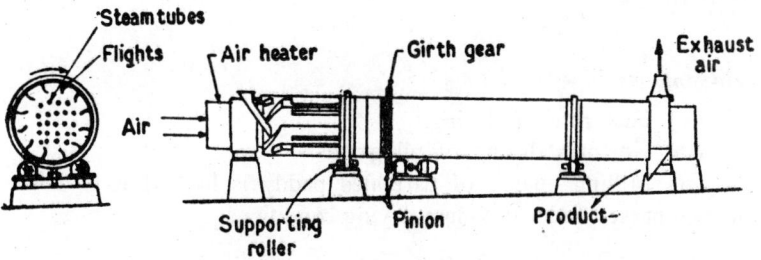

Fig. 5.23. Steam tube rotary dryer.

in two concentric rows inside the shell in combination with common steam inlet and condensate outlet fittings. The shell is equipped with six longitudinal flights of 9.15 m long and 15.24 cm wide for lifting and forward movement of the parboiled paddy towards the discharge end while it is being dried. Over the feed end breeching box there are feed hopper and screw conveyor with an adjustable sliding gate. The dryer is equipped with an air blower and a small steam tube heat exchanger for supplying heated air at the entrance of the feed end breeching box. The cylindrical shell of the dryer is rotated at 2 to 6 rpm by a motor through speed reduction gear, pulley and belt drive system.

Operation

The soaked and steamed paddy is fed to the dryer by the screw feeder. Heated air at about 80° C is blown (from the feed end) through the dryer in the same direction as the paddy moves and exhausted through the exhaust pipe. Heated air acts here mainly as a carrier of moisture from the dryer. While travelling from the feed end to the discharge end of the dryer, the parboiled paddy comes in contact with the steam heated pipes for a very short time in each rotation and is gradually dried to about 16 per cent moisture content in a single pass. Therefore, drying is accomplished mainly by the conduction of heat from the steam pipe to the grain. The travelling time of the grain in the dryer is adjusted to 30 to 45 min by adjusting inclination and rpm of the dryer. The hot paddy discharged from the dryer is then aerated by passing it through a cup and cone type cooler.

Advantages

(1) Fast rate of drying.
(2) Uniform drying of all grains.
(3) Milling quality of parboiled paddy is high if it is dried in two passes under optimum drying conditions.

Disadvantages

(1) Complicated design.
(2) Needs careful attention.
(3) Higher capital investment.
(4) Higher power requirement.
(5) Operating cost may be high due to higher consumption of electricity and steam.

(6) The dryer being horizontal larger floor space is required.

(7) Generally only 30 per cent of the dryer volume is utilised.

(8) It cannot be used for all types of freshly harvested grains.

CHAPTER 6

Selection, Design, Specifications and Testing of Grain Dryers

Selection of Dryers

Many factors have to be considered before the final selection of the most suitable type of dryer for a given application. Such a selection is further complicated by the availability of a large number of different types of dryers. Commercial dryers are not usually flexible enough to compensate for design inaccuracies or for problems associated with the handling of different types of food materials that have not been previously considered. For this reason, it is particularly important that all pertinent points be considered and that drying tests be conducted prior to the final selection of a dryer for a given problem. The following procedure is recommended for the selection of the most suitable dryer to produce the desirable product, economically.

PRELIMINARY DRYER SELECTION

The important factors to be considered in the preliminary selection of a crop dryer are as follows :

(1) Physicochemical properties of the crop being handled.

(2) Drying characteristics of the crop : (a) Type of moisture ; (b) Initial, final and equilibrium moisture contents ; (c) Permissible drying temperature ; and (d) Drying curves and drying times for different crops with different dryers.

(3) Flow of the crop to and from the dryer : (a) Quantity to be handled per hour ; (b) Continuous or batch operation ; and (c) Processes during drying and subsequent to drying.

(4) Product qualities : (a) Colour ; (b) Flavour ; (c) Shrinkage ; (d) Contamination : (e) Uniformity of drying ; (f) Decomposition or conversion of product constituents ;

(g) Overdrying; (h) State of subdivision; (i) Product temperature; (j) Bulk density ; (k) Case hardening ; and (1) Cracking and other desirable qualities of the end products. (5) Dust recovery problems.

(6) Facilities available at the site of proposed installation : (a) Space ; (b) Temperature, humidity and cleanliness of air ; (c) Available fuels ; (d) Available electric power ; (e) Permissible noise, vibration, dust or heat losses ; (f) Source of wet feed ; and (g) Exhaust-gas outlets.

Comparison of dryers

The dryers so selected are to be evaluated on the basis of drying performance and cost data.

DRYING TEST

Drying tests described in this chapter for a given crop have to be carried out with the dryers under consideration to determine the drying performance, operating conditions and the product characteristics. An approximate cost analysis is also useful for evaluation of the dryers.

Final selection of dryer

From the results of the drying tests and cost analyses the final selection of the most suitable dryer can be made.

For successful introduction of any grain dryer at the farm level, a few additional points are to be borne in mind in the selection and design of grain drying system. They are as follows :

(1) The dryer should be of proper size matching with the demand of a farmer, miller or any organisation ;

(2) The price of the dryer should be reasonable ;

(3) The dryer should be simple in design and should be made of different cheap and locally available materials so that it can be manufactured locally ;

(4) It should be easy to operate ;

(5) It should be possible to make the dryer portable, if necessary ;

(6) The operating cost should be minimum. Solar-cum-

furnace (fired with agricultural waste like husk, shells, etc.) air heating system should be introduced in grain drying to minimise the cost of drying ;

(7) The repair and maintenance requirements should be minimum ;

(8) It should be possible to use the dryer for different grains and to be used as a storage bin later for its maximum utilisation.

Design of Grain Dryers

As indicated earlier, heated air grain dryers can be divided into three major groups :

(1) Static deep bed batch dryers ;

(2) Continuous-flow-batch dryer (either mixing or non-mixing type) ; and

(3) Continuous dryer

Grain dryers mainly consist of : (a) drying chamber, (b) air distribution system, (c) direct or indirect air heating system, (d) blower, (e) control system (if any), and (f) grain conveying system (for flow dryers).

The following important factors are taken into consideration in the design of heated air grain dryers :

(1) DRYER FACTORS

(a) Size, shape and type of dryer ;

(b) Grain feeding rate ;

(c) Total drying time ;

(d) Air flow pattern and air distribution system ;

(e) Depth of grain bed in the dryer ; and

(f) System of cooling grain (if any).

(2) AIR FACTORS

(a) Velocity and air flow rate per unit mass of the grain.

(b) Temperatures and relative humidities of the heated air and exhaust air.

(c) Static pressure of the air at which it is blown, and

(d) Average ambient conditions.

(3) GRAIN FACTORS

    (a) Type, variety and condition of grain ;
    (b) Initial and final moisture contents of grain ;
    (c) The *usuage* of dried grain ; and
    (d) Latent heat of vaporisation of grain moisture.

(4) HEATING SYSTEM

    (a) Type of fuel and rate of fuel supply
    (b) Type of burner (for liquid fuel) or type of furnace (for solid fuel) ; and
    (c) Type of heat exchanger (for indirect heating system).

Some of the important design factors have been discussed very briefly in subsequent paragraphs.

Size, shape and type of dryer

Size or capacity of a dryer is decided by the amount and variety of grain to be dried per day or for the whole season.

Sizes of the dryer are expressed either in terms of holding capacity or amount of grain to be dried per unit time or the amount of grain passing through the dryer per unit time (throughput capacity).

Thickness of grain layer exposed to the heated air is generally restricted to 20 cm for continuous flow dryers. The designs of the continuous flow dryers are based on thin layer drying principles whereas static batch dryers are designed on deep bed drying principles. Air flow requirements for different depths and for different grains are given in Table 8 (Appendix). Total drying time required for various air temperatures for different grains are obtained from the drying curves given in Chapter 3 on Theory of Grain Drying.

Choice of a grain dryer largely depends on the situation. Continuous flow dryers are normally used for commercial purposes whereas static deep bed batch dryers are used for on-farm drying. Constructructional features of different types of heated air dryers have been described in Chapter 5. Farm level batch dryers can be made of locally available materials, namely, wood, bamboo, etc., if necessary. But commercial big dryers are made of mild steel sheet, angle iron, channel section supports.

Calculation of air, heat and fuel requirements for heated air dryers

The air flow rate required for heated air drying systems can be calculated as follows :

The rate of air flow required for drying may be calculated by making heat balance. The heated air drying system is represented by :

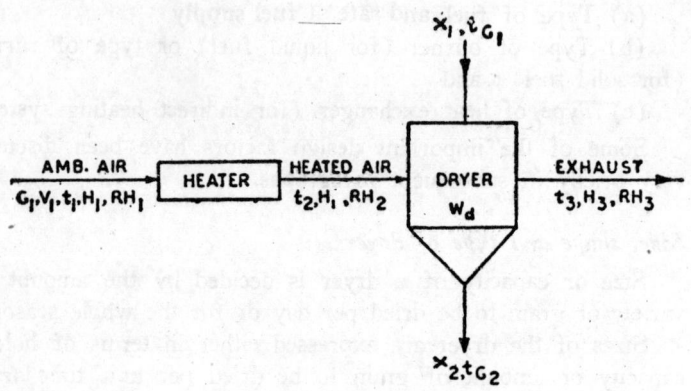

where

G = air flow rate, m^3/min.

H_1, H_2 = humidities of ambient and heated air, kg/kg.

H_3 = humidity of exhaust air, kg/kg.

RH_1, RH_2 & RH_3 = relative humidities of ambient, heated and exhaust air, respectively, per cent.

t_1, t_2 & t_3 = dry bulb temperatures of ambient, heated and exhaust air respectively, ° C.

W_d = total weight of bone dry grain in the dryer, kg.

X_1, X_2 = initial and final moisture contents of grain, (d.b.) kg/kg.

t_{G_1}, t_{G_2} = initial and final grain temperatures, ° C.

v_1 = initial humid volume, m^3/kg.

Heat supplied by drying air, q_a, kcals :

$$q_a = (0.24 + 0.45\, H_1)\, G'\, (t_2 - t_3)\theta$$

Where G' = rate of air supply, kg/min.

θ = total drying time, min.

Amount of heat required :

Heat required for evaporation of moisture from the grain, q_1, kcals :

$$q_1 = W_d \ (X_1 - X_2) \ \lambda$$

where,

λ = average value of latent heat of vaporisation of moisture from the grain, kcals/kg.

Sensible heat required to raise the temperature of the grain and its moisture, q, kcals :

$$q = W_d C_g (t_{G_2} - t_{G_1}) + W_d \ C_w \ (t_{G_2} - t_{G_1}) \ X_1$$

where

C_g, C_w = specific heats of grain and water respectively, Kcal/kg °C

Therefore

$$q_a = q_1 + q$$

or $\quad G' = (0.24 + 0.45 \ H_1) \ (t_2 - t_3) \theta$

$$= W_d \ [(X_1 - X_2)\lambda + C_g (t_{G_2} - t_{G_1}) + C_w (t_{G_2} - t_{G_1}) \ X_1]$$

or $\quad G' = \dfrac{W_d \ [(X_1 - X_2)\lambda + C_g (t_{G_2} - t_{G_1}) + C_w (t_{G_2} - t_{G_1}) \ X_1]}{(0.24 + 0.45 \ H_1)(t_2 - t_3) \ \theta}$

$\therefore \quad G = G' \times v_1$

where v_1 = humid volume.

Fuel consumption :

The rate of fuel consumption can be calculated as follows :

$$f = \dfrac{q'_a}{\eta . \eta_b . \eta_{ex} . C_n}$$

where $\quad f$ = fuel rate, kg/hr.

q'_a = total heat required to heat the drying air, kcal/hr.

C_n = Calorific value of fuel, kcal/kg of fuel.

η = efficiency of the heating system.

η_{ex} = efficiency of the heat exchanger.

η_6 = efficiency of the boiler, if any.

Drying air temperature

Correct choice of drying air temperature for a given type of grain is very important as it has effects on the quality of the dried product. The highest allowable air temperature for drying of grain depends on the type and condition of grain and the usage of dried grain. The upper limit of drying air temperatures for different grains to be used for food, feed and seed purposes are different and are given in Table 8 (Appendix).

Grain parameters

The grain factors which affect the rate of drying are as follows :

(a) Type, variety and condition of grain ;

(b) Initial/harvest moisture content, final moisture and equilibrium moisture contents of the grain ;

(c) Structure and chemical composition of the kernel, seed coat, husk etc., and

(d) Foreign materials present in the grain.

The above stated factors, are, therefore, to be considered in the design of grain dryers. Over and above, data on physical properties such as bulk density, angle of repose, porosity, angle of internal friction, flow properties of grain, aerodynamic properties and thermal properties (specific heat, thermal conductivity, etc.) are required in the design of a grain dryer and are thus taken into consideration. Some of these properties are tabulated in Tables 3 to 6 (Appendix).

AIR FLOW PATTERN AND AIR DISTRIBUTION

Any one of the three systems of air flow namely cross flow, counter flow and co-current flow can be adopted in flow type grain dryers. Generally cross flow of air is preferred. Double screen (say RPEC type) and baffle types of columnar dryers have a plenum chamber and LSU dryer has inverted V shaped air channels for uniform distribution of air throughout the drying chamber. The deep bed batch dryer has the plenums at the bottom of the grain drying chamber. These systems have been shown in Chapter 5 on Grain Dryers.

CONVEYING AND HANDLING SYSTEM

Suitable conveying equipments for loading, discharging, recirculating and shifting of grain before, during and after drying of grain are necessary for the grain drying system. Bucket elevators, vertical screw lifts for feeding, hopper bottom with proper inclination for grain discharging are commonly used. Forced discharge mechanism with slowly rotating fluted rolls are used for better control of the feed rate and drying rate. Dried grain from the dryer is usually conveyed to different places by belt conveyor or screw conveyor and bucket elevator.

AIR HEATING SYSTEM

Generally direct firing systems are used for gaseous and liquid fuels and indirect heating system using heat exchangers is employed for solid fuels. But direct flue gas from the husk fired furnace can also be efficiently used for grain drying. In view of the present energy crisis, the liquid or gaseous fuel burning system should be immediately replaced by the agricultural waste (husk, shells, bagasse, etc.) fired furnace for the supply of heated air economically. The drying cost can be further reduced by introducing solar-cum-husk fired grain drying system.

SPECIFICATIONS
Table—Specifications of dryer and its accessories.

Name of the unit/part	Sl. No.	Items
Dryer	1.	Name of the dryer
	2.	Type of the dryer
	3.	Model of dryer
	4.	Manufacturer's name and address
	5.	Holding capacity of dryer (tonnes)
	6.	Dimensions of dryer (cm)
	7.	Total height of dryer, and ground clearance (cm)
	8.	Total weight of dryer (kg)
	9.	Safety measures of dryer (if any)
	10.	H.P. required for feed rolls
	11.	Total H.P. requirement
	12	Total power requirement (KW)
	13.	Price of the dryer (Rs.)
Drying chamber	1.	Type of drying section (screen, baffle, etc.)
	2.	Dimensions (cm)
	3.	Grain holding capacity (kg)
	4.	Dimensions of the plenum (for double screen and baffle type)
	5.	Size and number of air ports (for LSU type)
	6.	Ratio of plenum volume to the whole drying chamber volume
	7.	Thickness of grain layer (grain depth) in drying section
	8.	Mesh No. of the screen (for double screen)
	9.	Dimensions and position of hopper
	10.	Grain distribution mechanism
	11.	Grain discharging mechanism
Blower	1.	Blower type
	2.	Dimensions (cm)
	3.	Rated capacity of blower (m³/min)
	4.	Static pressure (mm water)
	5.	Diameter of discharge outlet (cm)
	6.	Diameter of inlet port (cm)
	7.	Rated H.P. of the blower motor
	8.	Recommended speed of blower (rpm)
	9.	No. of rotary blades/impeller vanes
	10.	Diameter of rotary blades/impeller (cm)

Name of the unit/part	Sl. No.	Items
Control System	1.	Drying air temperature range and control
	2.	Air flow rate control
	3.	Grain flow rate control
	4.	Any other control

Handling Equipments

Bucket elevator	1.	Capacity (tonnes/hr)
	2.	Total height (cm)
	3.	Height from the ground level (cm)
	4.	Shape and size of bucket
	5.	Number of buckets
	6.	Position of grain inlet and outlet
	7.	Rated speed of main shaft (rpm)
	8.	Material of construction
	9.	Power requirement
Screw Conveyor	1.	Capacity (tonnes/hr)
	2.	Speed of shaft (rpm)
	3.	Outer diameter of screw (cm)
	4.	Outer diameter of shaft (cm)
	5.	Pitch (cm)
	6.	Length of the screw (cm)
	7.	Clearance between the screw tip and housing troughs (mm)
	8.	Material and thickness of flight (cm)
	9.	Power requirement

Air Heating System

Oil Burner		Type of fuel used and its calorific value (kcals/kg)
		Direct or indirect firing
	1.	Dimensions (cm)
	2.	Built-in type or separate
	3.	Type of burner
	4.	Nozzle diameter (cm)
	5.	Burner rating (kg/min)
	6.	Fuel and air ratio (kg/kg)
	7.	Required pressure for atomising (kg/cm^2)
	8.	Fuel feeding method and control
	9.	Material of construction
	10.	Capacity of the fuel storage tank (litres)
	11.	Method of temperature control
	12.	Method of ignition and extinguishing
	13.	Safety device

Testing of Grain Dryers

No generalised test procedure can be adopted for all types of grain dryers. The testing method for static deep bed batch dryer cannot be same as that of continuous flow thin layer dryers. It is always preferable that test procedure for each type of dryer be designed separately.

However, for convenience, the dryer testing method can be broadly divided into two major heads : simple method and rigorous method. Either of these two methods can be adopted in accordance with the objectives of the test.

SIMPLE METHOD

A simple test procedure is so designed as to determine the approximate performance of the grain dryer.

The simple test procedure for a batch dryer is tabulated as follows :

Test Procedures for the Performance of the Static Deep Bed Batch dryer

	Type and model No. of dryer : Type of grain and variety
Grain	1. Initial weight of wet grain (kg) 2. Final weight of dried grain (kg) 3. Initial moisture content (per cent) 4. Final moisture content (per cent) 5. Dryer loading time (hr) 6. Dryer unloading time (hr) 7. Average drying grain temperature (°C)

Type of grain and variety

	1. Air flow rate (maximum) (m³/min)
	2. Air flow rate (minimum) (m³/min)
	3. Max. static pressure (mm water)
	4. Min. static pressure (mm water)
Air	5. Average ambient d.b. temp. (° C)
	6. Average ambient w.b. temp. (°C)
	7. Average heated air d.b. temp. (° C)
	8. Average heated air w.b. temp. (° C)
	9 Average exhaust air d.b. temp. (° C)
	10 Average exhaust air w.b. temp (° C)
	1. Total drying time (hr)
	2. Cooling time (if any) (hr)
Drying capacity	3. Total moisture evaporation (kg)
	4. Rate of moisture evaporation (kg/hr)
	5. Rate of dried grain productions (tonnes/hr)
	1. Air heating method (oil fired burner/husk fired furnace/steam heat exchanger)
	2. Type of air heating (direct/indirect)
	3. When oil fired burner/husk fired furnace is used
	(a) type of fuel and cal. value
	(b) total fuel consumption (kg)
Heater and Fuel	(c) rate of fuel consumption (kg/hr)
	4. When steam heat exchanger is used
	(a) incoming steam pressure (kg/cm²)
	(b) rate of condensate outflow (kg/hr)
	(c) Temp. of condensate (° C)

Type of grain and variety	
Power	1. Power consumption for blowing air to burner (KW) 2. Power consumption for pumping oil to burner (KW) 3. Power consumption for blowing heated air (KW) 4. Power consumption for loading and unloading grain (KW) 5. Power consumption for running feed rolls (KW)
Quality of dried grain	1. Germination of grain before drying (per cent) 2. Germination after drying (per cent) 3. Head yield before drying (per cent—for paddy) 4. Total yield before drying (per cent) 5. Head yield after drying (per cent) 6. Total yield after drying (per cent) 7. Other quality factors

The simple test procedure for continuous flow dryer

Besides the test items tabulated in the above Table, the following items are to be taken into consideration for continuous flow dryers :

(1) Moisture content after each pass (per cent) ;
(2) Residence time in the dryer for each circulation (hr) ;
(3) Number of passes ;
(4) Tempering time (hr) ;
(5) Average rate of moisture reduction or rate of moisture evaporation in each circulation (kg/hr) ;
(6) Rate of grain recirculation (tonnes/hr) ;
(7) Drying air temperature at each pass ($^\circ$ C) ;
(8) Weight of remaining grain in the dryer, elevator, etc. (kg).

Rigorous method

Rigorous test procedures for some batch and continuous flow dryers are given as follows. The whole test procedure can be grouped into the following major heads :

(1) Checking of construction ;
(2) Drying performance test ;
(3) Fan/blower performance test ;
(4) Control system performance test ;
(5) Handling equipments performance test ; and
(6) Checking of different dryer–parts after disassembling (after the drying tests).

(1) CHECKING OF CONSTRUCTION

The purpose of this test is to ascertain the major dimensions, material of construction and other necessary specifications of the dryer and its accessories.

Investigation items

Specifications of : (a) dryer as a whole, (b) drying chamber with air distribution system, (c) blower, (d) heating system and (e) conveying units such as bucket elevator, grain distributor, screw conveyor, belt conveyor, etc. .

The specifications of the above items have already been discussed earlier.

(2) DRYING PERFORMANCE TEST

The objectives of this test are to determine the drying performance of a dryer on the basis of rate of drying, rate of consumption of fuel and electricity, heat utilisation, quality of the dried grain and other operating conditions.

The investigation items have already been tabulated.

(3) BLOWER PERFORMANCE TEST

The objective of this test is to determine the performance of the fan/blower attached with the dryer.

Investigation items

(a) Power input, kw, (b) air flow rate, m^3/min., (3) static and total pressure, mm water, (d) static pressure efficiency, and (e) vibration, noise and other working conditions of the blower.

(4). PERFORMANCE OF THE CONTROL SYSTEM

The objective of this test is to find out the accuracy of :
(a) The control of drying air temperature and the temperature
of heating unit, (b) control of air flow rate etc., and (c) other
working conditions of the whole control system.

Investigation items

(a) Accuracy of the temperature control with the heating
unit, (b) accuracy of the temperature control of the drying air,
(c) variation of heated air temperature at different points,
(d) air flow rate control and any other control system, and
(e) any mechanical trouble with the system.

(5) PERFORMANCE OF THE HANDLING EQUIPMENT

The rated and actual capacities and other working conditions
of the conveying and handling equipments are to be found out.
This has already been discussed earlier.

(6) INVESTIGATION AFTER DISASSEMLING

This is necessary to investigate the conditions of different
parts of various units after completion of the drying test.

PROBLEMS ON DRYER DESIGN

Solved problems

(1) Design a PHTC–recirculating batch dryer having
holding capacity of 2 tonnes of paddy with 15 per cent m.c.
(w.b.).

Assume the following data :

Ambient air temp. = 30° C
Relative humidity of ambient air = 70 per cent
Initial m.c. of paddy = 30 per cent (w.b.)
Final m.c. of paddy = 15 per cent (w.b.)
Grain inlet temp. = 30° C
Grain outlet temp. = 70° C
Heated air temp. = 85° C
Exhaust air temp. = 40° C
Latent heat of water vapour = 600 kcal/kg
Angle of repose = 45°

Thickness of grain bed to be dried $= 20$ cm
Bulk density of paddy grain at 15 per cent m.c.
    $= 575$ kg/m^3
Diameter of plenum chamber $= 135$ cm
Diameter of dryer $= 175$ cm
Hopper angle $= 50°$
Drying time $= 3$ hrs.

Solution

Assumptions

(1) Distance between top of dryer and top of plenum chamber $= 15$ cm
(2) Angle of conical portion of plenum chamber $= 45°$
(3) Diameter of grain outlet $= 15$ cm
(4) Specific heat of grain $= 0.4$ kcal/(kg) ($°$ C)

Height of the dryer

Height, $H = H_1 + H_3$

$$H_1 = H_2 + \frac{135}{2} \tan 45° + 15 = H_2 + 82.5$$

$$H_3 = \frac{175 - 15}{2} \tan 50° = 95.34 = 96 \text{ cm}$$

Volume of plenum chamber

$V_1 =$ volume of inner cylinder + volume of inner cones

$$V_1 = \frac{\pi}{4}(135)^2 H_2 + 2 \cdot \frac{1}{3} \cdot \pi \left(\frac{135}{2}\right)^2 \left(\frac{135}{2} \tan 45°\right)$$

or $V_1 = 14313.88 H_1 - 536770.53$ (1)

Suppose $V_2 =$ Volume of outer cylinder and hopper bottom

$$\therefore \quad V_2 = \frac{\pi}{4} \times (175)^2 \times H_1 + \frac{1}{3} \cdot \pi \cdot \tan 50° \left[\left(\frac{175}{2}\right)^3 - \left(\frac{15}{2}\right)^3\right]$$ (2)

$$= 24055.9 H_1 + 831557 \text{ cm}^3$$

Volume of drying chamber $= V_2 - V_1$

$$= 24055.9 H_1 + 831557 - 14313.88 H_1 + 536770$$

$$= 9742.02 H_1 + 1368327$$ (3)

Volume of the drying chamber $= \frac{2000}{575} = 3.478 \text{ m}^3$

$$= 3478000 \text{ cm}^3$$ (4)

Hence from equations (3) and (4)

$$9742.02H_1 + 1368327 = 3478000$$

$$H_1 = 216 \text{ cm}$$

$$H_1 \backsimeq 220 \text{ cm}$$

$$H_2 = 220 - 82.5 = 137.5 \text{ cm}$$

$$\therefore \quad H_2 \backsimeq 140 \text{ cm}$$

$$H_3 = 96 \text{ cm}$$

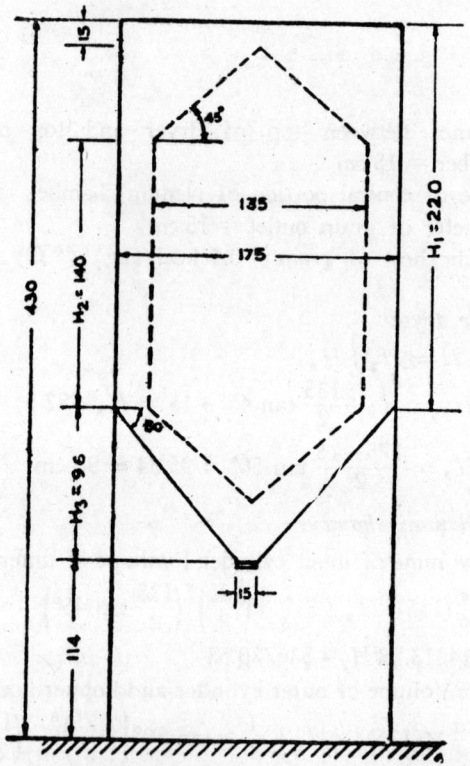

FIG. 6.1. Specifications of PHTC dryer as per
solution of problem 1.

Air requirement

Bone dry paddy = 2000 $(1-0.15)$ = 1700 kg.

Initial moisture content = 30 per cent w.b. = 42.857 per cent (d.b.)

Final moisture content = 15 per cent (w.b.) = 17.647 per cent (d.b.)

Weight of moisture evaporated

$$= \text{Wt. of bone dry paddy} \times (X_1 - X_2)$$
$$= 1700 \ (0.42857 - 0.17647)$$
$$= 428.57 \ \text{kg.}$$

From psychrometric chart

Absolute humidity of ambient air = 0.019 kg/kg
Humid heat of ambient air

$$S = 0.24 + 0.45 \ H$$
$$= 0.24 + 0.45 \times 0.019$$
$$= 0.24855 \ \text{kcal/(kg)} \ (^{\circ}C)$$

Let G be the rate of air supply in kg/min
Heat supplied by the air in 180 min

$$= G. \ S. \ (t_2 - t_1).\theta$$
$$= G \ (0.24855) \ (85 - 40) \times 3 \times 60$$
$$= 2013.255 \ G \tag{5}$$

Heat Utilised

(i) As sensible heat of grain

$$= \text{B.D. grain} \times \text{sp. heat of grain} \times \text{temp. rise}$$
$$= 1700 \times 0.4 \times (70 - 30)$$
$$= 27200 \ \text{kcal} \tag{6}$$

(ii) As sensible heat of water

$$= \text{total weight of water} \times \text{sp. heat of water} \times \text{temp. rise}$$
$$= 1700 \times 0.42857 \times 1.0 \times (70 - 30)$$
$$= 29140 \ \text{kcal} \tag{7}$$

(iii) As latent heat of water vapour

$$= \text{water evaporated} \times \text{latent heat of water}$$
$$= 428.57 \times 600$$
$$= 2,57,100 \ \text{kcal} \tag{8}$$

Total heat utilised = sum of (6), (7) and (8)
$$= 3,13,440 \ \text{kcal} \tag{9}$$

Suppose, heat loss = 10 per cent

$$\text{Net heat required} = \frac{313440}{0.9} = 3,48,266.6 \ \text{kcal}$$

Hence, 2013.255 $G = 3,48,266.6$

$\qquad\qquad G\ = 172.987$ kg/min

From psychrometric chart, humid volume of the ambient air

$\qquad\qquad\qquad\qquad = 0.88$ m^3/kg

So air required $\qquad = 172.987 \times 0.884$

$\qquad\qquad\qquad\qquad = 152.92$ m^3/min

Air requirement $\quad = 155$ m^3/min

Static pressure drop

$\qquad$ Surface area of plenum chamber

$$= \pi \times 135 \times 140 + \left[\frac{1}{2}\pi \times 135 \times \left(\frac{135}{2}\ \sec\ 45°\right)\right] \times 2$$

$$= 59383.8 + 28627.76$$

$$= 88011.56\ \text{cm}^2$$

Since maximum 50 per cent of the area is perforated, area through which air passes $= 44005.78$ cm^2

Air requirement per $m^2 = \dfrac{155}{4.400578}$

$$= 35.1\ \text{m}^3/\text{min/m}^2$$

From Shedd's curve (Agri. Engg. Handbook) static pressure drop for 32.12 m^3/min/m^2 = 8.13 cm of water per 30.48 cm grain depth.

Depth of grain = 20 cm

So pressure drop $= \dfrac{8.13}{30.48} \times 20 = 5.42$ cm of water

Density of air = 1.13/kg/m^3

Pressure drop in terms of air column $= \dfrac{5.42}{100} \times \dfrac{1000}{1.13}$

$$= 47.95\ \text{m}$$

H.P. required

$$= \frac{\text{Height of air column (m)} \times \text{air flow rate (kg/min)}}{4500}$$

$$= \frac{47.95}{4500} \times 172.987$$

$$= 1.868\ \text{hp}$$

$$\backsimeq 2\ \text{hp}.$$

(2) Design a LSU Dryer of 2 tonnes holding capacity with

paddy at 15 per cent m.c. (w.b.). Data for grain and air parameters are same as in the previous problem. Additional data are given below.

Cross-section of the dryer $= 1.2 \times 1.2$ m^2
Air velocity in the air ports $= 5$ m/sec
Pitch of the air ports $= 40$ cm
Row to row spacing $= 20$ cm
Grain residence time $= 30$ minutes

Solution

The heat and mass balance for the dryer are same as those in the previous problem.
Hence, air required $= 155$ m^3/min
Since velocity of air inside the air port or duct is 5 m/sec total cross-sectional area of ducts required

$$= \frac{155}{5 \times 60} = 0.5167 \text{ m}^2$$

Let the height of drying chamber be h cm
Therefore, volume of drying chamber

$V = $ Volume of the drying chamber $-$ Volume of ducts
$= 1.2 \times 1.2 \times h - 0.5167 \times 1.2$
$V = (1.44\,h - 0.62)\,\text{m}^3$ (1)

The holding capacity of the dryer is given as 2 tonnes of paddy at 15 per cent m.c. (w.b.) and the bulk density of paddy at 15% m.c. is $= 575$ kg/m^3

Hence, volume $V = \dfrac{2000}{575} = 3.478$ m^3 (2)

Substituting for V in equation (1)
1.44 $h - 0.620 = 3.478$
1.44 $h = 4.098$
$h = 2.846$ m

Height of the grain holding bin $= 35$ cm (assumed)
Height of the hopper bottom $= 60$ cm (approx.)
According to spacing, number of ducts in a row $= 3$
and number of rows in 2.85 m $= 14$
Total number of ducts $= 39$ (leaving 1 row for discharge rolls)

Cross-sectional area of each duct $= \dfrac{0.5167}{39} \times 10^4$ cm^2

$\qquad\qquad\qquad\qquad\qquad\qquad = 132.5$ cm^2

Cross-sectional area of each duct $= \dfrac{1}{2}\, b \cdot \dfrac{b}{2}$

or $\dfrac{b^2}{4} = 132.5$

or $\quad b = 23.02 = 23$ cm

Let there be three discharge rolls having shaft diameter 2.5 cm and flute diameter 7.5 cm

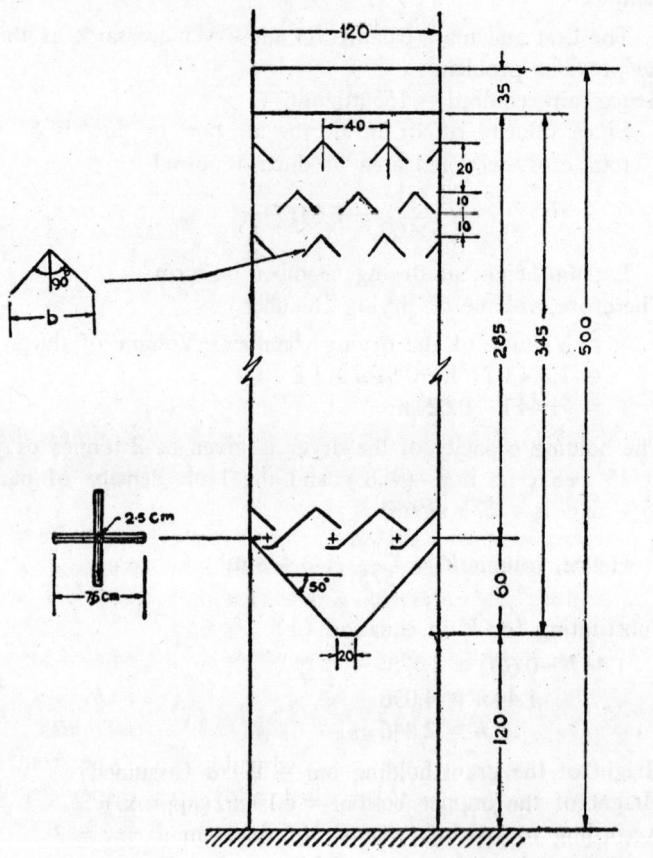

All dimensions in cm

FIG. 6.2 Specifications of LSU dryer as per solution of problem 2.

Volume discharged by each roll in one revolution

$$= \frac{\pi}{4}(D_o{}^2 - D_i{}^2)L$$

$$= \frac{\pi}{4}(7.5^2 - 2.5^2) \, 120$$

$$= 4712.39 \text{ cm}^3.$$

$\therefore$ Volume discharged by 3 rolls = 0.014137 m³/revolution
Wt. of paddy discharged = 0.014137×575 = 8.129 kg/revolution
Since the grain retention time in the dryer is 30 minutes,

grain discharge rate $= \frac{2000}{30} = 66.67$ kg/min

$\therefore$ Roller speed $= \frac{66.67}{8.129} = 8.2$ rpm ≈ 8 rpm

Specifications of the LSU dryer of 2 tonnes grain holding capacity :

Total height of the dryer = 3.8 m
Height of drying chamber = 2.85
Height of the holding bin = 0.35 m
Height of the hopper bottom = 0.60 m
Number of feed rolls = 3
Grain outlet diameter = 20 cm
Space between inlet and outlet duct = 20 cm
Pitch of ducts in a row = 40 cm
Blower capacity = 155 m³/min with static
pressure 5 cm (W.G)
Blower motor hp = 2
Duct dimensions : height = 11.5 cm, width = 23 cm
Speed of the discharge roll = 8.0 rpm

Exercises

(1) From the following data determine the rate of air supply in a grain dryer :

(a) Holding capacity of the dryer   — 6 Tonnes
(b) Initial m.c. of the parboiled paddy — 30 per cent (w.b.)
(c) Final m.c. of the parboiled paddy   — 15 per cent (w.b.)
(d) Ambient air temp.   — 30° C
(e) Heated air temp.   — 85° C
(f) Exhaust air temp.   — 40° C

8

(g) Grain temp. (at inlet)   — 30° C
(h) Grain temp. (at outlet)   — 70° C
(i) Relative humidity of air before
    heating   — 70 per cent
(j) Total drying time   — 3 hrs
(k) Loss of heat to the surroundings — 20 per cent

(2) Design a recirculating RPEC dryer of 1.25 tonnes holding capacity. Diameter of the plenum chamber (inner cylinder) is 90 cm. Assuming other necessary data as in Example No. 1, determine (i) height of the inner and outer cylinders, (ii) total height of the dryer, (iii) air flow rate, and (iv) H.P. requirement of the blower.

(3) Design a L.S.U. dryer of 2 tonnes/hr capacity. The square cross section of the rectangular chamber is 2.02×2.02 m². Assume other necessary data as in Example No. 2. Calculate (i) total height of the dryer, (ii) number of air ports required, (iii) speed of the discharge roll, and (iv) H.P. of the motor for the discharge rolls.

(4) Assuming all necessary data, design a baffle type grain dryer of 1.25 tonnes holding capacity.

(5) A static deep bed rectangular batch dryer of 1 tonne holding capacity has to be designed. The temperature of the ambient and drying air are 25° C and 40° C respectively. Assuming other necessary data determine (i) the dimensions of the drying chamber and plenum chamber and (ii) capacity of the blower.

SYMBOLS

C_g = specific heat of grain, kcal/kg° C
C_w = specific heat of water, kcal/kg° C
C_n = calorific value of fuel, kcal/kg
f = rate of fuel consumption, kg/min
G = volumetric air flow rate, m³/min
G' = air flow rate, kg/min
H_1 = humidity of ambient air, kg/kg
H_2 = humidity of heated air, kg/kg
H_3 = humidity of exhaust air, kg/kg
X_1 = initial moisture content of grain, (d.b), kg/kg

X_2	= final moisture content of grain (d.b), kg/kg
q	= heat required for heating the grain and moisture, kcal
q_1	= latent heat required for evaporating grain moisture, kcal
q_a	= total heat required for drying, kcal
q'_a	= heat required to heat the drying air, kcal
RH_1	= relative humidity of ambient air, per cent
RH_2	= relative humidity of drying air, per cent
RH_3	= relative humidity of exhaust air, per cent
t_1	= temperature of the ambient air, $^\circ$ C
t_2	= temperature of the drying air, $^\circ$ C
t_3	= temperature of the exhaust air, $^\circ$ C
v_1	= humid volume of the ambient air, m^3/kg
W_d	= weight of bone dry grain, kg

BIBLIOGRAPHY ON SECTION I

1. Allen, J. R., 1960, Application of grain drying theory to the drying of maize and rice, *J. Agr. Eng., Res.*, 5(4), 363-86.
2. American Society of Heating, Refrigerating and Air-Conditioning Engineers, 1965, ASHRAE Guide and Data Book. Fundamentals and equipments for 1965 and 1966, Ch. 3, pp. 29-48.
3. American Society of Heating, Refrigerating and Air-Conditioning Engineers, 1967, ASHRAE Handbook of Fundamentals, ASHRAE, New York.
4. American Society of Agricultural Engineers, 1966, Agriculture Engineer's Year Book, St. Joseph, Michigan.
5. Angladette, A., Rice Drying Principles and Techniques, Informal Working Bulletin 23, pp. 52, Plate Pl. 6, Food and Agr. Org. of U. N. Rome, Italy.
6. Arnold, J. H., 1933, The theory of the psychrometer, *Physics*, 4, 334-40.
7. Babbit, E. A., 1945, The thermal properties of grain in bulk, *Can. J. Res.*, 23, 388-401.
8. Babbit, J. D., 1949, Observations on the adsorption of water vapour by wheat, *Can. J. of Res.*, 27(F), 55-72.

9. Chakraverty, A., 1978. Intermittent drying of paddy in thin layer, *J. of Agric. Engg.*, 15(1), 33-36.

10. Chakraverty, A., 1978. A derived mathematical equation for intermittent drying of paddy. XVIth I.S.A.E. convention, IIT, Kharagpur.

11. Chakraverty, A. 1978. Analytical approach to thin layer drying of paddy. RPEC Reporter, 4(2).

12. Chakraverty, A., 1988, Bulletin of Paddy and other grain drying systems, IIT, Kharagpur.

13. Chakraverty, A., (Princ. Inv.). Development of farm level grain dryers. Report on ICAR Scheme, IIT, Kharagpur.

14. Chakraverty, A. (Princ. Inv.). Development of farm level solar-cum-husk fired grain dryers. Report on DST Scheme, IIT, Kharagpur.

15. Chakraverty, A. et al., 1976. Studies on thin layer drying of paddy. Rice Report, Spain.

16. Chakraverty, A. et al., 1984, Thin layer drying characteristics of cashew nuts in the Book 'Drying 84', H.P.C., U.S.A.

17. Chakraverty, A. et al., 1979, Thin layer drying characteristics of soybean, *Harvester*, 21.

18. Chakraverty, A. et al., 1983, Design development and testing of a simple baffle type of grain dryer. AMA, 14(1), 41-44.

19. Chakraverty, A. et al., 1987, Design and testing of a solar-cum-husk fired paddy dryer of IT/day cap. in 'Drying 87'. H.P.C., U.S.A.

20. Chakraverty, A. and Das, S.K., 1991, Development of a solar paddy dryer, Energy. Conv. Mgmt., U.S.A., 33(3), 183-190.

21. Chakraverty, A., 1975, Some aspects of intermittent drying of pady, *J. of Agric. Engg.*, 13 (1), 15-18.

22. Chakraverty, A. and Ojha, T. P., 1975, Effects of various air temperatures and exposure times on milling quality of rice, *J. of Agric. Engg.*, 13(2), 1-6.

23. Chakraverty, A., 1976, Effects of tempering on drying characteristics of paddy, *J. of Agric. Engg.*, 13(3), 130-33.

24. Chakraverty, A., 1978, Effects of continuous and intermittent drying on drying characteristics of paddy, *RPEC Reporter*, 4(1).

25. Chung, D. S. asd Pfost, H. B., 1967, Adsorption and desorption of water vapour by cereal grains and their products, *Trans. ASAE*, 10, 552-75.

26. Coleman, D. A. and Fellows, H. C., 1925, Hygroscopic moisture of cereal grains and flaxseed exposed to different relative humidities, *Cereal Chem.*, 2, 275-87.

27. Dale, A. C. and Johnson, H. K., 1956, Heat required to vaporise moisture in wheat and shelled corn, *Purdue Engr. Res. Bul.*, 131.

28. Day, D. L. and Nelson, G. L., 1965, Predicting performance of cross-flow systems for drying grain in storage in deep cylindrical Bins., *Trans. ASAE*, 2(2), 288-92, 197.

29. Day, D. L. and Nelson, G. L., 1965, Desorption isotherm for wheat *Trans. ASAE*, 8, 293-97.

30. Disney, R. W., 1954, The specific heat of some cereal grains, *Cereal Chem.*, 31, 229-334.

31. Fenton, F. C., 1941, Storage of grain sorghums, *Agri. Engg*, 22, 185-88.

32. Flood, C. A., et al., 1972, Simulation of a natural-air corn drying system, *Trans. ASAE*, 15, 156-59, 162.

33. Foster, G. H., 1950, Methods of conditioning shelled corn, *Agri. Engg.*, 31, 407-502.

34. Foster, G. H., 1953, Minimum air flow requirements for drying grain with unheated air, *Agr. Engg.*, 34(10), 681-84.

35. Foster, G. H., 1964, Dryeration—A corn drying process, *USDA Agr. Marketing Service Bull.*, 532.

36. Foster, G. H., 1967, Moisture changes during aeration of grain, *Trans. ASAE*, 10, 344-47, 351.

37. Foster, G. H., 1973, Heated air grain drying (In Sinha, R. H. and Muir, W. E., 1973 *Grain Storage : Part of a system*) AVI Publishing Co., Westport Conn.
38. Gallahar, G. L., 1951, A method determining the latent heat of agricultural crops, *Agri. Engg.*, 32, 34, 38.
39. Gerzhoi, A. P. and Samochetov, V. F., 1958, *Grain Drying and Grain Dryers*, Third review and eni. ed. Edited by A. S. Ginzburg, Khleboizdat ; Moscow.
40. Goff, J. A. and Gratch, S., 1945, Thermodynamic properties of moist air, *Trans. ASHVE*, 55, 463-64.
    properties of moist air, *Trans. ASHVE*, 51, 125-64.
41. Goff, J. A., 1949, Standardization of thermodynamic properties of moist air, *Trans. ASHVE*, 55, 463-64.
42. Gustafson, R. J., 1972, Equilibrium moisture content of shelled corn from 50° F to 155° F, Master of Science Thesis University of Illinois, Urbana, 111.
43. Hall, C. W., 1957, *Drying Farm Crops*, AVI Publishing Co., Westport, Conn.
44. Hall, C. W. and Rodrignez-Arias, J. H., 1958, Equilibrium moisture content of shelled corn, *Agr. Engr.*, 39, 466-70.
45. Harkins, W. D. and Jura, G., 1944, A vapour adsorption method for the determination of the area of solid, *J. Am. Chem. Soc.*, 66, 1366-71.
46. Haswell, G. A., 1954, A note on the specific heat of rice, oats and their products, *Cereal Chem.*, 31, 341-43.
47. Haynes, B. C., 1961, Vapour pressure determination of seed hygroscopicity, *Tech. Bull.*, 1929, ARS, USDA, Washington, D. C.
48. Henderson, S. M., 1952, A basic concept of equilibrium moisture, *Agr. Eng.*, 33, 29-31.
49. Henderson, S. M., and Perry, R. L., 1955, *Agricultural Process Engineering*, John Willey and Sons, New York.
50. Henderson, S. M. and Pabis, S., 1961, Grain Drying Theory, I. Temperature effect on drying coefficient, *J. Agr. Engr. Res.*, 6(3), 169-74.
51. Henderson, S. M. and Pabis, S., 1962, Grain Drying Theory, IV, The effect of airflow rate on the drying Index, *J. of Agr. Esgr. Res.*, 7(2), 85-89.

52. Hogan, J. T., and Karon, Melvin, 1955 Hygroscopic of rough rice at elevated temperatures, *Amer. Chem. Soc. Meeting*, Mimeographed paper, Cincinnati.

53. Holman, L. E., 1948, Adapting cribs for corn drying, *Agri. Engg.*, 29, 149-51.

54. Holman, L. E., 1955, Aeration of stored grain, *Agri. Engg.*, 36, 667-68.

55. Houston, D. F. and Kester, E. B., 1954, Hygroscopic equilibrium of whole-grain edible forms of rice, *Food Tech.*, 8, 302-304.

56. Hukill, W. V., 1947, Basic principles in drying corn and grain sorghum, *Agri. Eng.*, 28, 335-38, 340.

57. Hukill, W. V., 1948, Types and performance of farm grain dryers, *Agri. Engg.*, 29, 53-54.

58. Hukill, W. V., 1954a, Grain drying with unheated air, *Agri. Engg.*, 35, 393-95.

59. Hukill, W. V., 1954b, Drying of grain, In *storage of Cereal Grain and Their Products*, J. A. Anderson and A. W. Alcock (Editors). *Am. Assoc. Cereal Chem.*, St., Paul, Minn.

60. Hukill, W. V. and Schmidt, J. L., 1966, Drying Rate of Fully Exposed Grain Kernels, *Trans. ASAE*, 3(2), 71-77, 80.

61. Hustrulid, A. and Flikke, A. M., 1959, Theoretical Drying Curve for Shelled Corn, *Trans. ASAE*, 2(1), 112-14.

62. Ives, N. C., Hukill, W. V., and Black, H. M., 1966, Wheat drying rates and counterflow steady state, *Trans. ASAE*, 9, 690-95, 701.

63. Ives, N. C., Hukill, W. V., and Black, H.M., 1968, Corn-drying time at counterflow steady state. *Trans, ASAE*, 11, 240-49.

64. Kachrew, R. P., Ojha, T. P. and Kurup, G. T., 1971, Equilibrium moisture content of Indian Paddy varieties, *Bulletin of Grain Technology*, (9)3, 186-96.

65. Kazarian, E. A. and Hall, C. W., 1965, Thermal properties of grains, *Trans. ASAE*, 8(1), 33-37, 48.

66. Kreyger, J., 1972, Drying and Storing Grains, Seeds and Pulses in Temperature Climates, Bulletin 205, Institute

for Storage and Processing of Agricultural Produce, Wageningen, The Netherlands.

67. Langmuir, I., 1918, The adsorption of gases on plane surfaces of glass and mica and platinum, *J. Am. Chem. Soc.*, 40, 1361-65.

68. Lorenzer, R. T., 1958, Effect of moisture on weight volume relationships of small grains, *ASAE* Paper, 58-111.

69. Lorenzen, C., 1959, Moisture effect on granular friction of small grain, *ASAE* Paper, 59-416.

70. Maddex, R. L., and Hall, Carl W., 1954, Drying grain with forced air, *Ext. Bul.*, 316, Michigan State University.

71. McEiven, E. and O'Callaghan, J. R., 1955, The effect of air humidity on through drying of wheat grain, *Trans. Inst. Chem. Engrs.*, (Br.), 33, 135-54.

72. Miles, S. R., 1937, Test weight of corn, *J. Am. Soc. Agron.*, 29, 412-18.

73. Miller, D. F., 1958, Composition of cereal grains and forages *Natl. Acad. Sci.*, Natl. Res. Council Publ. 585.

74. Mohsenin, N. N., 1970, Physical properties of plant and animal materials, Gordon and Breach, New York.

75. Nelson, G. L., 1960, A new analysis of batch grain-dryer performance, *Trans. ASAE*, 3(2), 81-85, 88.

76. Newman, A. B., 1931, The drying of porous solids, diffusion and surface emission equations, *Trans. Am. Inst. Chem. Engr.*, 27, 203-310.

77. Othmer, Donald, F., 1940, Correlating vapour pressure and latent heat data, *Industrial and Engineering Chemistry*, 32, 841-46

78. Pabis, S. and Henderson, S. M., 1961, Grain Drying Theory, II, A critical analysis of the drying curve for shelled maize, *J. of Agr. Engr. Res.*, 6(4), 272-77.

79. Pabis, S. and Henderson, S. M., 1962, Grain Drying Theory, III, The air-grain temperature relationship, 7(1), 21-26.

80. Perry, R. L., 1944, Heat and vapour transfer in the dehydration of prunes, *Trans. ASME*, 66, 447-56.

81. Peterson, G. M. and Simons, J. W., 1956, Heated air drying in storage, *Proc. Conf. on Field Shelling and Drying of Corn*, ARS-USDA, Chicago, Illinois.

82. Quackenbush, F. W., 1963, Corn Carrotenoid : effects of temperature and moisture losses during storage, *Cereal Chem.*, 40, 266-69.
83. Richey, C. B., Jacobson, P., and Hall, W. C., Agricultural Engineers' Hndbook, McGraw-Hill Book Company.
84. Schmidt, J. L., and Waite, P. J., 1962, Summaries of wet-bulb temperature and wet-bulb depressions for grain dryer design, *Trans. ASAE*, 5, 186-89.
85. Shedd, C. K., 1945, Resistance of ear corn to air flow, *Agri. Engg.*, 26, 19-20, 23.
86. Shedd, C. K., 1946, Drying ear corn in farm cribs by natural ventilation, *Agri. Engg.*, 27, 426-27.
87. Shedd, C. K., 1953, Resistance of grains and seeds to air flow, *Agr. Engg.*, 34, 616-19.
88. Shove, G. C., and Olver, E. F., 1967, Temperature gradients in grain drying, *Trans. ASAE*, 10, 152, 153, 156.
89. Simmonds, W. H. C., Ward, G. T., and McEwen, E., 1953a, The drying of wheat grain, Part I, The mechanism of drying, *Trans. Instn. Chem. Engr.*, 31, 265-78.
90. Simmonds, W. H. C., Ward, G. T., and McEwen E., Drying of Wheat Grain, Part II, Through-drying of deep beds, *Trans. Instn. Chem. Engr.*, 31, 279-88.
91. Smith, J. E., 1947, The sorption of water vapour by high polymers, *J. of Amer. Chem. Soc.*, 69, 646-51.
92. Sorenson, J. W., Jr., et al., 1949, Drying and its effects on the milling characteristics of sorghum grain, *Bul. 710*, Texas Agricultural Erperiment Station, Texas, A and M.
93. Stanton, M., 1954, Drying rice unheated air, *Agr. Engg.*, 35, 735-36.
94. Steele, J. F., Saul, R. A., and Hukill, W. V., 1969, Deterioration rate of shelled corn as measured by carbon dioxide production, *Trans. ASAE*, 12, 685-89.
95. Thompson, H. J., and Shedd, C. K., 1954, Equilibrium moisture and heat of vaporization of shelled corn and wheat, *Agr. Eng.*, 35, 786-88.
96. Thompson, R. A., and Foster, G. H., 1963, Stress cracks and breakage in ertificially dried corn, *Marketing Research Report No. 631, USDA*, Washington, D. C.
97. Thompson, T. L., Peart, R. M., and Foster, G. H., 1968,

Methematical simulation of corn drying—a new model, *Trans. ASAE*, 11, 582-86.

98. Thompson, T. L., Foster, B. H., and Peart, R. M., 1969, Comparison of concurrent flow, cross flow, and counter flow grain drying methods, *USDA, Marketing Research Report 841.*

99. Toshizo, Ban, 1965, Drying of rice in Japan, *Institute of Agr. Mach.*, Japan.

100. Troeger, J. M. and Hukill, W. V., 1971, Mathematical description of the drying rate of fully exposed corn, *Trans. ASAE*, 14, 1153-56, 1162.

101. Treybal, R. E., 1955, *Mass Transfer Operations*, McGraw-Hill Book Company.

102. USDA, 1952a, Drying shelled corn and small grain with unheated air, *Leaf-let*, 332.

103. USDA, 1962b, Drying shelled corn and small grain with heated air, *Leaf-let*, 331.

104. USDA, 1952c, Drying ear corn with heated air, *Leaf-let*, 333.

105. USDA, 1952d, Drying ear corn with unheated air, *Leaf-let*, 334.

106. USDA, 1959, Research on conditioning and storoge of rough and milled rice, Review Through 1958, ARS 20-27.

107. Van Arsdel, W. B., 1947, Approximate diffusion calculations for the falling rate phase of drying, *Trans. Amer. Instn. Chem. Engr.*, 43, 13-24.

108. Wasserman, T., et al., 1956, Drying characteristics of western rice, Part I, Equal moisture removal and constant drying air temperature in all phases, *Rice Journal*, 59(3), 12-16.

109. Wasserman, T., et al., 1956, Drying characteristics of western rice, *Rice journal*, 59(4), 41-45.

110. Wasserman, T., et al., 1957, Commercial drying of western rice, *Cereal Science To-day*, 2(9), 251-54.

111. Young, J. H. and Nelson, G. L., 1967, Research of hysteresis between sorption and desorption isotherms of wheat, *Trans. ASAE.* 10, 756-61.

SECTION II
PARBOILING

CHAPTER 7

Principle of Parboiling of Paddy

Parboiling is a hydrothermal treatment followed by drying before milling for the production of milled parboiled grain. Parboiling of paddy has been known in the orient for centuries. Nearly 50 per cent of the paddy produced in India at present is parboiled.

The parboiling process finds extensive application in the Eastern and part of Southern India, Eastern Madhya Pradesh and Uttar Pradesh. It is also well known in western Uttar Pradesh, Punjab and Hariyana in the form of Sela process of parboiling. The process is also being used in Bangladesh, Pakistan, Burma, Ceylon, Malaysia and Thailand. Parboiling has been practiced in the United States, Italy and British Guiana on a commercial scale since 1940.

Physico-chemical changes during parboiling

The endosperm of the grain contains mainly polygonal starch granules. The voids or intergranular spaces are filled with air and moisture. That is why it looks opaque. Moreover, there are fissures and or cracks in the grain, developed during maturity, which can cause breakage of rice during milling. The most important change during parboiling is the gelatinisation of starch and disintegration of protein bodies in the endosperm (S. N. Raghavendra Rao, and B. O. Juliano, 1970). The starch and protein expand and fill the internal air spaces. The fissures and cracks in the endosperm are sealed making the grain translucent and hard as a result of which the breakage of grain during milling is minimised.

The colour of the rice changes to yellow or yellowish brown depending upon the paddy variety, soaking time and temperature.

steaming time and temperature (pressure of steam), drying time and temperature and many other post harvest factors.

Parboiled rice takes a longer time to cook to the same degree of softness than raw rice of the same variety. The loss of protein and starch from parboiled rice in the cooking water is low. Water soluble B-vitamins and other water soluble nutrients diffuse into the endosperm during parboiling and hence the loss of nutrients is less in parboiled rice even after polishing. The presence of vitamin E is particularly noted in parboiled rice (L. Bosario, and F. Gariboldi, 1965). Slight dextrinisation and destruction of lipase occurs during parboiling. The heat treatment during parboiling causes destruction of some natural antioxidants and may result in increased rancidity of parboiled rice during storage.

In general, the three major steps in parboiling, i.e. soaking, steaming and drying, have a great influence on the final characteristics and quality of parboiled rice. Soaking of paddy is done at or below the gelatinisation temperature. The lower the temperature the slower is the process of soaking and vice versa (K. R. Bhattacharya, and V. P. Subba Rao, 1966).

Soaking time can be reduced by subjecting the paddy to vacuum before soaking and or soaking under pressure in hot water. Steaming helps in the gelatinisation of starch in the paddy. The higher the temperature of steam and longer the steaming time, the harder is the rice and darker the colour. Drying of parboiled paddy may be done in the shade, in the sun, or with hot air. Shade drying takes a longer time but results in excellent milling quality. Rapid drying in the sun or with hot air causes higher breakage during milling. In continuous drying, breakage starts as the moisture content reaches about 18 per cent and increases rapidly with further drying (K. R. Bhattacharya and Y. M. Indudharaswamy 1967). Hence the recommended practice would be to dry in two passes with a tempering in between at about a moisture content of 20 per cent. Normally, the varieties of paddy which are more brittle are preferred for parboiling. The long and slender varieties which are more fragile compared with short and medium length grains are usually parboiled. Scented and tiny varieties which have good milling quality are generally not parboiled.

SOAKING

The process of water absorption is known as soaking, steeping or imbibation. It is a diffusion process. As a result of water absorption the paddy swells. The water moves inside the paddy as long as the water vapour pressure inside the grain is less than that of soak water and stops when equilibrium is reached. Soaking is the result of molecular absorption, capillary absorption and hydration. Initially, during soaking, water penetrates the rice kernel and fills up the intergranular spaces due to capillary absorption. Some of the water molecules are absorbed by starch granules while some will enter into the lattice of starch molecule where they will be held as water of hydration (N. N. Mohsenin, 1968).

The volume of paddy increases due to soaking. But the volume of soaked paddy is always less than the sum of the initial volume of paddy and the volume of water absorbed (N. Ali, and T. P. Ojha, 1975 a). The soaking process is always accompanied by release of heat. A considerable amount of kinetic energy is lost as heat when water molecules are absorbed.

Soaking is done to provide the starch with a quantity of water

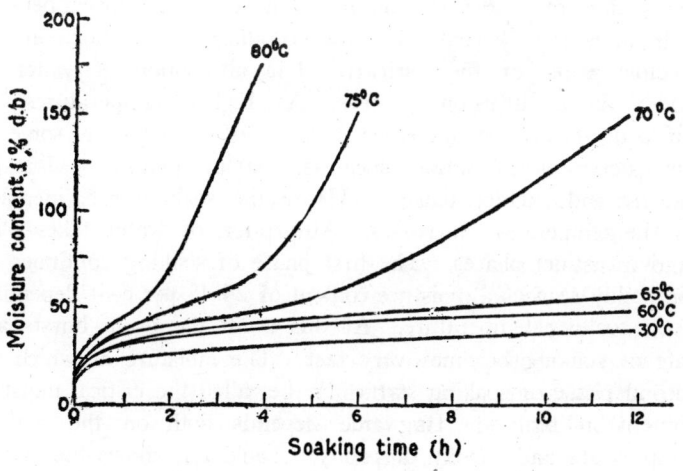

FIG. 7.1 Soaking curves for I R-8 at different temperatures
(Ali and Ojha, 1975a)

sufficient for gelatinisation. The rate of soaking is also dependent on temperature of soaking (Fig. 7.1).

The rate of soaking is high initially but it decreases with
time until bursting of the grain takes place when the soaking
rate increases particularly at the temperature of gelatinisation
and higher (Fig. 7.2).

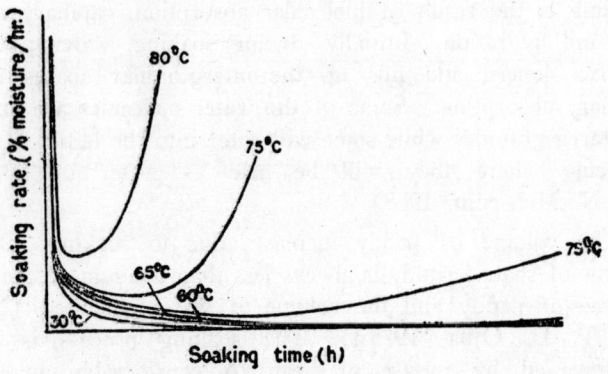

FIG. 7.2 Soaking rate versus time for IR-8 at different
temperatures (Ali and Ojha, 1975a)

The initial high rate of soaking is mainly due to quick
absorption of water by the hull the filling of space between
hull and rice kernal and the capillary absorption in the
shallow pores of the pericarp. The absorption of water by
paddy is a diffusion process. At higher temperatures the
diffusion coefficient increases because of changes in some of
the properties of water, such as, vapour pressure, viscosity,
density and surface tension. Hence the soaking rate increases
as the temperature increases. Absorption of water takes place
in two distinct phases. The first phase of soaking continues till
the paddy reaches a moisture content of 24-45 per cent depending
upon soaking temperature. At this point the grain bursts and
rate of soaking becomes very fast. The moisture at which the
second phase of soaking starts may be called the critical moisture
content in soaking. Its value depends both on the soaking
temperature and variety of paddy. Table 7.1. shows the critical
moisture content (dry basis) of some varieties of paddy during
soaking at various temperatures.

PARBOILING 129

TABLE 7.1 Average value of critical moisture content (dry basis) of different varieties of paddy during soaking at various temperatures (Ail and Ojha, 1975a)

Soaking temp (°C)	IR-8	Patnai-23	Sitasal
30	40	40	36
40	45	42	42
65	59	43	45
70	60	45	45
75	60	58	57
80	53	57	52

The soaking characteristics of different varieties of paddy are usually different because of the differences in the gelatinisation temperatures. The gelatinisation temperatures are normally within 65-75° C. The water absorption also depends on the superincumbent pressure in the soaking tank. In some modern processes vacuum and hydrostatic pressure are used to reduce soaking time, keeping the temperature within desirable limits. Figure 7.3 shows the moisture uptake of paddy at different conditions of pressure.

The soaking of paddy is associated with an increase in volume.

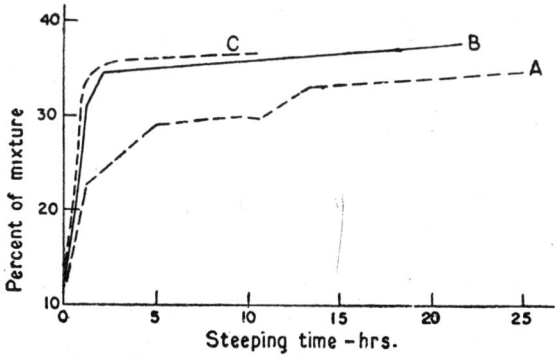

A - At ambient pressure , B - Vacuum treatment before steeping
C - Vacuum treatment steeping followed by hydrostatic pressure (8 kg/cm²)

FIG. 7.3 Water absorption by the same paddy steeped at 45°C

9

Swelling of paddy grains as a function of time and temperature of soaking is shown in Fig. 7.4

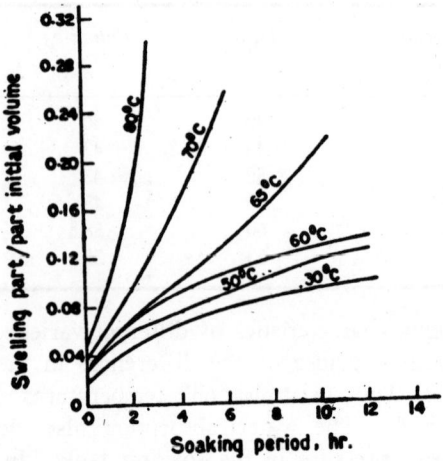

FIG. 7.4   Swelling of grain as a function of time and
temperature

Figure 7.5 (S. Bandyopadhyay and N. C. Roy 1977) further shows the relationship between swelling and moisture content of paddy.

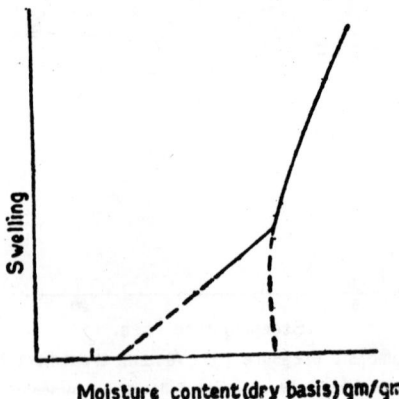

FIG. 7.5   Moisture content
versus Swelling

There is a sharp change in the slope after a break at a moisture content of about 0.5 gm/gm basis. The air space inside the husk allows the kernel to hydrate and expand without appreciable change in external grain volume. Hence initially the volume change is low. Thereafter the grain bursts and swelling is perceptible, as reflected in the break in the swelling line. A further coroboration of this result can be obtained if the analysis is based on the diffusion equation proposed by Ghosh et al, (Bandyopadhyay B. & T. K. Ghose, 1975). The break in the Arrhenius plot of log Km versus the reciprocal of absolute temperature around 62-69° C, took place in the vicinity of gelatinisation temperature as shown in Fig. 7.6.

This indicated the rapid hydration process due to gelatinisation with higher activation energy (25-31.7 kcal/mole).

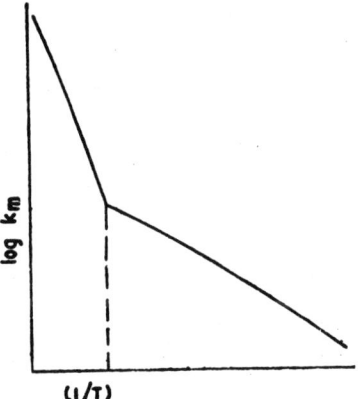

FIG. 7.6 Log K_m as a function of reciprocal of the absolute temperature (variety: *Pankaj*)

STEAMING

Steam is used to complete the gelatinisation process as it does not remove moisture from the paddy rather it adds moisture by condensation. Moreover it has high heat content. During steaming the spread of the water soluble substances inside the paddy grain which is begun during soaking is continued and increased ;

the granular texture of endosperm becomes pasty due to gelatinisation ; any crack in the caryopsis is sealed ; the endosperm becomes compact and translulcent ; most of the biological processes are completely annihilated and the enzymes are also inactivated. If the starch is not fully gelatinised, there will remain white cores in the endosperm. So steaming should be sufficient to cause complete gelatinisation. If there is a higher degree of gelatinisation, it will be reflected in the hardness of the grain, the deepness of colour, the greater amount of cohesion between the layers of perisperm and between the germ scutellum and the endosperm. The time and temperature of steaming are to be controlled in order to get the desirable characteristics in the final product. Figure. 7.7 shows the effect of steaming temperature on the expanded volume. It shows that big increase in volume occurs between steam temperature of 100-120° C.

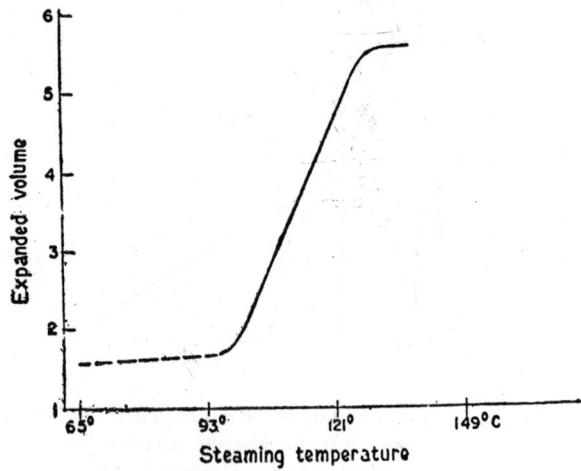

FIG. 7.7 Swelling of grain as a function of time and temperature (variety : *Padma*)

DRYING

The parboiled paddy is required to be dried to a moisture of 14-16 per cent to obtain the desirable milling and storing properties.

In India, drying is generally carried out on large paved yards

in the rice mills. The paddy is dried to a moisture of about
18-20 per cent and then heaped and tempered for few hours and
then again dried for 1-2 hrs to bring down the moisture to
14-16 per cent.
The drying is also carried out in mechanical driers in some
mills with hot air. The most important aspect in drying is that
the process should be carried in two stages. If the drying is
continued in one stage below a moisture of 18 per cent there is
considerable amount of breakage. But if it is conditioned at
that level and again dried to 14-16 per cent moisture, the breakage
is considerably reduced.

Effects of parboiling on milling, nutritional and cooking qualities of rice

It has been shown (Bhattacharya, 1969) that breakage of rice
during milling is mostly due to inherent cracks and fissures
per cent in the kernel. Parboiling seals the cracks and hardens
the grain. The breakage also depends on the milling conditions
and the type of milling machinery used. Rice varieties with
short grains are usually more resistant to breakage compared
to the long slender varieties. The head yield of rice is considerably improved by parboiling particularly for the varieties
having very poor milling quality.
Parboiled rice takes longer time compared to raw rice for
the same degree of polish. Moreover, parboiled rice requires
three to four times as much abrasive load as raw rice to attain
the same degree of polish (Raghavendra Rao, et al., 1967).
However to achieve an equal degree of surface bran removal,
parboiled rice must be subjected to less polishing than raw rice.
For example, for 80 per cent bran removal, parboiled rice must
be polished to about 3 per cent whereas raw rice must be polished
to about 4 per cent.
If the degree of polish is done to a level required for
minimum consumer acceptability (80 per cent of bran colour
removal) parboiling increases the total yield by 1 to 1.5 per cent
and the yield of marketable rice (containing brokens not larger
than one quarter the size of the original rice) by about
3.5 per cent.
The nutrive value of rice and its byproducts is shown in

Table 7.2. It shows that concentration of nutrients in the bran is higher than in endosperm. During parboiling many nutrients are diffused inside the endosperm and hence loss during polishing is minimised. Moreover, the improved methols of parboiling retains more nutrients compared to the traditional one. As much as 70 per cent vitamin B is retained in the parboiled rice produced by improved method, whereas the traditional parboiled rice retains only 30 per cent (Mazumdar, et al., 1960).

The cooking quality of rice is expressed in terms of time of cooking, swelling capacity, expansion ratio, colour, solids in gruel and pastiness.

Raw rice takes about 15-20 min to become fully cooked in boiling water, whereas parboiled rice requires about 30-40 min for a comparable degree of softness. Raw rice cooked beyond 20 min becomes pasty (Mahadevappa and Desikachar, 1968a).

Swelling capacity is expressed as the ratio of the final to the initial volume or weight of rice. The water absorption capacity, as expressed by the swelling ratio is significantly lower for parboiled rice than for raw rice cooked for the same period. But if raw rice and parboiled rice are cooked to an equivalent degree of softness, then parboiled rice can absorb more water without losing its shape (Mahadevappa and Desikacsar 1968a).

Expansion ratio is the ratio of the dimensions of cooked and uncooked rice both along the length and breadth. At the equivalent degree of softness parboiled rice expands more along the bredth than raw rice, whereas the expansion along the length is not significantly different.

The loss of solids into the gruel is greater in raw rice than in parboiled rice.

Discolouration of rice during parboiling is mainly due to non-enzymatic Maillard type browning, that can be inhibited by bisulphite. The husk pigment may also contribute colour by diffusion into the endosperm.

Advantages

(1) The process imparts to the grain a hard texture and a smooth surface finish, as a result the brokens in the milled rice is minimised. While 90 per cent of the parboiled grains may remain unbroken; the brokens in raw rice could be as high as

50 per cent. The reduction in broken rice results in an increase of 3-5 per cent in the total yield of rice.

(2) Insects find it more difficult to bite and eat their way through the hard and smooth surface of parboiled rice.

(3) The loss of solids in the gruel during cooking is also less in parboiled than in raw rice.

(4) Milled parboiled rice contains more of B-vitamins than milled raw rice.

(5) Loss of B-vitamins is less in parboiled rice, during washing and cooking, compared to that in raw rice.

(6) The cooking quality is different from that of raw rice. Parboiled rice is non-sticky and non-glutinous.

(7) The parboiled paddy on milling produces a bran higher in oil content (about 25-30 per cent oil) compared to raw rice bran (about 10-20 per cent oil).

(8) Parboiled rice bran is relatively stabilised compared to raw rice.

Disadvantages

(1) It develops a relatively darker colour compared to raw rice.

(2) The traditional parboiling process produces an undesirable smell.

(3) Parboiled rice takes more time to cook to the same degree of softness than raw rice.

(4) Because of long soaking in traditional process, mycotoxins may develop in parboiled rice and cause health hazard.

(5) Heat treatment during parboiling destroys some natural antioxidants and hence parboiled rice develops more rancidity than raw rice during storage.

(6) Shelled parboiled rice requires more power for polishing.

(7) Parboiled paddy may choke the polisher because of the higher oil content of the bran.

(8) Parboiling process requires an additional investment of capital.

However, in spite of these disadvantages, the higher outturn of rice (about 1-2 per cent) and higher return from high oil content bran ensures lower price to the consumer and higher return to the miller.

CHAPTER 8

Practice of Parboiling of Paddy

Rice parboiling process consists of five major steps-soaking, steaming, drying, conditioning and cooling. During soaking the water should penetrate the centre of the grain. The water content of paddy after soaking increases to about 50-55 per cent on dry basis. During the steaming process the rice is gelatinised. Finally the paddy is dried to a desirable moisture content so that it toughens enough and does not break easily during milling.

A few Traditional Methods of the traditional premilling treatments to improve the milling, nutritional, cooking and keeping qualities are :

Atapa

This treatment originated in Bengal. The paddy is soaked in water at room temperature for 24 hours and then dried in the sun (hence the name *atapa* or sun-dried). The dried paddy is then milled by traditional methods. The relative breakage of rice is more in this process.

Balam

This treatment also originated in Bengal. It is slightly better than *atapa*. Here the paddy is sprinkled with water, which inflates the grain. When the paddy is dried in the sun and milled, the hull is easier to remove.

Josh

This treatment was developed in Larkhana, Pakistan. Large earthen pots filled with paddy and water are placed on 15 cm layer of hull which is used as fuel. The pots remain on the fire overnight. The next day the water is drained and the paddy is placed on shallow iron pans and heated over fire for one hour. The paddy is then dried in sun.

Sela

This treatment was originated in Saharanpur, India. Paddy is soaked in water at room temperature for 24-48 hours and then gently roasted in hot sand (80-90° C). The roasted paddy is then further dried in sun and milled.

Siddha

This treatment originated in Bengal. Paddy is soaked in water at room temperature for 20 hours, and then boiled for few minutes. It is finally dried in sun. In this method, rice from over-soaked paddy becomes coarse in appearance, and rice from over-dried paddy shows poor milling quality.

Parboiling

Parboiling is the latest premilling treatment which improves the quality of rice. The traditional parboiling process in India is carried out in different ways. The principal methods are single-boiling and double-boiling process.

The double boiling method (Dobhapa) : This involves double steaming in its sequence of operations. The vertical steaming kettles, generally two in number, are made of mild steel plates. The size of each kettle is generally 700-900 mm in diameter and 1.2-2 metres in height with about 600 mm deep conical bottom having a 300 mm diameter flanged outlet, fitted with a sliding valve. The flat top cover is fitted with a 300 mm diameter central opening for feeding the raw paddy. The kettles are provided with steam pipe extending vertically through the centre about half way down through the top cover. When the direct steam from the boiler at 6 to 7 kg/cm² is used, a 20 to 25 mm diameter steam pipe is supplied.

The soaking is done in large masonry water tanks constructed on the ground floor. These are generally two in number working each in line with a steaming kettle. Each tank usually of 23 metres in depth holds 20 to 35 tonnes of paddy. The water level in the tank is maintained such as to cover the paddy completely during the soaking period.

The process involves filling the dry paddy in the steaming kettle and opening the steam valve. During steaming the top opening of the kettle is covered with a gunny bag. Depending on the size of the batch the steam starts blowing out through the bag on the top in three to eight minutes. Steam is turned off and the paddy is discharged from the bottom and then quickly dumped into the water in the soaking tank. The temperature in the tank rises, as more and more paddy is dumped. Finally at the end the temperature of soak water is around 70 to 80° C. But because of large exposed surface, the temperature of soak water drops to 50-60° C within two hours. The paddy is allowed to soak for 24 to 72 hours after which the water is drained off. The colour of the soak water turns brown. In most cases signs of fermentation have been observed within 18 hours. These result in a bad odour and brown colour in the milled rice.

The soaked paddy is then lifted back into the steaming kettles for the second steaming or actual parboiling operation. The procedure followed is the same as is done in case of the first steaming. The parboiled paddy is discharged from the kettles and allowed to dry in the drying yard or in a mechanical drier.

The single boiling method : The paddy is soaked in cold water in the cement tanks for a few days and then steamed in the usual manner. The soaking time is generally more in the case of the single boiling process.

In both these methods, during prolonged soaking of the paddy, the rice prepared out of it produces a bad odour, as a result of fermentation during soaking.

These difficulties are eliminated by the improved methods of parboiling developed in India at the Central Food Technological Research Institute, Mysore, Jadavpur University, Calcutta and in certain other parts of the world.

In the modern methods of parboiling, the long steeping and steaming cycle using low temperatures is replaced by those with short cycles using high temperatures and pressures and the process is carried out either in a batch plant or a semi-continuous or continuous plant.

The treatment will depend on the variety and quality of paddy and the characteristics of the final product desired. The choice of any parboiling technique will also depend on the initial investment, running costs, local conditions and amount of automation desired.

IMPROVED PARBOILING METHOD OF CFTRI, MYSORE, INDIA (BATCH)

The system developed by CFTRI (Central Food Technological Research Institute) was primarily aimed at improving the yield and quality of rice with a lower capital investment. The soaking and steaming is done in the same mild steel cylindrical tank. Steam enters through the perforated pipe at the centre and there are more perforated pipes arranged radially at the bottom of the tank. The base of the tank is cone-shaped and is closed at the bottom by a water tight hatch. At the side of the hatch there is a valve for draining of the steeping water.

During parboiling the tank is filled with water heated by steam injection to 85° C. The paddy is then poured inside the tank. The temperature of water drops to 70-75° C. After two to three and a half hours steeping, the water is drained off. Pressurised steam is then passed through the perforated pipes until the husks just begin to crack open. After steaming the hot paddy is unloaded through the bottom hatch and then spread over the drying floor.

SCHULE PROCESS (Federal Republic of Germany) (Batch)

The process was developed by the well-known German firm, a rice machinery manufacturer. In this process the steam is used only to heat the water. The paddy is put into a pressure tank and is first soaked 120-160 minutes in medium temperature water kept in circulation. When the paddy has reached the temperature of soaking water the water supply is turned off and hydrostatic pressure of 4 to 6 kg/cm^2 is applied introducing compressed air in the tanks. The second heating or cooking period is started by releasing pressure and readmitting water at a very high temperature to ensure that the starch gelatinises completely. The water is then drained off and the paddy is dried in a predrier and then in a column drier. The paddy is finally dried to a moisture content of 13 per cent in another column drier after proper tempering.

CRYSTAL RICE PROCESS (Italy) (Batch)

In this process the paddy is first soaked in cold water to remove impurities and lighter grains. Steeping is done in a stationary autoclave where vacuum is applied first and water is injected and then high hydrostatic pressure is maintained at controlled temperature. Steaming and drying are done in a rotary autoclave which is also fitted with a steam jacket. The drying is done under vacuum.

RICE CONVERSION PROCESS (U.K.) (Batch)

The process was patented in the United Kingdom. This was also the first parboiling process adopted in the United States and came into use in 1941-42. Steeping is done in an autoclave after the paddy is deaerated by vaccum. This facilitates water absorption. Then pressure is applied to the steeping water. The combination of vacuum and pressure reduces steeping time to less than three hours. Steaming is done in a rotating steam jacketted autoclave with a pressure of about 1 kg/cm² for about one hour after which a vacuum is applied to free the grain of excess water. Final drying is done in the same autoclave by applying vacuum keeping the paddy hot by contact with steam heated surfaces. The process is completed in a rotary drier utilising medium temperature air.

IMPROVED PARABOILING METHOD OF JADAVPUR UNIVERSITY. (Semi-continuous)

This process is partly continuous. Steeping is done at 70° C within two and a half to three hours in vertical cylindrical batch tanks. Steaming is carried out in the same tank having perforated steam pipes and is continued only for three to five minutes. After steaming the paddy is rapidly cooled in vertical cup and cone type arrangements. The cooling helps to maintain a lighter colour in the finished rice. After the cooling the paddy is then dried in a steam tube rotary drier at a temperature of about 90° C. The paddy is then tempered and cooled before milling.

Maek process (United States) (Semi-continuous)

The above process was patented in the United States. The parboiled rice so produced is amber coloured and fully gelatinised. The grains are very hard. The steeping is done at a high temperature for three to six hours in batch tanks. It is then steamed into a vertical cylindrical autoclave, which has a conical base. The drying is done continuously in a steamheated rotary cylindrical drier and then also continuously in a vertical through flow drier.

Rice Growers' Association of California Parboiling process (USA), (Semi-continuous)

The process involves a continuous pressure steaming unit. The raw rice is soaked in tepid water for several hours in a tank and then in higher temperature water (varying from 40—90° C depending on the variety) for one to ten hours. It is then steamed continuously under pressure for a short period (15 secs to three minutes) at a pressure between one and five kg/cm². Drying is done initially at high temperature followed by a batch type column drier. The paddy is tempered before final pass in the column drier. The main features of this process are the long soaking time and the extremely short exposure to steam at high pressure. As a result the product is very pale in colour and gives a good milling yield.

Avorio process (Italy) (Continuous)

The process was patented in Italy in 1936. The parboiling procedure is completely mechanised and continuous. Steeping is done by mechanically submerging baskets filled with paddy through a tank. The water is kept in continuous circulation and aerated by blowing in air. Steeping time is between 50 and 120 minutes and is adjusted by controlling the speed at which the baskets pass through the tank. After steeping the paddy is steamed in continuous pressure autoclave containing rotating perforated cylinders. The paddy is loaded and unloaded through special valves which functions alternately. Pressure may be raised up to 1 kg/cm². Before drying the steamed paddy is cooled by a stream of cold air in a rotary cylinder, after which it is transferred to a series of vertical column drier utilising air at 45-50° C. The rice is amber in colour. In fact, the Italian word, *avorio* means ivory, referring to the colour of the product.

FERNANDES PROCESS (Suriam) (Continuous)

The process was patented in 1952. The soaking, steaming and drying operations are carried out in three similarly constructed horizontal rotating cylinders, having internal helical conveyors for movement of paddy. At the centre of each cylinder, a perforated pipe extends along the length. This tube carries hot water for soaking in the first cylinder, steam for cooking in the second and hot air for drying in the third cylinder.

INTERNATIONAL RICE RESEARCH INSTITUTE PROCESS (Method under study)

A process is under development whereby freshly harvested paddy is dried using high temperature sand (exceeding 200° C). The drier extracts moisture as well as gelatinises part of the starchy endosperm.

TRUE CONTINUOUS PARBOILING PROCESS OF JADAVPUR UNIVERSITY, INDIA (Method under study)

This process is based on a true continuous system of parboiling consisting of a continuous vertical soaker, continuous horizontal steamer, a continuous fluid bed drier, a continous vertical conditioner and a continuous vertical throughflow cooler. The time and temperature of soaking and steaming can be controlled by controlling the star valve at the bottom of soaker and the steam flow at the soak water tank and the speed of the screw conveyor in the steamer. The residence time in drier, conditioner and cooler can also be adjusted. The drier is a horizontal fluid bed drier where positive movement of paddy bed is made by a flight conveyor.

RPEC METHOD (Indian) (Method under study)

This was developed by Rice Process Engineering Centre, Indian Institute of Technology, Kharagpur during 1970-73. The paddy is soaked in water at or a little above the gelantinisation temperature. The parboiling process is completed by the heat and moisture. No steaming is required. The swelling index of the parboiled rice so produced is similar to the one from conventionally produced parboiled rice. Most important advantage would be that the boiler can be eliminated in a rice mill as no steam is required in the process. Hot water can be generated by suitable husk or coal fired furnace.

SODIUM CHROMATE METHOD (Indian) (Method under study)

This was developed at Tiruvarur in 1972 (V. Subrahmanyan, 1972)

Oxidising agent like sodium chromate (0.05 per cent solution) is used in soaking the paddy for 40-48 hrs. This controls putrifactive changes for three days as also reduces the loss of dry matter during cold soaking.

BRINE SOLUTION METHOD (Indian) (Method under study)

This is a modified CFTRI method. The modifications and developments were done at the R&D laboratory of the Modern Rice Mill at Tiruvarur, India in 1969. In this method a 15 per cent brine solution is circulated for 10-20 minutes through hot paddy that has been soaked at 65° C and has attained a moisture content of 45 per cent (dry basis). The paddy is then steamed at 3-5 kg/cm² for 15-20 minutes. During drying paddy loses moisture to a level of 14-16 per cent. The main advantage of this method is the reduction in drying time.

KISAN CONTINUOUS PARBOILING METHOD (Indian) (Method under study)

This was developed by Kisan Krishi Yantra Udyog in 1972 (M. A. Kuppuswamy, 1972). A hexagonal tank with 12 compartments is used for soaking in sequential order starting with No. 1. By the time the 12th compartment is filied the first one is ready for steaming. The steaming is continuously done in the annular chamber of a vertical cylinder. The steam is injected into the perforated inner chamber.

PRESSURE PARBOILING METHOD (Indian) (Method under study)

This method was also developed at Tiruvarur in 1969

TABLE 8.1. Composition of rice and its milling products (Houston and Kohler 1970)

	Water (%)	Protein (%)	Fat (%)	Ash (%)	Carbohydrate		Minerals and vitamins (mg/100 g)							
					Total (%)	Fibre (%)	Cal-cium	Phos-phorus	Iron	Sodium	Potas-sium	Thia-mine	Ribo-flavin	Niacin
Brown	12.0	7.5	1.9	1.2	77.4	0.9	32	111	1.6	9	214	0.34	0.05	4.7
White fully milled (common)	12.0	6.7	0.4	0.5	80.4	0.3	24	94	0.8	5	92	0.07	0.03	1.6
White fully milled (waxy)	13.2	5.6	0.9	0.5	79.8	0.3	36	100	2.0	10	130	0.07	0.04	2.0
Enriched, all types	12.0	6.7	0.4	0.5	80.4	0.3	24	94	(2.9)	5	92	(0.44)	(—)	(3.5)
Long grain, parboiled	10.3	7.4	0.3	0.7	81.3	0.2	60	200	(2.9)	9	150	(0.44)	(—)	(3.5)
Long grain, precooked	9.6	7.5	0.2	0.2	82.5	0.4	5	65	(2.9)	1	—	(0.44)	(—)	(3.5)
Rice bran	9.7	13.3	15.8	10.0	50.8	11.5	76	1386	19.4	trace	1495	2.26	0.25	29.8
Rice polish	9.8	12.1	12.8	7.6	57.7	2.4	69	1106	16.1	trace	714	1.84	0.18	28.2

Note : Values in parentheses for iron, thiamine, and niacin are based on minimum level of enrichment specified in standards of identity. Those required for riboflavin are presently not in effect.

(C. S. Shivanna, 1971). The paddy is soaked for nearly 40 mins at a temperature of 80-90° C in a vertical closed tank and then steamed under pressure for 18 minutes. The parboiling is completed in 1 to 1.5 hrs. The rice has a pleasing, slightly yellowish, uniform colour. Main advantages are reduction in soaking time and drying time as also an increase in shelling efficiency (nearly 80 per cent of paddy hull splits during steaming) and an increase in milling out-turn because the grains are resistant to breakage. Several plants have already been installed for commercial production.

10

CHAPTER 9

Parboiling of Wheat

Introduction

Debranned (polished) and cracked parboiled wheat is known as *bulgur*. Bulgur is one of the special products of wheat. Various cooked foods, quick cooking products, breakfast cereals etc., can be prepared using bulgar. It is mainly used as a substitute of rice. Parboiled wheat resembles rice when it is debranned and split into two or more pieces. It takes about 25 to 30 minutes to cook fully.

Bulgar is consumed in many countries, namely, Australia, Argentina, Canada and the U.S.A. Bulgar wheat has been successfully produced on a commercial scale in India also.

The process of bulgur wheat production is more or less same as that of parboiled rice. It consists of soaking followed by steaming, drying and milling (i.e., debranning and cracking). However, in this chapter, only parboiling and drying of wheat have been discussed in detail and others in brief.

Principle of Parboiling of Wheat

SOAKING

For complete gelatinisation of starchy endosperm by open steaming, the moisture content of raw wheat has to be raised to the level of 80 per cent (d.b) by soaking prior to steaming.

Figure 9.1 shows the hydration characteristics of a local variety of wheat at soaking temperature of 75° C. It may be seen from the figure that at 75° C it takes about 2.5 hours to increase the moisture content of wheat from 15 to 83 per cent (d.b). Soaking temperatures above 75° C should not be used so as to minimise the bursting of kernals and leaching losses as well.

Sτ, AMING (Cooking)

Open steaming for about 15 to 20 minutes is necessary for complete gelatinisation of the soaked wheat of 83 per cent

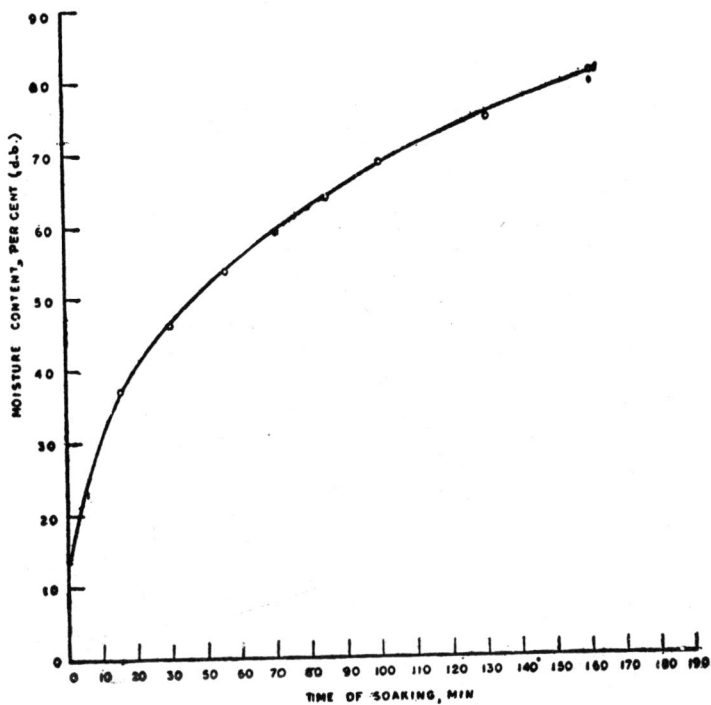

FIG. 9.1. Hydration Characteristics of wheat
(Temperature of water—75°C)

moisture content (d.b). It may be pointed out that only 3 to 5 per cent moisture is added during steaming of soaked wheat containing 83 per cent (d.b) moisture.

DRYING

The effects of drying air temperatures on the thin layer (one grain thick) drying characteristics of parboiled wheat and on the quality of the dried product are shown in Figs. 9.2 and 9.3 respectively.

It should be kept in mind that at a constant air tempera-

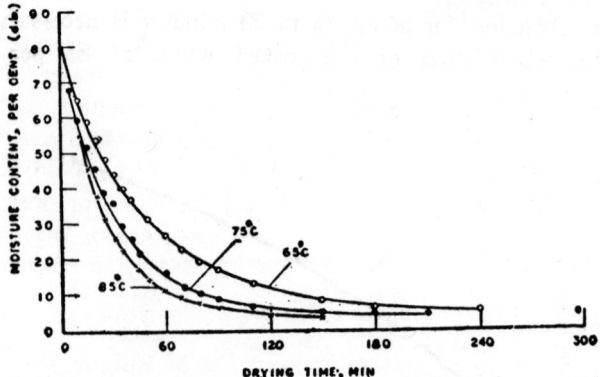

FIG. 9.2. Relation between moisture content and drying time at air temperatures of 65° C, 75° C and 85° C at an air velocity 12 m/min.

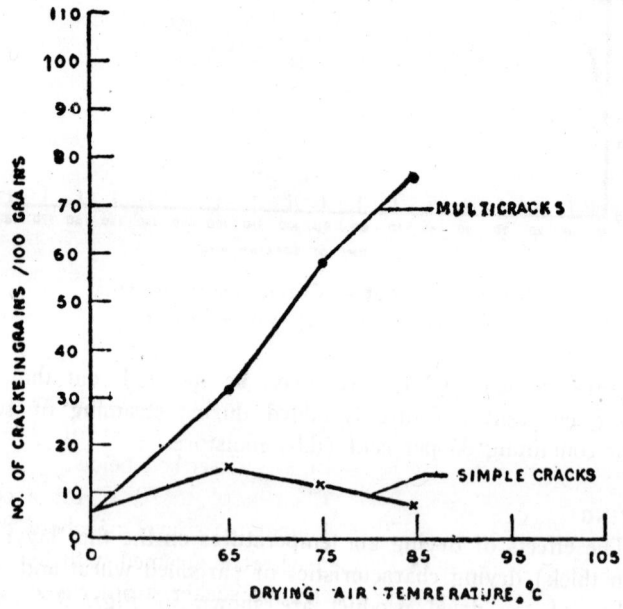

FIG. 9.3. Effect of drying air Temperature on Development of cracks in dried Parboiled wheat

ture, the rate of drying decreases significantly as the thickness of grain increases. Fig. 9.3 shows that the percentage of multicracks increases as drying air temperature increases. Multicracks are not desirable when the dried debranned parboiled wheat is to be split into two pieces to give appearance resembling rice. Moreover multicracks in the grain always lead to the production of higher percentage of fines in the product after debranning and cracking. From the stand-point of drying time and quality (percentage of multicracks) the drying air temperature of 75° C appears to be optimum.

Methods of Parboiling and Production of Bulgur

The methods of production of bulgur wheat can be grouped into three major heads, namely, traditional batch method, modern method and chemical lye peeling method.

The *traditional batch method* consists of soaking and open steaming in a kettle, drying in dryers, partial debranning in a polisher and cracking in under runner disc type or any other type cracking machine.

The *Modern method* involves soaking and pressure cooking (steaming) in modern parboiling units, drying in dryers, debranning and cracking in modern milling machines.

The *Chemical lye peeling method* includes continuous soaking and pressure cooking, lye peeling, drying and cracking.

A few special processes developed in India (Method-1) and the U.S.A. (Method II-IV, Roger, 1970) have been described in the subsequent paragraphs.

I. BATCH METHOD

In India, the bulgur wheat has been produced on a commercial scale successfully under the supervision of Jadavpur University, Calcutta. The process is described below.

The clean raw wheat is soaked at 65 to 70° C for a certain period to raise the moisture content to a level of about 85 per cent (d.b.) and then the soaked wheat is steamed with live steam for about 20 minutes in a batch type soaker-steamer (i.e., paddy parboiling tank developed in India). The parboiled wheat is then dried to the proper moisture content with heated air in a LSU dryer.

The clean and dry-parboiled wheat is partially debranned in a Satake-horizontal abrasive type polisher. The debranned grain is then allowed to pass through the small clearance between the two rotating steel rolls of a Satake type husker for cracking. Now the bulgur is ready for consumption.

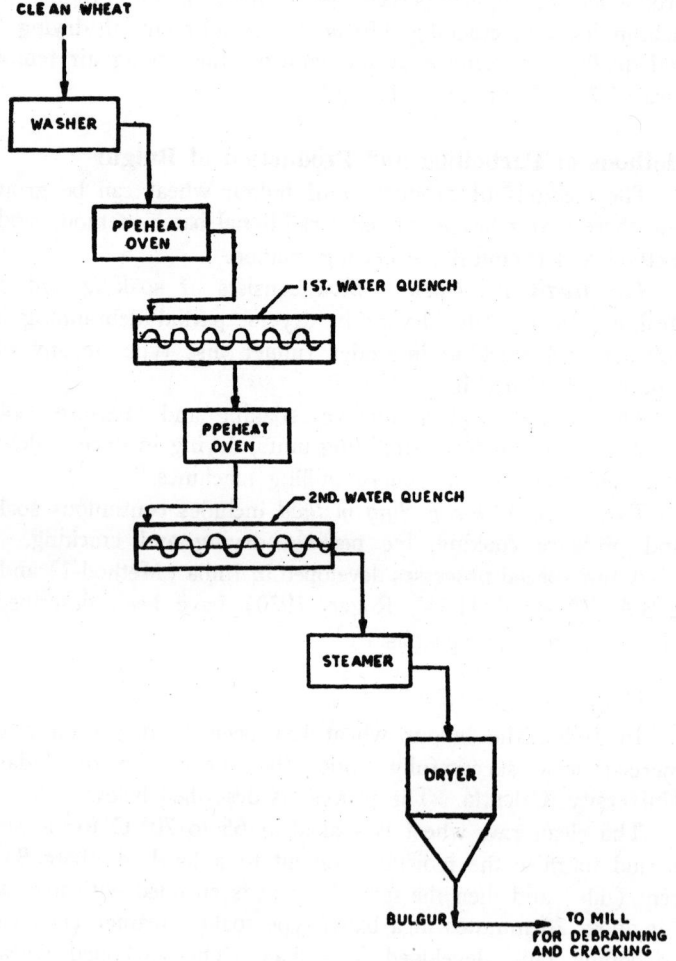

FIG. 9.4. Flow diagram of pre-heat process

ÏI. PREHEAT TREATMENT PROCESS

In this process, the clean and washed wheat is first preheated in an oven at a temperature between 93 and 105° C and the preheated grain is then introduced into a first water quench. During this operation the moisture content of wheat is raised from 10 to about 50 per cent (d.b). The partially soaked wheat is led to the second reheat oven, wherein, the grain is again heated to a temperature between 65 and 75° C. The reheated wheat grain is then fed to the second water quench to increase its moisture content to a level of about 90 per cent (d.b). The total time required for the above operations is approximately one hour.

The soaked wheat is then cooked by steaming at a pressure of 2 kg/cm². The cooked grain (gelatinised grain) is dried to 10 per cent moisture content (d.b) by the dryers.

The dried parboiled wheat may then be conveyed to the mill for debranning and cracking. The flow diagram for the heat treatment process is shown in Fig. 9.4.

IIï. CONTINUOUS PROCESS

In a continuous process, the clean and washed wheat is treated with a spray of water while moving through a series of three screw conveyors, steam is also injected into each of the three conveyors so as to raise the temperature of wheat to 65° C and increases the moisture content to the desired level. The heated and moistened wheat from the first screw conveyor is discharged into the first steeping tank. The wheat is partially steeped while moving from the top to the bottom of the tank. The partially steeped wheat is then conveyed to the top of the second steeping tank by the second screw conveyor wherein, it is again subject to a spray of water and open steam. In the final step also the wheat is moistened and heated in the third screw conveyor and steeped to the proper moisture level in the third steeping tank. The above sequence of operations require about 12 hours.

The steeped wheat is blanched in the blanchers and then introduced into a continuous steamer wherein it is cooked for about 2 minutes by steam under a pressure of 2 kg/cm². After cooling in a cooler, the cooked (gelatinised) wheat is dried to

10 per cent (d.b) with hot air in a series of two columnar dryers.

The dried product may be debranned and cracked as usual. The out-turn of the cracked bulgur and fines are abont 85 and 15 per cent respectively.

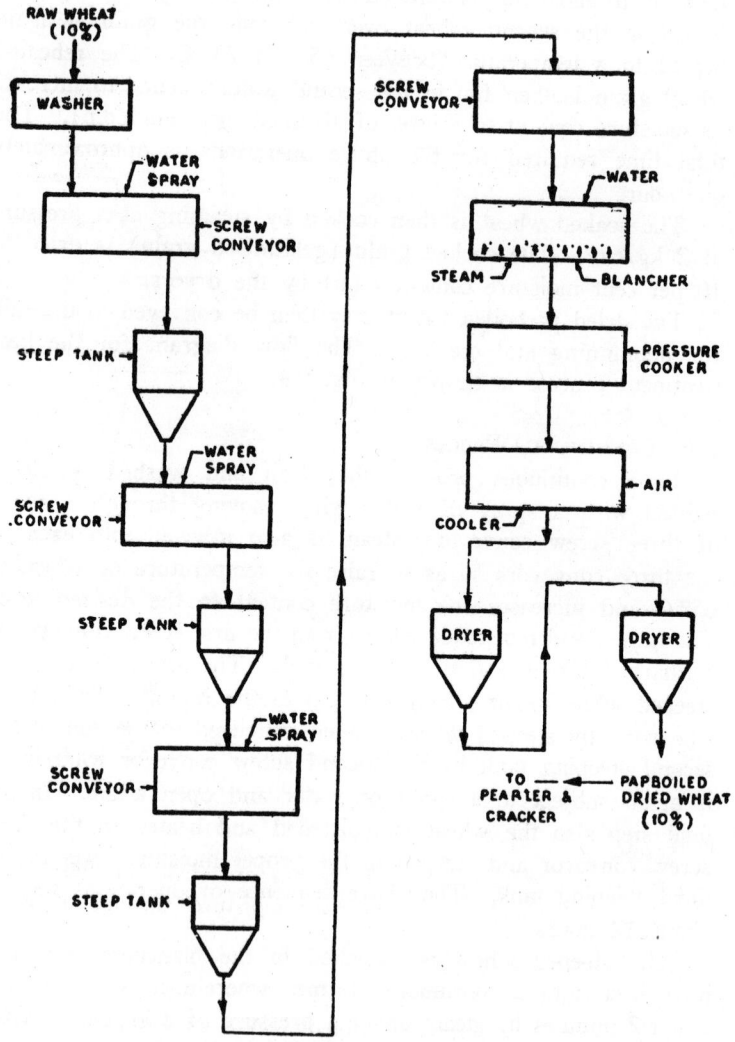

FIG. 9.5. Flow sheet for Continuous Process

The flow diagram for the continuous process is shown in Fig. 9.5.
The process is particularly suitable for soft white wheat berry.

IV. CHEMICAL LYE PEELING PROCESS

The lye peeling process has been discussed below.
The process is illustrated in Fig. 9.6.

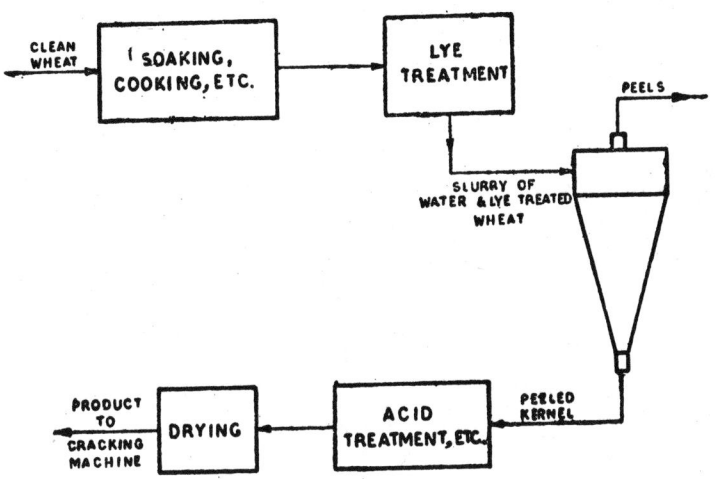

FIG. 9.6 Flow diagram for Continuous Lye Peeling Process

Soaking
Raw wheat is allowed to pass through a screw conveyor filled with hot water. Heating jackets are provided to maintain the temperature of grain and water mixture at 82° C at the exit. The soaking period in the conveyor adjusted to one hour.

Tempering
The soaked wheat is fed to a bin and held in there for 30 minutes at 82° C to equilibriate moisture throughout the kernel.

Cooking
The soaked and tempered wheat is passed through a reel in which it is steamed at 100° C for about minutes.

Lye treatment

The cooked wheat while in the reel is treated with hot dilute aqueous solution of caustic soda (NaOH) at 85° C and the lye coated wheat is held in the reel for about 3 minutes. Then the lye solution is removed from the lye treated wheat by a spray of cold water in a rotating screen.

Peeling

The lye treated wheat along with water is pumped through a hydrocyclone at a pressure of 3 kg/cm². The peeled kernels issuing from the discharge tip is washed thoroughly with water.

Acid treatment

The washed and peeled wheat kernel is then treated with 1 per cent aqueous acetic acid solution at 50° C for 5 minutes in a worm to neutralise the last trace of caustic soda adhering to the lye peeled wheat kernels.

Drying

The lye peeled wheat kernel is then dried to 10 to 14 per cent moisture content (d.b) by dryers.

Advantages

(1) The light coloured product gives an appearance resembling rice.

(2) The product is suitable for quick cooking cereals, breakfast cereals and as an ingredient of baby food.

Disadvantage

(1) The production cost is comparatively high.

BIBLIOGRAPHY ON SECTION II

1. Agrawala, N. S., 1963, Parboiling of rice in India, *Bull. Grain Technology*, 1(3) : 55-60.
2. Ali, N., and Ojha, T. P., 1975a, Soaking characteristics of paddy, *J. Agric Eng. Res.*, In press-1975b. A new concept in parboiling technology, *J. Agric. Eng. Res.*, In press.

3. Ali, N., and Pandya, A. C., 1974, Basic concept of parboiling of paddy, *J. Agric. Eng. Res.*, 19(2) : 111.

4. Bal, S., Ali, N., and Ojha, T. P., 1974, Parboiling of paddy, *RPEC Publication No. 745.* Indian Institute of Technology, Kharagpur, India.

5. Bandyopadhyay, B., and Ghosh, T. K., 1965, Studies on the hydration of Indian paddy, I. A. rate equation of the soaking equation, *Indian J. Technology*, 3(11) 360.

6. Bandyopadhyoy, S., and Roy, N. C., 1977, Studies on swelling and hydration of paddy by hot soaking, *J. Food Sci. & Tech.*, 14, 3 : 95-98.

7. Bhattacharya, K. R., 1969, Breakage of rice during milling and the effect of parboiling., *Cereal Chem.*, 37 : 478-85.

8. Bhattacharya, K. R., and Indudharaswamy, Y. M., 1967, Conditions of drying parboiled paddy for optimum milling quality, *Cereal Chem.*, 44(6) : 592-600.

9. Bhattacharya, K. R., and Subba Rao, V. P., 1966a, Processing conditions and milling yield in parboiling of rice, *J. Agric. Food Chem.* 14(5) : 473-1966b. Effect of processing conditions on quality of parboiled rice, *J. Agric. Food Chem*, 14(5) : 475.

10. Borasio, L., and Gariboldi, F., 1965a. Parboiled rice-production and use ; Part I production, *Rice J.* 68(5) : 32-35, 41.- ......1965b, Parboiled rice-production and use part II, *Use. Rice J.*, 68(8) : 23-27.

11. Chakravarty, A. et al., 1982. Determination of optimum drying conditions for drying of parbiolid wheat. AMA, 13, Japan.

12. Desikachar, H. S. R., Bhashyam, M. K., and Parpia, H. A. B., 1967, Relative yields of total and head rice from raw and parboiled paddy, *J. Food Sci. Technology*, 4 : 156.

13. Desikachar, H. S. R., Sowbhagya, C. M., Viraktamath, C. S., Indudharaswamy, Y. M., and Bhashyam, M. K., 1969, Steaming of paddy for improved culinary, milling and storage properties, *J. Food Sci. Technology*, 6(2) : 117-21.

14. Food and Agriculture Organisation, 1954; Rice and Rice diets —a nutritional survery (revised), FAO, Rome, Italy, 1967-1968. Pilot study on paddy losses in Thailand during har-

156   POST HARVEST TECHNOLOGY

vesting, drying, and threshing, FAO, Rome Italy.
15. Gariboldi, F., 1954, It surriscaldamento del riso, *Riso*, 3(1) : 17-20.
16. Ghose, T. K., 1963, Development of an improved and fully mechanized method for the production of parboiled rice, Jadavpur University, Calcutta, India.
17. Ghosh, R.L.M., Ghatge, M.B., and Subrahmanyan, V., 1960, Rice in India (revised), *ICAR*, New Delhi, India.
18. Houston, D. F., (ed.), 1972, Rice chemistry and technology, American Association of Cereal chemists, Inc., St. Paul, Minnesota.
19. Houston, D. F., and Kohler, G.O., 1970, Nutritional properties of rice,. *National Academy of Science*, Washington, D. C.
20. Houston, D. F., Hunter, I. R., and Kester, E. B., 1956. Storage changes in parboiled rice, *J. Agric. Food Chem.*, 4(11) : 964.
21. Houston, D. F., Hunter, I. R., McComb, E. A., And Kester, E. B., 1954, Deteriorative changes in the oil fraction of stored parboiled rice, *J. Agric. Food Chem* 2(23) : 1185.
22. Jayanarayana, E. K., Influence of processing conditions on the browning of parboiled rice, *Rice J.*, 62(12) : 16-17.
23. Jones, J. W., and Taylor, J. W. 1933. Effect of parboiling rough rice on milling quality, U.S. Department of Agriculture, Circular No. 340.
24, Jones, J. W., Zeleny, L., and Taylor, J. W., 1946, Effect of parboiling and related treatments on the milling nutritional and cooking quality of rice, U.S. Department of Agriculture, Circular No. 752.
25. Kisan Krishi Yantra Udyog, Kanpur, 1972, Automatic parboiling and drying of paddy, prospect and promises—a performance study, Government of India.
26. Kausal, R. T., 1979, M. Tech. Thesis. PHTC, IIT, Kharagpur.
27. Kuppuswamy, M.A., 1972, Mathematical model for a continuous system of paddy parboiling, *J. Agric. Eng. Res*, 9(3) : 53.
28. Kurien, P. P., Radhakrishnamurthy, R., Desikashar, H.S.R., and Subrahmanyan, V., 1964, Effect of parboiling on the swelling quality of rice; *Cereal Chem.* 41(1) : 16-22.
29. Mahadevappa. M., and Desikachar, H. S. R., 1968a, Expan-

sion and swelling of raw and parboiled rice during cooking, *J. Food Sci. Technology*, 5(2) : 59-62.,

......1968b.   Some observations on the histology of raw and parboiled rice, *J. Food Sci. Technology*, 5(2) : 72-73.

30. Matz, S. A., 1959, *The Chemistry and Technology of Cereals as Food and Feed*, The AVI Publishing Co,. Inc., West Port, Conn.

31. Mozumdar, A. C., Bose, A. N., Ganguli N. C., and Guha, B. C., 1960, I—Soaking and gelatinization ; II—Dehydration ; III—Effect of hot soaking and mechanical drying on the nutritive value of parboiled rice, *J. Biochem. Microbiol. Technol Eng.* 2(4) :431.

32. Mecham, D. K., Kester, E. B., and Pence, J. W., 1961, Parboiling characteristics of California medium-grain rice, *Food Technology*, 15(11) : 475-79.

33. Mohesenin, N. N., 1968, Physical properties of plant and animal materials : Part I Department of Agric. Penn. State Univ., University Park, Penn.

34. Radhey, L., and Wimberly, J. E. 1970, Notes on modern parboiling plants, Rice process Eng. Centre, Indian Institute of Technology, Kharagpur, India.

35. Raghavendra Rao, S. N., and Juliano, B. O., 1970, Effect of parboiling on some physiochemical properties of rice, *Food Chem.* 18(2) : 289.

36. Raghavendra Rao, S. N., Narayana, M. N., and Desikachar, H.S.R., 1967. Studies on some comparative milling properties of raw and parboiled rice, *J. Food Sci. Technology*, 4(4) : 150-55.

37. Rama Rao, V. V., and Bal, S., 1973, Design and layout of a modern parboiling and drying plant, Unpublished report, Rice Process Eng. Centre, Indian Institute of Technology, Kharagpur, India.

38. Roberts, R. L., Potter, A. L., Kester, E. B., and Keneaster, K. K., 1954, Effect of processing conditions on the expanded volume, colour, and soluble starch of parboiled rice, *Cereal Chem.* 31(2) : 121-29.

39. Roger, D., 1970. Editor, Rice and Bulgur Quick-Cooking Processes, Food processing review No. 16, New Jersey U.S.A.

40. Rajkondawar, R. R., 1984, Development and testing of soaking steaming system for the production of crystal rice, M. Tech. Thesis, IIT, Kharagpur.
41. Rao, J. P. V. K., 1991. Pneumatic parboiling of paddy, M. Tech, Thesis, IIT, Kharagpur.
42. Shivanna, C. S., 1971, Traditional and modern methods of parboiling and drying, *Food Industries. J.*, 4(5):1-12, 24-25.
43. Shyamal, D. K., Chakraverty, A. and Banerjee, H. D., 1994, thermal properties of wheat and wheat bulgur, Energy convirs. Mgmt., U.K.
44. Shyamanuj, D., Mukharjee, R. K. and Chakraverty, A., 1989, Production technique for crystalline parboiled rice, *J.Agric. Engg.*, 26(1), 55-58.

SECTION III
MILLING

CHAPTER 10

General Grain Milling Operations

Food grains are naturally endowed with outer protective husk/bran layers, composed of rough, fibrous, pigmented and waxy substances which are undesirable for edible purposes. It also consists of oily germs which are undesirable for storage purposes. Removal of these parts constitutes the most fundamental prerequisite in grain milling or flour milling technology of cereals. In grain milling the outer husk/bran layers are removed from the grain with its shape retained whereas in flour milling, flour without or with negligible bran content is prepared without the grain shape.

In general, milling refers to the size reduction and separation operations used for processing of food grains into edible form by removing and separating the inedible and undesirable portions from them. Milling may involve cleaning/separation, husking, sorting, whitening, polishing, grinding, sifting, etc.

To increase the milling quality of the food grains or to improve the quality and quantity of their end products or to facilitate milling operations for the desired products, food grains are sometimes subjected to hydrothermal treatment prior to milling called conditioning.

Basic milling operations and hydrothermal treatment involved in cereal milling technology have been discussed.

CLEANING/SEPARATION

Classification of separation methods

Any mixture of solid materials can be separated into different fractions according to their difference in length, width, thickness, density, roughness, drag in moving air, electrical conductivity, colour and other physical properties.

Each of the various types of separators employed in flour and grain milling is designed on the basis of the difference in the following physical characteristics of grain : (1) Width and thickness of the grain for sieves, screen cleaners, sifters, thickness graders, grading reels, inclined sifters, etc. ; (2) Length of the grain for indented type or disc type pocket separators ; (3) Aerodynamic properties for husk aspirators, cyclone separators . (4) Form and state of the surface for separators for coarse grain, spiral separators, belt type separators ; (5) Specific gravity and coefficient of friction for separating tables, stone separator ; (6) Ferromagnetic properties for magnetic and electromagnetic separators ; (7) Electrical properties for electrostatic separators and (8) Colour for electronic separators.

Separation According to Aerodynamic Properties

The pneumatic separation is based on the difference in aerodynamic properties of the different components. The aerodynamic properties of a particle depends on the shape, dimensions and weight of the particle, the state and position of the particle with respect to the air current.

The aerodynamic properties have been discussed in detail in other section

Separation According to Specific Gravity

If the components of a mixture are different in densities and subjected to a reciprocating movement of an inclined table or screen then the components of the mixture are readily separated into different fractions according to their densities.

This type of separator works on the principle of self sorting or stratification. The heavier particles of the mixture sink to the bottom by the to and fro movement of the inclined table and are then separated by any suitable method.

In a mixture of components of same density, the finer particles sink while in a mixture of components of equal dimensions but of different densities, the heavier particles sink to the bottom. This is the principle of operation of stone separators.

Composite stone separators of pneumatic grading-table type are used to enhance settling of stone. The stone separator has been discussed in detail in Rice Milling Chapter. The effectiveness of operation of a stone separator depends on many factors. Of them kinematic parameters are most important. Continuous and uniform feeding of mixture are also important.

SEPARATION ACCORDING TO MAGNETIC PROPERTIES

Metallic impurities in the grain accelerates wear and tear of different parts of the milling machinery. Moreover, even minute quantity of metallic impurities present in the milling products can make them unfit for human consumption.

The magnetic impurities like steel, pig iron, nickel and cobalt particles present in a grain mixture can be separated on the basis of their differences in magnetic properties.

Since effectiveness of removal of metallic impurities depends on the force of attraction of the magnet, an electromagnet is preferred to an ordinary permanent magnet as the force of attraction of the former can be increased by increasing the strength of electric current only. Magnetic separation consists of three steps : (a) distribution of feed over the magnet, (b) collection and retention of the ferromagnetic impurities by the magnet, and (c) cleaning of the magnet from the impurities.

SEPARATION ACCORDING TO ELECTROSTATIC PROPERTIES

When different particles are charged with statical electricity and are passed through another electric field, then the action of the outer electric field on the electric field of the charged parti-

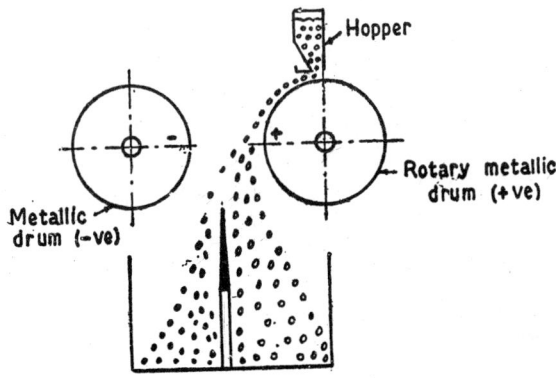

FIG. 10.1 Electrostatic Separator

cles produces some mechanical work which is used for separation (Fig. 10.1).

The electrical separation consists of two stages : Preliminary charging of the particles with electricity and separation of the charged particles by electrostatic forces in accordance with the magnitude and nature of the charges on the particles.

Magnitude of the preliminary charge is determined by the following factors : electrical conductivity, dielectric constant, and other properties of the particles such as particle size and shape, specific gravity and design of the separators also.

ELECTRONIC SEPARATORS

Separation according to colours

Difference in colour can be used for separation. With the help of an electronic separator some fruits, vegetables and cereal grains can be sorted from the discoloured or defective ones in accordance with their differences in colour.

In an electronic separator (Fig. 10.2) the seeds are uniformly fed to the optical chamber. Two photo cells are set at a certain angle in order to direct both beams to one point of the parabolic trajectory of the seeds.

A needle connected to a high voltage source is placed on the other

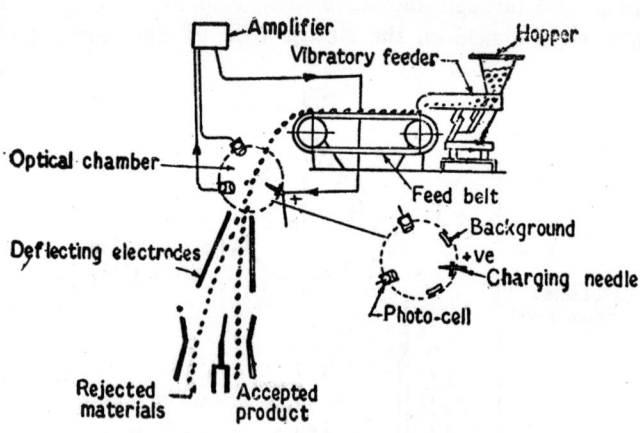

FIG. 10.2 Flow Diagram of an Electronic
Colour Sorter

side. When a beam through photoelectric cells falls on a dark object, a current is generated on the needle. The end of the needle receives a charge and imparts it to the dark seeds. The grains are then allowed to pass between two electrodes with a high potential difference between them. As a result two fractions of the mixture are separated according to difference in colours.

Electronic separators have been used in various industries for a long time. Recently electronic sorters are being used for the separation of discoloured grains in some advanced countries. But the sorting capacity of these units is limited resulting in very high cost of separation.

FRICTIONAL SEPARATORS

Separation according to surface properties : The frictional properties can be utilised for the separation of a mixture of grains of almost same size. Sizes of oats and hulled oats, millets and bind weed are almost the same. These mixtures can be separated by frictional separators (Fig. 10.3) consisting of an inclined plane surface. The operation of the separators is based on the differences between the friction angles of two types of grain.

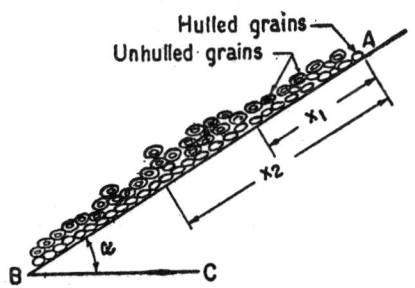

FIG. 10.3   Inclined Plane Frictional
Separators

When grains are allowed to move along an inclined plane, frictional forces of different magnitudes act upon these particles. Therefore, different particles move on inclined surface at different velocities.

In this case also heavier particles will sink at the lower layer and move at a lower velocity, while lighter particles will float at the top and move downward at a higher velocity.

The velocity of the particle at any point on the inclined plane can be found out as follows :

$$v_1 = \sqrt{2g\,K_1 x_1}$$

where $K_1 = \sin \alpha - \mu_1 \cos \alpha$

   $x_1 =$ distance travelled by a body which has initial velocity zero

   $\alpha =$ angle of inclination

   $\mu_1 =$ coefficient of friction

When coefficient of friction of the dehusked grain is greater than the coefficient of friction of the unhusked grain, the movement of the lower layer of husked grain will be retarded. The unhusked grain will move above the lower layer with higher velocity, v_0

$$v_0 = v_1\ (1 + K_2/K_1)$$

   $v_0 =$ absolute velocity of the upper layer

   $v_0 > v_1$ by the factor K_2/K_1

These properties of free flowing particles can be used in separation of husked and unhusked grains.

Effectiveness of the separation

$$
\begin{array}{c|c|c}
\text{Feed} & & \text{Product} \uparrow \\
\xrightarrow{} & & \overline{\text{C, kg/hr}} \\
\text{F, kg/hr} & & \text{Reject} \\
& & \text{D, kg/hr} \downarrow
\end{array}
$$

$$\varepsilon_A = \frac{(X_F - X_D)X_C(X_F - X_C)(1 - X_D)}{(X_D - X_C)^2 X_F(1 - X_F)}$$

where $\varepsilon_A =$ Separating effectiveness for a mixture of two components A and B.

   $F =$ Rate of feeding to the separator, kg/hr

   $C =$ Rate of separating the product, kg/hr

   $D =$ Rate of reject, kg/hr

$X_F,\ X_C,\ X_D =$ Fractions of Component A in the feed, separated product and reject respectively.

HUSKING/SCOURING/HULLING OF GRAIN

In general, husking refers to the removal of outer seed coat from the grain kernel. The terms hulling and scouring are also used in cereal milling. In grain milling, husk is removed from the grain retaining its original shape whereas in flour milling bran is removed from the grain to produce flour without any emphasis on its shape. Husking and scouring are the most important operations in grain milling or flour milling technology of cereals.

Different types of machines are employed for husking and scouring operations because of the differences in anatomical structure, type of bonds and strength properties among husk, bran and kernel of different grains.

Methods of husking

The operation of husking and scouring machines can be divided according to the following three basic principles :

(1) Compression and shear : Compression and shear can compress, split and strip off the husk from grain. Concave type of husking machine, rubber roll husker, etc., are designed on the basis of this principle.

(2) Abrasion and friction : Hollanders are based on the friction of grain on an abrasive surface (emery).

(3) Impact and friction : Husk can be stripped off by the action of impact and frictional force. Centrifugal type paddy sheller comes under this group.

Figure 10.4 shows different methods of husking.

CONCAVE TYPE HUSKER

This machine consists of a horizontal rotating cylinder, called roll, and a stationary cylindrical surface known as concave (Fig. 10.5).

The husk/bran layer can be removed from buck wheat and millets keeping the original shape of the kernel by applying mild shear and compression. These types of machines are fairly efficient and require low power.

On feeding into the mill the grain is first caught up by the rolls and passed through the husking zone between the roll and

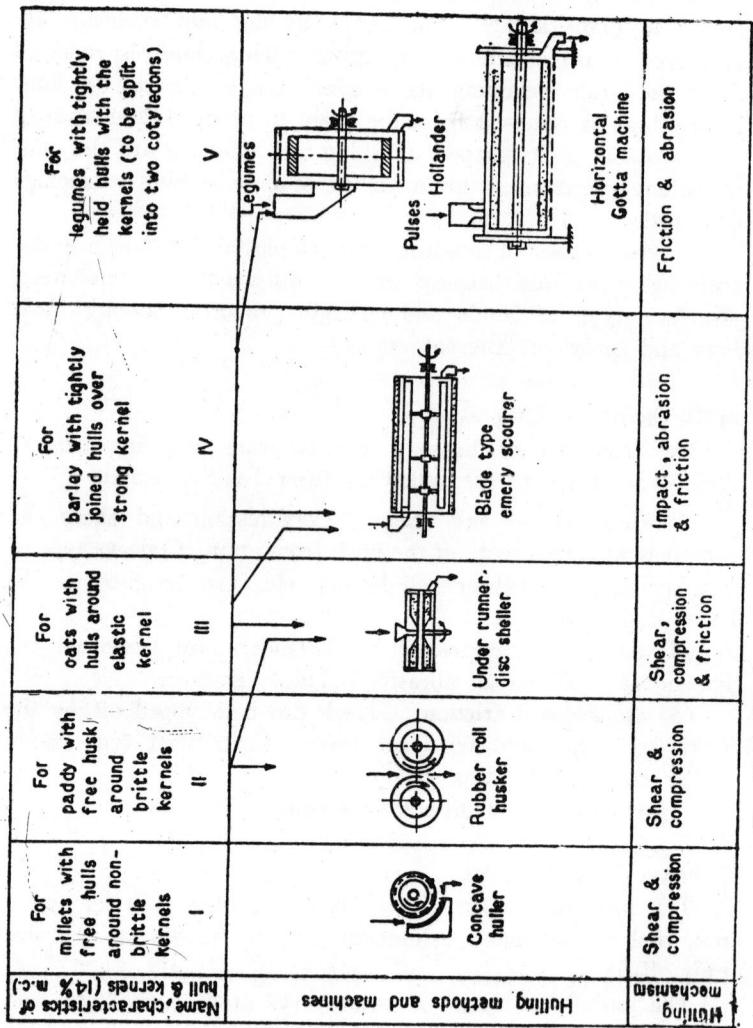

Name, characteristics of hull & kernels (14% m.c.)	Hulling methods and machines	Hulling mechanism
I — For millets with free hulls around non-brittle kernels	Concave huller	Shear & compression
II — For paddy with free husk around brittle kernels	Rubber roll husker	Shear & compression
III — For oats with hulls around elastic kernel	Under runner disc sheller	Shear, compression & friction
IV — For barley with tightly joined hulls over strong kernel	Blade type emery scourer	Impact, abrasion & friction
V — For legumes with tightly held hulls with the kernels (to be split into two cotyledons)	Horizontal Gotta machine (Legumes, Pulses, Hollander)	Friction & abrasion

Fig. 10.4 Classification of Husking/Scouring/Hulling Methods

the concave where it is subjected to shear and compression simultaneously.   One part of the husk is sheared by the rotating

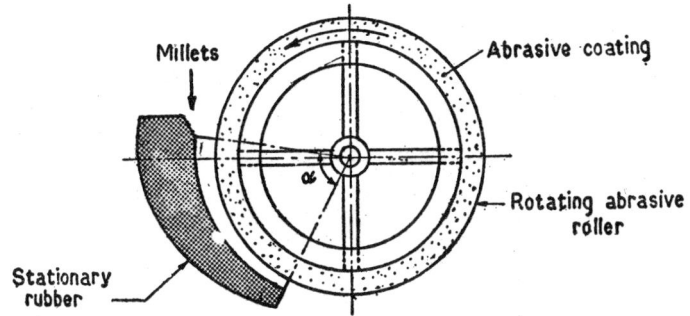

Fig. 10.5 Principle of Hulling by concave Type Huller

roll while the other part is pressed against the stationary concave and subjected to breaking forces.

The minimum clearance between the roll and the concave must be greater than the dimensions of the grain kernel, otherwise the kernel will be crushed. The radius of curvature of the concave is usually the same as the radius of the roll.

Composition of roll and concave varies with the type of grain to be husked. As for example roll made of abrasive material and concave made of commercial rubber are used for millets.

Usually the following specifications of rolls and concaves (Kuprits, 1967) are used :

Diameter of concave	—50 to 60 cm
Length of concave	—19 to 30 cm
Angle of contact	—40° to 70°
Peripheral speed	—10 to 15 m/sec

HUSKING BY THE ACTION OF RUBBER ROLLS

In case of paddy, deformation caused by shear and compression of the two rotating rubber surfaces are sufficient to split and separate the husk from the grains. The paddy is passed through the clearance between two rubber rolls, rotating in opposite directions at different speed. The clearance between them is smaller than the mean thickness of the paddy. One part of the husk is subjected to shearing forces whereas the other part in contact with the slower roll is under compression and is thus subjected to breaking forces. Husking is done by the action of these forces.

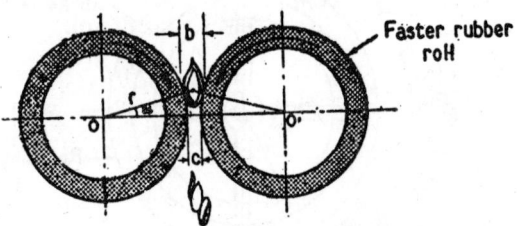

FIG. 10.6   Husking Principle of Rubber Roll Husker

Suppose a grain having thickness b (Fig. 10.6) is brought into contact with the rolls at points A and A_1. The grain is then acted upon by the rolls until it leaves the working zone. If α_1 is the angle between the line connecting the centres the rolls and the radius drawn through the point at which the grain contacts the roll,

Then $\cos \alpha_1 = \dfrac{r + (C/2)}{r + (b/2)} = \dfrac{d+C}{d+b}$

where r = radiaus of the rolls, cm.

          d = diameter of the rolls, cm.

          C = clearance between the rolls, cm.

          b = size of the grain, cm.

Hence, $\alpha_1 = \cos^{-1}\left(\dfrac{d+C}{d+b}\right)$

The full length of the husking zone from the point at which the grain is caught by the rolls to the point where the grain is no longer in contact with the roll will correspond to the length of the arc, l_h and angle $2\alpha_1$

Length of the husking zone, l_h can be expressed as follows :

$$l_h = \frac{2\pi d}{360} \cos^{-1}\left(\frac{d+C}{d+b}\right)$$

The length of the husking zone l_h depends on the diameter of the rolls, the thickness of grain to be husked, and the linear distance between the centres of the rolls.

When the size of the grain, b and the clearance, C are fixed, then the length of the husking zone increases with the increase in diameter of the roll.

The period of husking, $t = \dfrac{l_h}{V_f}$ (faster roll)

The period of husking, $t = (l_h - l_{ad})/V_s$ (slower roll)

where l_{ad} = difference between the paths of faster and slower roll.

$$l_{ad} = \frac{l_h(V_f - V_s)}{V_f}$$

This equation shows that the difference between the paths of the two rolls depends not only on the geometrical parameters but also on the peripheral speeds of the rolls, their relative velocities and the differential speeds.

If V_f = 15 to 17.5 m/sec and
V_s = 12.5 to 15 m/sec,

The $V_f - V_s$ should not be less than 2.5 m/sec (Kuprits, 1967).

HUSKING BY UNDER RUNNER DISC HUSKER (disc sheller)

Paddy may be husked by the under runner disc sheller. Oats can also be husked by this machine. Previously it was used for millets.

Principle

The under runner disc husker consists of two horizontal and coaxial cast iron discs, partly coated with abrasive material. The top disc is stationary and provided with an opening at the centre for feeding while the bottom disc is rotating. The clearance between the two discs can be adjusted by changing the position of the lower rotating disc vertically.

The grains which fall on the lower disc through the central opening are pulled along by its rotation and move outwards by centrifugal force. During rotation around the axis of the disc and simultaneous movement towards the edge, grains tend to take a vertical position. At this point, their tips strike against the hard surface of the top disc which exerts pressure and slight friction resulting in splitting of husk apart.

The effective width of the abrasive coating should not be more than 1/6th of the stone diameter and the optimum peripheral speeds should be about 14 m/sec and 20 m/sec for paddy and oats respectively.

The trajectory of the grain with respect to the working zone of the stationary and rotating discs is a curve directed from the inner radius, r of the rotating disc to its outer radius R. The grain moves with increasing velocity

The velocity, $V = w.r'$

where w is the angular velocity of the rotating disc

r' is the variable radius vector for the moving grain

$$(r < r' < R)$$

The centrifugal force $C = mw^2 r'$

Under the influence of these forces the grain describes a curve stretching from the centre to the periphery of the discs. The force acting on the grain increases as it travels from the centre to the periphery, since the peripheral speed as well as the relative velocity are simultaneously increased. This increase in the velocities leads to complex deformations of the husk (deformation by compression, shearing and slip). As a result the husk is split and stripped off from the kernel.

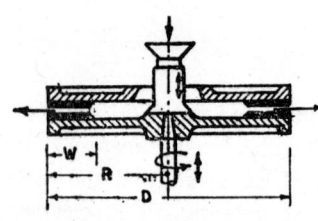

FIG. 10.7 Under Runner Disc Husker

Construction

Figure 10.7 shows the constructional features : The main parts of this machine are : The feed control device, the upper stationary disc, the lower rotating disc fitted to the shaft, and the pulley mounted on shaft. The shaft can be moved up and down.

Advantages

(1) Construction and operation of the machine are simple.

(2) Life of the machine is long.

(3) Running cost is low.

(4) The performance of the machine is satisfactory for raw and parboiled paddy of uniform size.

Disadvantages

(1) Compared to rubber roll husker the head and total yields are less.

(2) Damage to the rice kernel is done due to the formation of scratches on it by the hard abrasive coating.

HUSKING BY SCOURERS AND BLADE TYPE HUSKERS

Impact huskers can be used for barley, wheat and oats having moisture content of about 13 per cent

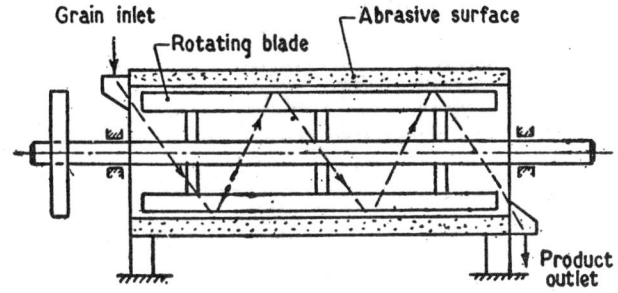

FIG. 10.8   Principle of Husking by Blade type
Emery Scourer

It consists of a rotating horizontal shaft fitted with blades encaged in a cylinder. When grains are fed to the cylinder (Fig. 10.8) they come in contact with the revolving blades and are thrown to the internal abrasive surface of cylinder which rebounds them. The grains impinge on the blade again. Two impacts per revolution between the grain and the abrasive cylinder and friction amongst the grains result in removal of husk from the grain.

The holding time of the grain in the scourer depends on the peripheral speed of the abrasive cylinder and the blade-angle. The effective inclination of the blade is 3 to 6 sec only.

Advantages

(1) The machine is easy to operate.

(2) It does not require much attention.

Disadvantages
   (1) Yield of cracked and crushed grain is high,

HULLING BY AN ABRASSIVE DRUM IN A CYLINDRICAL STEEL SHELL
   Grains with hull firmly attached to the kernel such as barley,
wheat, etc., can be husked by a more drastic treatment.

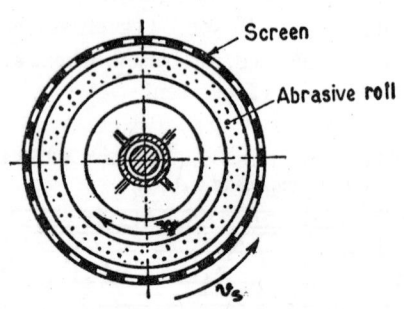

FIG. 10.9 Working Principle of
Batch type Hollander

   Hollander (Fig. 10.9) can be used for the above purpose
It comprises of rapidly rotating abrasive roll encaged in a slowly
rotating steel shell. In a batch huller the grains enter into the
space between the abrasive roll and the perforated cylindrical
shell and take a considerable period to travel from one end to
the other. The shell rotates slowly in the opposite direction. In
Hollanders the hull is removed from the grain because of the
friction among the grain, abrasive roll and perforated steel shell
and friction between grain and grain.
   On account of the following disadvantages of batch type
Hollanders, continuous Hollanders are being increasingly used :
   (1) The machine is heavy and bulky,
   (2) It consumes high power, and
   (3) Due to batch system, continuous production is not
possible and operational schedule becomes complicated.

Factors which affect the effectiveness of hulling/husking/ scouring
   The effectiveness of hulling depends on the properties of the
grain and the type of huller.

Amount of desired and undesired products obtained from cereal milling depends on the following grain parameters :

(1) Type of the grain and its special properties ;

(2) Bond strength between kernel and husk, strength of the kernel and strength of the husk ;

(3) Sound or cracked grain, grain size and uniformity of size ;

(4) Moisture content of grain and difference in moisture content between husk and kernel ;

(5) Extent of hydrothermal treatment given to the grain ;

(6) Proportion of husked kernel in the grain ; and

(7) The ease of separation.

Effectiveness of hulling/husking/scouring

The coefficient of hulling $E_{hulling}$ is defined by the percentage of husked grain obtained from the total amount of grain input.

$$E_{hulling} = \left(\frac{n_1 - n_2}{n_1}\right) = \left(1 - \frac{n_2}{n_1}\right)$$

where n_1 = amount of grain before hulling

n_2 = amount of unhulled grain after hulling.

The coefficient of wholeness of the kernels, E_{wk} is defined by the proportion of whole kernels to the total amount of kernels (kernel+crushed grain+mealy waste) extracted by the given system.

$$E_{wk} = \frac{k_2 - k_1}{(k_2 - k_1) + (d_2 - d_1) + (m_2 - m_1)}$$

where $k_2 - k_1$ = Yield of whole kernels

$d_2 - d_1$ = Yield of crushed kernels

$m_2 - m_1$ = Yield of mealy waste in the product

k_2 = Contents of the whole kernels after hulling

k_1 = Contents of the whole kernels before hulling

d_2 = Contents of the crushed kernels after hulling

d_1 = Contents of the crushed kernels before hulling

m_2 = Contents of the mealy waste in the product after hulling

m_1 = Contents of the mealy waste in the product before hulling

The efficiency of operation of hullers can be expressed by an overall 'coefficient, which takes into account both the qualitative and quantitative aspects of the operations carried out

$$\eta \text{ hulling} = E \text{ hulling } E_{wk}$$

GRINDING

Cereal grinding system can be divided into two groups : plain grinding and selective grinding.

In plain grinding hard bodies are ground to a free flowing material consisting of particles of sufficiently uniform size. This material is either the final product or a product ready for further processing.

In selective grinding, the grinding operation is carried out in a number of stages successively using differences in structural and mechanical properties of the components of the body.

It should be noted that the power consumption for grinding is about 50 to 80 per cent of the total power required for all operations.

Therefore, the following important points are to be considered for power design of the grinding system : rational utilisation of the raw material, quality of the products, size and colour of the products, efficiency of the grinders, specific power consumption and costs of production.

The characteristics of grinding operation is affected by the following grain parameters :

(i) Type of cereal grain, (ii) Variety, (iii) moisture content, (iv) extent of hydrothermal treatment given to the grain, (v) mechanical properties.

Each type of grain has an optimum moisture content for highest efficiency of grinding. The maximum formation of new surface for each type of wheat is related to the optimum moisture content. Moreover, power consumption is also dependent on moisture content. The starch granules are separated from the proteins due to deformation of hard wheat.

Hardness of rice and barley endosperms are 11.5 to 14.5 kg/mm², and 6.0 to 9.0 Kg/mm² respectively (Kuprits, 1967).

Effectiveness of grinding

The main criteria for evaluation of effectiveness of grinding of any solid body, including grain are : degree of grinding, specific power consumption and the specific load of the initial product on the working tool of the grinder. Degree of grinding, i is expressed as follows :

$$i = \frac{Sa}{Sb},$$

where Sa = overall surface area of the product after grinding, in cm^2

Sb = overall surface area of the product before grinding, in cm^2

The term overall extraction, Ex expressed in per cent refers to the difference between the percentage of undersized particles, C_1 in the final ground product and the percentage of undersized particles I in the initial feed entering the grinder

$$Ex = C_1 - I$$

$$C_1 = \left(\frac{u_1}{u_1 + O_1}\right) \cdot 100$$

$$I = \left(\frac{u_2}{u_2 + O_2}\right) \cdot 100$$

where u_1 = weight of undersized particles obtained by sifting the ground product

O_1 = weight of oversized particles obtained by sifting the ground product

u_2 = weight of the undersized particles in the initial product to be ground

O_2 = weight of oversized particles in the initial product to be ground

Ex depends upon : structural-mechanical properties of the material, dimensions of the rolls (i.e.. dia etc.), geometry of the surface of the rolls, kinematic parameters of the rolls, specific load on the rolls.

Machinery used in cereal grinding

Depending on the objective of grinding and mechanical properties of cereal grain, effects of the following are utilised for grinding : Compression and simultaneous shear of the

12

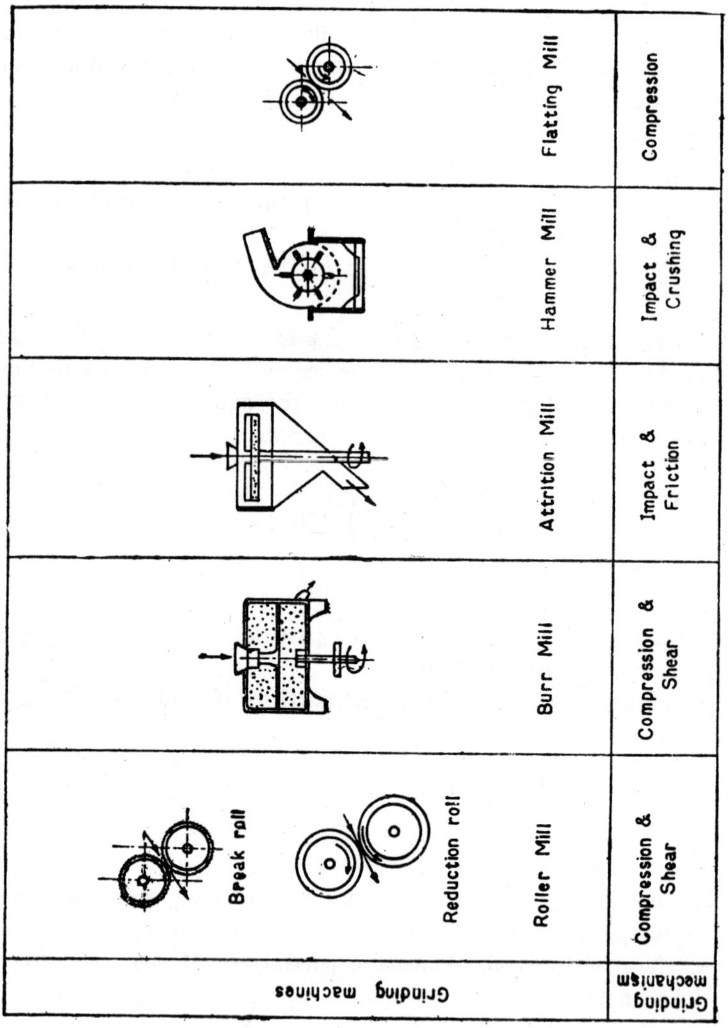

Grinding mechanism	Roller Mill	Burr Mill	Attrition Mill	Hammer Mill	Flatting Mill
	Compression & Shear	Compression & Shear	Impact & Friction	Impact & Crushing	Compression

FIG. 10.10 Classification of Grinding Machinery

material, impact followed by crushing of the material etc. The classification of grinding machines is shown in Fig. 10.10.

Grinding of grain in roller mills

The roller mill consists of two cylindrical steel rolls revolving in opposite directions at different speeds. In the roller mill the grain or its parts are ruptured in a space, which is narrowed towards the bottom.

Certain degree of grain rupturing starts at above the line connecting the centres of the rolls. The slow roll holds the grain during the action of the fast roll. In the grinding zone, the grain or its parts are simultaneously subjected to compression and shear resulting in deformation of grain. Rupturing of endosperm without much grinding the bran of wheat under grinding conditions is the characteristic of the first breaking system.

Factors affecting the effectiveness of roller mills

Clearance between rolls : Even a small variation in rollers' clearance leads to considerable variations in the products.

Geometrical parameters of rolls : Conditions of rupture of the particles to be ground depend upon the roll diameter, clearance and initial size of the particle.

Shape, number, slope, mutual position and shape of the cross-section of corrugations of the rolls have significant effects on the quality and yield of flour, total output and specific power consumption of the roller mills. Position of the corrugation edges have also the same effects on the product.

Kinematic parameters of the rolls : The important kinematic parameters of the rolls are speed of the fast roll, Vf and ratio of the speeds between fast and slow rolls $\left(\text{i.e., } k = \frac{Vf}{Vs}\right)$

The efficiency of grinding depends upon the kinematic parameters. *Capacity of the roller mills and power consumption for their operation*

The capacity of a roller mill is the amount of product in kilogrammes, ground per unit time.

The theoretical capacity of a pair of rolls can be determined from the formula (Kuprits, 1967) :

$$Qr = 3.6 \; \rho_1 \, l \, V_z \, b \, \psi$$

where Qr is the theoretical capacity of the roll pair, kg/hr

     ρ_1 = the bulk density of the product before grinding, kg/cm^3

     l = the length of the rolls, cm,

     V_z = the mean calculated velocity of the product in the grinding zone, cm/hr

     b = the clearance between the rolls, cm

     ψ = the coefficient of filling of the grinding zone, where

$$\psi = \frac{Qa}{Qr} \; (Qa \text{ is the actual capacity of the roll pair}).$$

The capacity of a roller will is also dependent upon type of grain and the moisture content of the grain.

Grinding grain in hammer mills

Grinding in a hammer mill involves impact on the material followed by crushing. The main working tools of this type of mill are hammers made of high quality steel, screens, and metal lines.

The output of hammer mill depends on the peripheral speeds of the hammer, the clearance between the screen and hammers, the area of the screen, the size of the screen openings, and the structural-mechanical properties of the material.

CHAPTER 11

Hydrothermal Treatment/Conditioning of Cereal Grains

Some times cereals, pulses and other food grains are subjected to hydrothermal treatment. Hydrothermal treatment of grains refers to the addition of moisture and heat to the grains for improving the quality and quantity of their end products or to facilitate different milling operations for the desired products. Hydrothermal treatment is commonly called conditioning and considered as a pre-milling treatment. It can be carried out either at room temperature or at a little elevated temperature or at high temperature.

Hydrothermal treatment is used for various purposes. It can be used for improving shelling efficiency, nutritional quality and milling quality of paddy and for facilitating degermination and dehulling of corn and wheat. Pulses are conditioned by alternate wetting and drying. It helps in the dehusking and splitting of the kernels during milling. Even toxins of *khesri* pulses which causes paralysis, can be removed by soaking it in hot water. Green vegetables are blanched with hot water for retention of the green colour and removing disagreeable odour. Disagreeable odour of soybean can also be removed by blanching. Therefore, simultaneous addition of moisture and heat to the grains and other crops is an important step in cereal milling and crop processing.

Hydrothermal treatment brings about several changes in the properties of cereal grains. They are grouped into three major heads, namely, changes in physicothermal, physicochemical and biochemical properties. These changes, and the effects of basic parameters on them have been discussed.

Physicothermal properties

Strength/hardness

Generally hardness of cereal grains decreases with the increase of their moisture content. Among all crops, the hardness of corn is highest, followed by highly-vitreous wheat variety.

Density and hardness

Bulk density of grain decreases as moisture content increases. With the increase of moisture softness of grains increases. Therefore, increase of moisture is related to the strength properties of the grain, and to the power consumption for grinding as well. Hence the role of hydrothermal treatment of grains is very important.

Hysteresis

Hysteresis of grain plays an important role in grain milling. When grains are subjected to alternate wetting and drying processes, their primary hardness decreases. Husk is also loosened from the kernel resulting in higher efficiency of shelling.

Thermal properties

Thermal properties, namely, specific heat, thermal conductivity, and thermal diffusivity of grains increase with the increase of either temperature or moisture content or both. Rate of hydration and chemical reactions also increases as temperature increases.

Biochemical properties

Biochemical properties of grains are largely dependent upon their protein and amylose contents. In case of wheat both qualitative and quantitative changes in crude gluten take place during hydrothermal treatment. Changes in the proteolytic and amylolytic complexes determine the physical properties of the dough and the bread-making properties to a considerable extent.

Thus changes in biochemical properties affect primarily the bread-making properties, i.e., colour and structure of the crumb and especially the volume of the bread produced. During parboiling of paddy it inactivates the lypase and stabilises the rice bran.

Physicochemical properties

The germ and bran layers can be removed more easily without much reduction in their sizes if the grains are subjected to hydrothermal treatment prior to milling.

Changes in the physicochemical properties of the grain during hydrothermal treatment of wheat mainly affects the flour milling properties, i.e., whiteness of flour, and specific power consumption for grinding, etc.

Effects of various factors on the changes of different properties

The three important factors, namely, grain moisture content, heating temperature and heating time have significant effect on the above changes.

There is an optimum moisture content for each type of grain at which it should be milled. This optimum moisture content is determined by the initial and final properties of grain, and the atmospheric conditions.

The maximum temperature rise and heating time of grain are determined mainly by its biochemical properties which are ultimately dependent upon its protein complex.

Effects of moisture content

The moisture content of any grain for milling is determined on the basis of its physical properties (mainly hardness). The physical properties of the grain are dependent upon the type, variety, region, harvesting condition, biochemical properties and the type of grinding machines used. The optimum moisture content for milling of parboiled paddy, soft and hard varieties of wheat are about 15, 14, and 17 per cent respectively.

Husk, germ and endosperm are hydrated and swelled by hydrothermal treatment. But plastic deformation takes place only in the case of husk and germ making them more rubberlike and less brittle. As a result, during degermination and bolting husk and germ are easily separated from the endosperm and specific power requirement for grinding is also minimum at the optimum moisture content of grain.

Effects of temperature

The best results are obtained when heat is added along with the addition of moisture. As for example, wheat should be soaked to the desired moisture level at about 40—60°C for a desired period of time only.

Thermal properties

Moisture moves in the same direction as heat flows. This phenomenon is known as thermal moisture—conductivity. It is characterised by a value numerically equal to the moisture transfer at a temperature difference of 1° C through arbitrary sections under constant operating conditions. Both specific heat and thermal conductivity of grain increase with the increase of temperature.

Chemical kinetics

The rate of moisture absorption, moisture equilibration and chemical reaction increases as temperature increases. Therefore, duration of hydrothermal treatment depends on temperature.

This explains why the effect of steam is considerable. It affects temperature and moisture gradients simultaneously.

Coefficient of expansion

During hydrothermal treatment, expansion of cellulose of husk is different from that of proteins and starch of the endosperm. As a result, internal slip occurs which has a favourable effect on the separation of husk, on formation of middlings and on power requirement during grinding.

Biochemical properties

Proteins : Temperature has a great influence on the quality and quantity of gluten. When soaked wheat is conditioned at a temperature between 40 and 50°C, the yield of crude gluten is higher than that of wheat conditioned at ordinary temperature.

The most remarkable changes which occur in the qualitative

characteristics of the gluten are flexibility and extensibility. At a higher temperature denaturation of protein takes place. *Enzymes* : Within limits, enzymatic activities increases with temperature. But most of the enzymes are inactivated at temperatures above 80° C. Catalase is one of the heat-sensitive enzymes.

Optimum conditions
Therefore, it is necessary to find out an optimum combination of heating temperature and time and moisture content for successful hydrothermal treatment of each type of grain for effective milling and desired bread-making quality, if any.

CHAPTER 12

Rice Milling

Rice milling machinery used in different countries range from crude hand pounding equipment and small scale hullers to highly sophisticated and capital intensive units. However, the rice milling machinery can be broadly classified into two groups : traditional and modern rice milling machinery.

Traditional rice milling machinery

Traditional rice mills include hand pounding equipments, single huller and battery of hullers, sheller-cum-huller and sheller mills.

Hand pounding

A variety of implements are used for the purpose of hand pounding, the more common being ; (a) mortar and pestle, (b) Dhenki and (c) hand stone (*chakki*).

Single huller

Construction

The common type of Engleberg huller consists of an iron ribbed cylinder mounted on a rotating shaft on ball bearings and fitted in a concentric cylindrical housing (shown in Fig. 12.1). The inner ribbed cylinder has helical ribs upto one-fourth of its length and four to six number of straight ribs for rest of the length. The cylindrical casing can be divided into two halves. The bottom half of the cylinder is replaceable and made of slotted sheet so that the bran removed during milling may pass through the slots by the pressure generated in the cylinder. The ribbed cylinder is rotated at a speed of 600 to 900 rpm.

Principle

The paddy is husked and whitened in the huller by friction and pressure generated in the milling chamber. Both husking

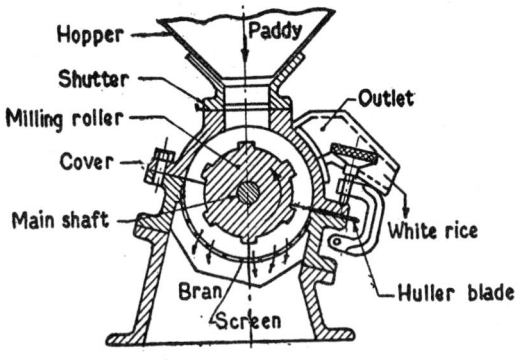

FIG. 12.1 Engelburg Type huller

and whitening are done by the same machine. The milling can be carried out either in a single pass or in multipasses.

Operation

An iron bar called knife or blade is protruded to resist the movement of grain in the milling chamber and to control the degree of whitening. The blade can be moved forward and backward manually to adjust the clearance. Paddy is fed at one end of the upper half and discharged from the other end of the half of the housing. Paddy handling capacities of the huller from 0.25 to 0.75 tonnes/hr are common. Generally in a single huller paddy is husked and whitened in a single operation by applying high pressure resulting in a high degree of whitening and high percentage of broken in the processed rice. The total and head yields can be slightly increased by milling paddy in a number of passes. Single hullers of small capacity are located in the village for custom milling. But rice mills consisting of two to six hullers are located in towns, market areas and cities. The total rice out turns are about 56 and 64 per cent for raw and parboiled paddy respectively.

Advantages

(1) The initial investment and operating cost are small.

(2) The huller can be manufactured locally and operated with unskilled labour.

(3) The huller can be utilised for whitening of parboiled rice as it produces uniformly whitened rice.

Disadvantages

(1) Both total and head yields are low (in comparison to any other milling machine) as the degree of whitening cannot be adjusted to a low value.

(2) The huller bran, contaminated with large amount of husk, cannot be utilised for oil extraction and for feed purposes.

The huller bran is sometimes used for boiler fuel. From the conservation of food materials and other points of view, the huller is an uneconomic and wasteful machine. Therefore, the huller should be discarded in all countries as soon as possible.

Some more problems are also associated with the huller milling system. It is reported that in the villages of many Asian countries, the hand pounding system is being replaced by the single huller milling system. The single huller meets the immediate need of the villagers by doing custom milling of a few kilogrammes of paddy at a time. It is also beyond the capacity of a single huller owner to switch over to the capital intensive modern rice mills. Therefore, unless and until a low cost mini- modern rice mill of equivalent capacity as that of a single huller is introduced, it will be very difficult to abolish the huller system completely from the underdeveloped countries.

In India, the centrifugal type of husker in combination with a rubber disc type rice whitener has been introduced to replace the huller unit.

HULLER MILL

The huller mill consists of battery of hullers, sieves for cleaning paddy, reciprocating sieves for removing brokens, etc. and bucket elevators. Sometime, aspirator is also employed for removing husk. The machines are arranged in proper sequence. Sun dried raw or parboiled paddy is first cleaned to remove foreign materials. The clean paddy is fed to the first huller, used mainly for husking. Then the mixture of husled rice, paddy and husk is fed in equal amount to the second and third hullers which are operated with narrower clearance between the blade and rotating ribbed roll. In the second and third hullers complete husking and whitening takes place. The mixture of whitened rice, husk and some bran obtained from these two hullers are separated in the sieve sifter.

SHELLER-CUM-HULLER MILL

Under runner disc husker is used for husking and the huller is used for whitening of rice. After cleaning of paddy in a sieve, the cleaned paddy is husked in the under runner disc husker (sheller) (Fig. 12.2). The stock from the sheller is fed to hullers for whitening. The mixture is then sifted to remove bran brokens, etc., from the rice. The out turn of rice from this mill is higher than that of huller mill.

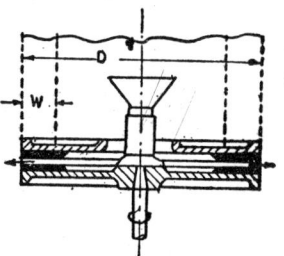

FIG. 12.2 Particulars of the under-runner disc sheller

SHELLER MILL

As far as basic milling operations are concerned, the sheller mill is almost identical to a modern mill except that the husking operation is done by the under runner disc husker (sheller) in place of modern rubber roll husker.

This type of mill consists of : (a) a cleaner, (b) one or more disc shellers, (c) aspirator (to remove husk), (d) one or more paddy separators, and (e) one or more cone type rice whitener. Commonly, the capacities and total power consumption vary from 1 to 2 tonnes/hr and 35 to 50 P.HP respectively.

Among all traditional rice mills, total and head yields are highest in sheller mill.

However, in huller and sheller-cum-huller and sheller mills, a certain amount of husked rice, smaller and lighter paddy escape along with the husk due to defective design of the aspiration system and small brokens are also lost with the bran. Moreover, imnature paddy cannot be separated in these mills and is mostly lost in the pile of husk.

Advantages

(1) Sheller bran can be used for oil extraction.
(2) Operating cost is low.
(3) Life of the machinery is long.
(4) The emery cone can be recoated at the mill sight.
(5) It works well with parboiled paddy.
(6) Sheller mill can be manufactured locally.

Disadvantages

(1) Head and total yields are less than the modern rice mills.

(2) Some scratches may be formed on the rice kernel which are undesirable for long storage.

Modern rice milling machinery

The modern rice milling machinery can be divided into two major groups :(1) rice milling machinery developed in Japan, and (2) rice milling machinery developed in Europe.

Both European and Japanese modern rice milling machines have been described in this chapter.

The major operations performed by modern rice mills (Fig 12.3) are as follows :

(1) storage, (2) cleaning, (3) husking, (4) separation, (5) whitening and (6) grading.

CLEANING

The paddy procured from the farmer is cleaned with the help of paddy cleaners. The removal of impurities from the grains is essential to protect the subsequent milling machinery from unusual wear and tear and to improve the quality of the final product.

If the procured paddy contains excessive amounts of foreign materials or if paddy is parboiled prior to milling then the procured paddy is sometimes precleaned in an open double sieve type precleaner or enscalper installed outside the mill room.

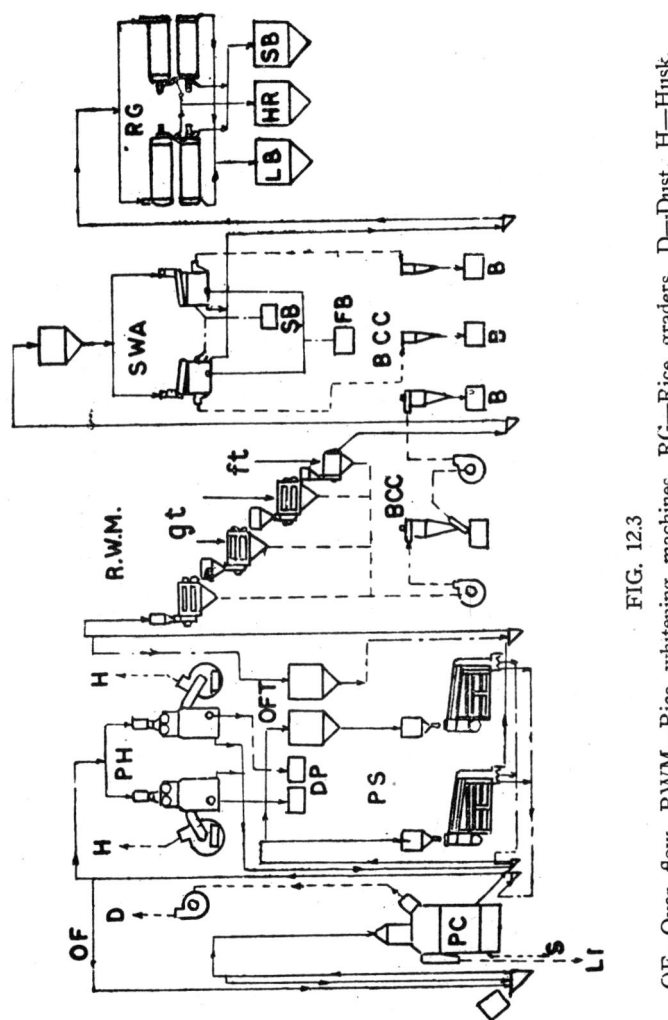

FIG. 12.3

OF—Over flow, RWM—Rice whitening machines, RG—Rice graders, D—Dust, H—Husk, PH—Paddy huskers, SWA—Sieve with aspirator, OFT—Over flow tank, DP—Defective paddy, SB—Small broken, LB—Large broken, HR—Head rice, FB—Fine broken, B—Bran, BCC—Bran collecting cyclones, PS—Paddy separators, P—Paddy, PC—Paddy cleaner, LI—Large impurities, gt—grinding type, ft—friction type.

General principles of cleaning

Differences in physical characteristics such as size, specific gravity, weight and sometimes length of the impurities compared to the paddy grain are being utilised in cleaning operations. Light impurities can be removed by aspiration and or by sieving. Impurities larger and smaller than paddy are removed by sieving, whereas impurities of the same size but heavier than paddy are removed by gravity separation.

Iron parts or particles can be removed with the help of sieve or magnetic separators.

Open Double-Sieve Precleaner

In many rice mills in India prior to parboiling, precleaning is performed through open single or double layer oscillating sieves. The precleaners are driven directly by an eccentric drive from the main transmission shaft. Sometime, single sieve type precleaners are equipped with suction fans also, for aspiration of light impurities.

Advantages

(1) Price is low.

(2) It can be manufactured locally

Disadvantages

(1) It is open sieve, dust formation in the mill premises is considerable.

(2) Without having a self-cleaning device the bottom sieves with small perforations are often clogged, resulting in lower separation efficiency.

(3) The separation of impurities of about the same size as the paddy grains is not possible.

Single Scalper drum cleaner (Japan)

This machine can be used for precleaning of either harvested paddy or rough paddy from the impurities such as straws, ears, chaffs, big stones, dust and light impurities, sands, etc. (Satake, 1973).

Construction and Operation

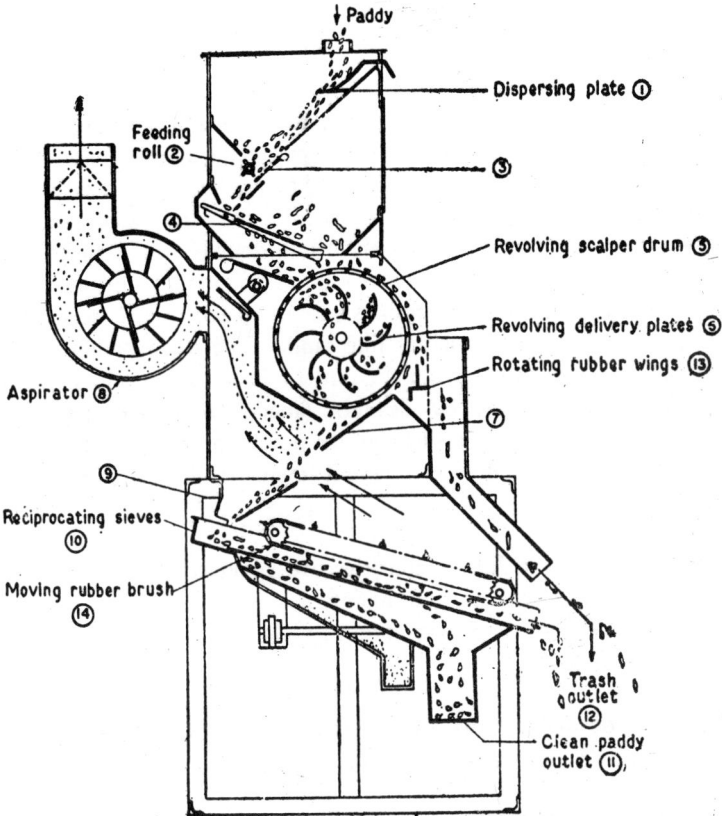

FIG. 12.4 Single Scalpur drum type precleaner (Japan)

Basically it consists of a horizontal rotating scalper drum, an aspirator and vibrating sieves (Fig. 12.4).

The dispersing plate (1) disperses the paddy evenly on the whole width of the vibrating screen. The paddy input is controlled by a feed roll (2), and a valve (3). An inclined vibrating screen (4) helps the paddy grain in getting them into loose form and removing large impurities. The paddy is then fed to the rotating scalper drum (5). The scalper drum, covered with hexagonal slotted screens, removes the large impurities such as

13

straw, ear chaffs, big stones, etc. The paddy with small impurities first enters through the hexagonal slots of the scalper drum and is then discharged from the drum uniformly with the help of the device (6). The speed of the falling grains is equalised by an inclined plate (7). When they fall from the inclined plate as a film, an air stream is sucked through the grain film by a suction fan (8) to aspirate the lighter impurities like, dust, etc., from the grains. The paddy with remaining impurities is fed through hopper (9) to the reciprocating sieve (10). The reciprocating sieve is a double layer type. The top sieve of large mesh removes large impurities through the outlet (12) while the bottom sieve of small mesh separates heavier and smaller impurities like sand. The clean paddy overflows and is discharged from the outlet (11). The scalper drum is continuously cleaned by cleaners (made of rubber) and the wide vibrating screen is cleaned by a special moving scraping device. These two devices prevent them from clogging.

Features
    (1) Straws and light impurities are removed effectively.
    (2) Easy to operate and maintain.
    (3) Sieve cleaning device prevents clogging.

Stoner
    Stones of about same size as paddy grains can be separated by the gravity separation method.

Stoner with aspirator (Japan)
    The main purpose of this machine is to remove dust and stone from paddy effectively. It separates immature paddy also. The system can be used independently or in combination with other cleaning systems (Satake, 1973).

Principle
    The machine consists of an inclined reciprocating tray having convex slots all over the surface. A large amount of air is blown from underneath through the slotted separating tray. When a mixture of grain, stone, etc., is fed at the top of the tray, the stones having higher specific gravity slowly go down

a:: occupy the bottom layer of the mixture and thus come in contact with the reciprocating tray.

The heavier stones are carried to the top of the tray by its movement. Since the direction of movement is more inclined than the inclination of the tray, the heavier particles in contact with the reciprocating tray are lifted. Paddy being lighter floats on the stone and moves downward by gravity. The strong air current through the slots of the tray, directed towards the movement of the paddy further facilitates in lifting and shifting

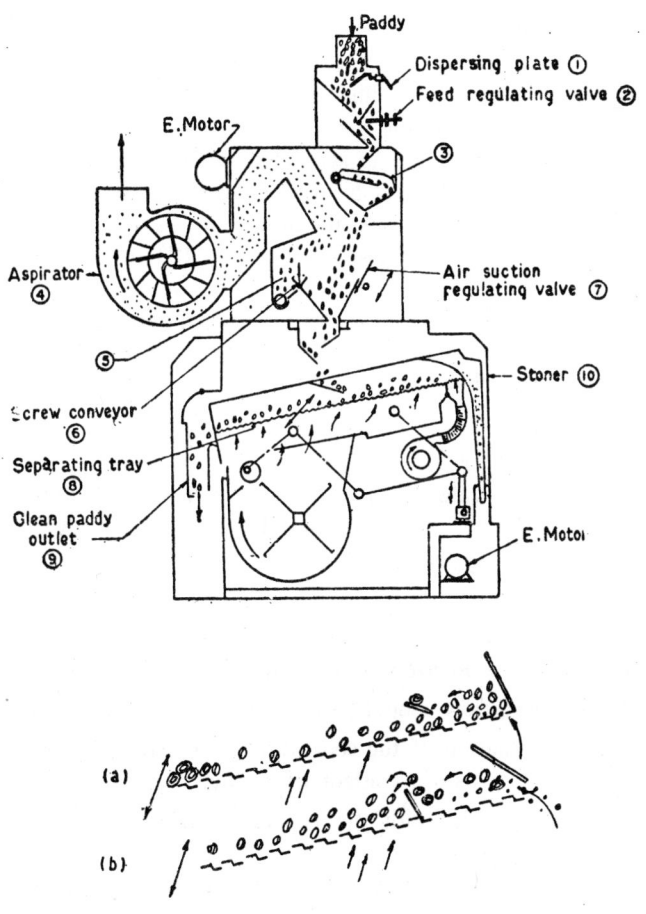

FIG. 12.5

them downwards. Any paddy grain in contact with the stones is separated and returned or blown back to the tray with the help of an another smaller blower installed underneath the tray. The stones collected under a flap can be unloaded either manually or by an automatic device.

Construction

The machine is shown in Fig. 12.5. The grain with impurites is distributed uniformly over the whole width of the machine by a dispersing plate (1). The flow of the mixture is controlled by a feed control valve (2). With the help of a device (3) the speed of the flow is reduced and equalised. Light and small impurities in the grain are aspirated by an aspirator (4). The immature grain is separated/settled in the expansion chamber (5) and discharged by a screw conveyor (6). The air flow rate is controlled by the air controlling device (7). Then the grain is delivered to the separating tray (8) in which stones and a few grains move upward while almost all grains move downward. The paddy grains are discharged through the grain outlet (9) while stones are discharged through the stone outlet as described earlier.

Operation

The stone separator is a very delicate machine. Its satisfactory performance can be achieved by a careful operation. The following suggestions may be given for satisfactory performance.

(a) The machine is to be labelled properly so that the separating tray is in the horizontal position perfectly.

(b) The grain flow should be uniform and in proper quantity.

(c) The inclination of the separating plate should be adjusted according to the moisture content of paddy.

(d) Blowers underneath the separating tray should be installed in the correct position.

(e) The chrome galvanised separating tray is to be kept in a rust-proof condition.

Advantages

(1) Stones, immature grains and light impurities are removed effectively.

(2) It can be used independently or with other type of cleaner.

(3) It can be used for the same purpose for brown rice also.

(4) The inclination of the separating tray is adjustable.

Disadvantages

(1) It can separate a small percentage of stone content from a mixture. Hence, the capacity of the stone separating part is limited.

(2) Careful maintenance and operation are necessary.

Paddy Cleaner with Stoner (Japan)

The purpose of this machine is to remove large impurities, light impurities, sand, stones and metallic parts from paddy.

Construction and operation

The machine consists of a rotating drum covered with sieve having hexagonal slots (rotoscalper), a suction fan and a slant vibrating tray with convex perforation. Under the separating tray a blower is installed. Large impurities are removed by the rotoscalper and light impurities is aspirated by the suction fan. stones and other heavy impurities of same size, etc., move upwards towards the upper part of the tray and are separated. Cleaned paddy moves downward by gravity and is discharged.

Advantages

(1) The rotoscalper and the aspirator is capable of removing about 30 per cent impurity content.

(2) Large impurities, light impurities, stones, sands, and metallic parts are separated by the same machine.

Disadvantages

(1) The separating capacity of the stone separating tray is limited up to 2 per cent stone content only.

(2) Careful operation and maintenance are necessary.

(3) The separating tray is to be imported from the manufacturer only.

Paddy Cleaner (West Germany)

The Fig. 12.6 illustrates the constructional features of a Schule grain cleaner.

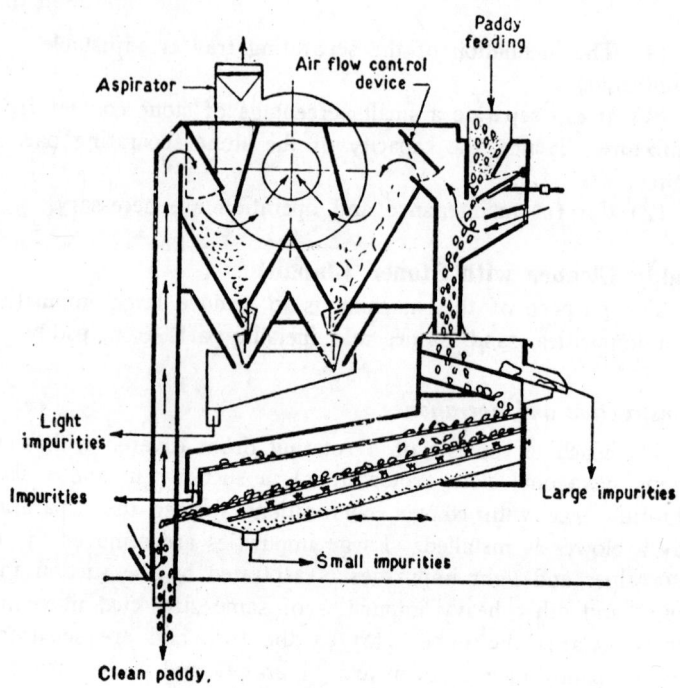

FIG. 12.6 Closed type double action aspirator Precleaner
(West Germany)

Unclean grain enters the machine through a balanced feed gate which ensures even distribution of grain. A suction fan situated in the upper portion, aspirates off lighter impurities and dust. Then the grain has to pass through an aspiration channel where the air current lifts off chaff and other lighter particles which are drawn into the settling chambers and delivered through gate flaps to inclined chute. Lighter immature grains are also collected in the chamber which otherwise go along with air current.

The mixture is then passed through the vibrating screen where large impurities such as straws, big stones, clods of dirt, etc., are removed. The following grain sieve overtails seeds and other admixtures larger than grains. On the sand sieve, the grain tails over while sand, etc., passes through it. Before being discharged, the last traces of light impurities are removed from the grains when they are subjected to a strong aspiration through a deep aspirating leg.

HUSKING

The purpose of a modern husking machine is to remove husk from paddy without damage to the bran layer and rice kernel.

Husking machines are known by different names such as huskers, dehuskers, shellers, and sometime hullers also.

Impact type paddy husker (Japan)

Principle

The working principle of the impact or centrifugal type of husker is based on the utilisation of impact and frictional force for husking of paddy. In the impact type husker, paddy is thrown against a rubber wall (Fig. 12.7) by a rotating disc. The impact on the rubber

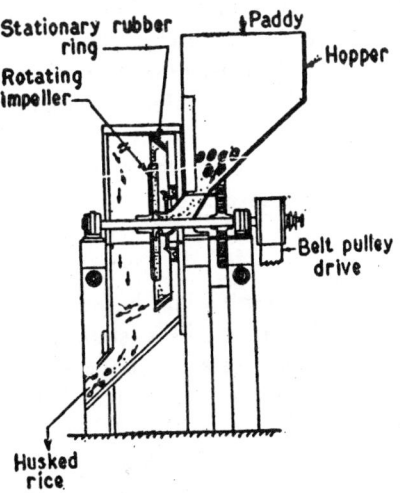

Fig. 12.7 Impact type husker

wall due to the centrifugal force of the rotating disc causes cracking of hulls with a minimum damage to the kernel.

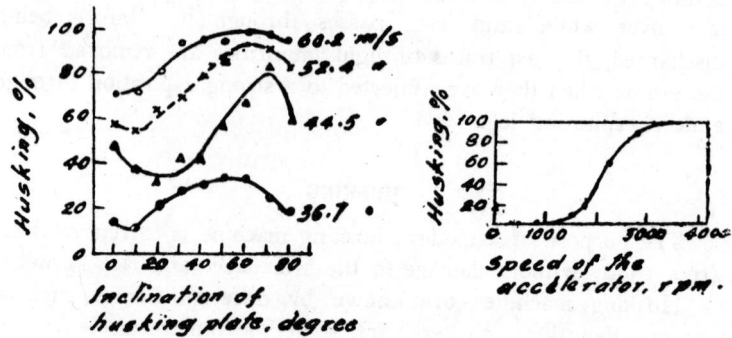

FIG. 12.8 Relation between husking% and the angle of inclination of husking plate
(Source : Ezaki, 1973)

FIG. 12.9 Relation between husking% and the speed of accelerator plate
(Source : Ezaki, 1973)

Relations between husking percentage and rpm of the disc, husking percentage and angle of inclination of the husking plate with Japonica varieties of paddy are shown in Fig. Nos. 12.9 and 12.8. Figure 12.9 shows that the husking percentage increased sharply from 2,000 rpm and reached its maximum at 4,300 rpm. But the head yield decreased as rpm increased. Therefore, optimum rpm of the disc for different varieties of paddy is very important. It was also observed that the most important factor affecting husking ratio was not the diameter of the rotating disc but the circumferential speed.

Construction

A common type of centrifugal husker consists of a rotating disc of diameter 28.5 cm within a stationary rim of synthetic rubber 30 cm in diameter centred at the same axle (Fig. 12.7). The thickness of the rubber rim is about 2.5 cm. The diameter of the rotating disc varies from 23 to 31 cm. The shore hardness of rubber rim is about 85°. The husking capacity of a machine with a disc of 30 cm in diameter is about 300 kg/hr.

Advantages

(1) Price is reasonably low.

(2) Operating cost is low due to small power requirement (1 HP/500 kg paddy/hr) and long life of the rubber rim.

(3) Total and head yields are higher in comparison to huller.

(4) Husking efficiency and head yields are quite satisfactory for parboiled paddy.

(5) The machine is compact and portable.

(6) It can be manufactured locallv.

Disadvantages

(1) Critical adjustment is required for different varieties and moisture contents of paddy.

(2) Breakage percentage inrreases with the increase of husking ratio.

(3) It is not possible to increase the husking capacity of the machine unless the number of husking disc on the same rotating shaft is increased.

Rubber Roll Husker (Japan)

Principle

If paddy is passed between two resilient surfaces rotating at different speeds in different directions, its husk will be split and stripped off. Fig. 12.10 shows the principle of husking. If paddy is allowed to pass through the gap (smaller than the thickness of paddy) between two rubber rolls rotating at different speeds then it makes contact with the two rolls for different periods of time. The contact of the faster revolving roll is longer than the slower revolving roll. As a result the paddy is sheared and compressed and its husk is stripped off and removed.

Construction

Figure 12.10 shows the constructional features of the Satake husker. It consists of two major parts, the upper part is the husking section and the lower part is the husk aspirating section (Satake, 1973).

Clean paddy is delivered through a shutter (1) and a feeding roll (2), fixed below the shutter. Feed rate is controlled by a

feed regulating valve (3). The paddy is then passed through
the gap between a fixed (stationary) roll (4) and an adjust-

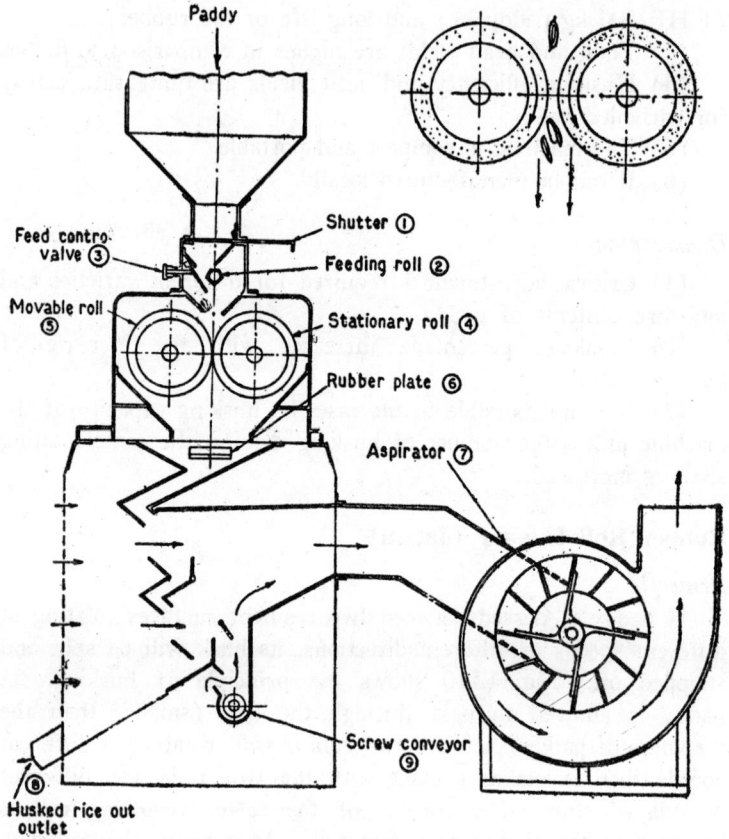

FIG. 12.10 Rubber roll husker (Japan)

able (movable) roll (5), and husked. After reducing the
grain speed with the help of resistance (rubber) plate (6), the
mixture is allowed to pass through the aspiration section (7) to
aspirate husk. Mature grain being heavy is collected in the
husked rice outlet (8). Immature grain being light is collected
and discharged by a screw conveyor (9). The husk is aspirated
and thrown out of the mill building by a fan (10).

Both rolls have the same diameter. Diameter of the rubber rolls varies from 150 to 250 mm depending on the capacity of the husker. Their differential speeds are shown below :

Roll diam (mm)	High speed (rpm)	Low speed (rpm)
150	1320	900
200	1200	900
250	1000	740

The wear of the rubber is considerable and with the reduction of the roll diameter, capacity is also reduced. The main reason for the capacity reduction is the decrease in the relative speed of the two rolls.

In general only 85 to 90 per cent of the paddy fed is husked due to variation in moisture content, size, degree of maturity of grain, eccentricity of the revolving rubber rolls and uneven wearing of rubber roll surfaces.

The clearance between the two rolls can be adjusted manually. A sophisticated pneumatic device for automatic adjustment of the clearance has been introduced in place of manual adjustment.

Now a days rubber roll huskers are equipped with a blower to blow air on the rubber rolls' surface and bring down their temperature rise due to friction between husk and roller during husking.

Operation

When the husker is in operation for a certain period, the faster revolving roll wears more than the slower revolving roll. As a result the diameter of the former becomes smaller than the latter and the difference in peripheral velocity between the two rolls becomes less. Though the speed ratio is kept constant, yet it causes lowering of husking efficiency. To encounter this difficulty application of high pressure is not the proper means as it would break the grains. However, the rubber rolls are to be interchanged at a regular interval of time.

Advantages

(1) Highest percentage of sound and whole husked rice is

produced as the risk of breaking the kernel is small and the chance of forming scratches on the kernel is also nil.

(2) The mixture of different sizes and varieties of paddy can be used without any significant increase of brokens in husked rice.

(3) Husking ratio can be increased to 0.9 without reduction in head yield.

(4) It does not remove germ.

Disadvantages

(1) Operating costs are high due to wear of rubber rolls.

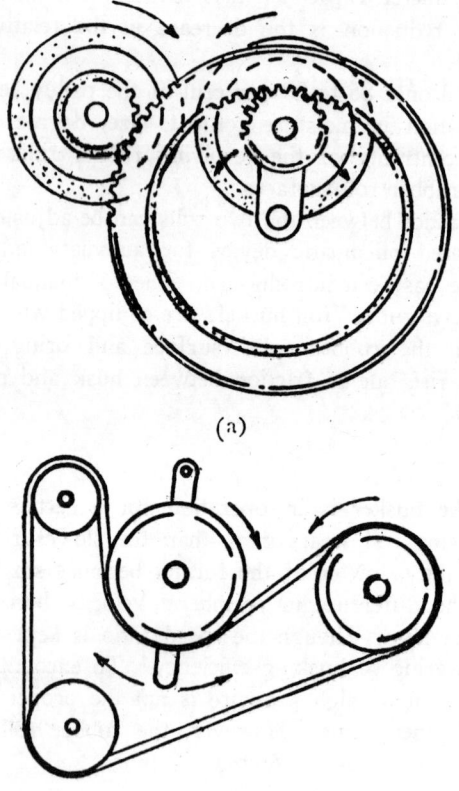

(a)

(b)

FIG. 12.11 Power transmission system for Rubber roll husker (Japan)

(2) Storage life of rubber roll is limited as storage deterio-rates its quality and in consequence shortens its working life.

(3) If the paddy separator fails to separate paddy completely and the husked rice is returned to the husker along with paddy, the constituent of the rubber may impart colour and odour to the rice.

(4) It requires skilled labour to operate the machine efficiently.

(5) Sometimes on account of uneven grain distribution and uneven thickness of rubber, the rolls surface wears out unevenly which adversely affects the efficiency and capacity. If the roll surfaces are corrected by turning, the life of the rubber rolls will be reduced considerably.

(6) In general the husking capacity of the rubber rolls in tropical countries is low due to : (a) high temperature and humi-dity of the atmospheric air, (b) structure, and (c) larger surface area of the long grain husk in contact with the rubber rolls.

Power transmission system

Figs. 12.11*a* and 12.11*b* show the power transmission system.

This type of power transmission system is most commonly used for the rubber roll husker. In the rubber roll husker with 25 cm rubber roll, a hexagonal belt is usually used (Fig. 12.11b).

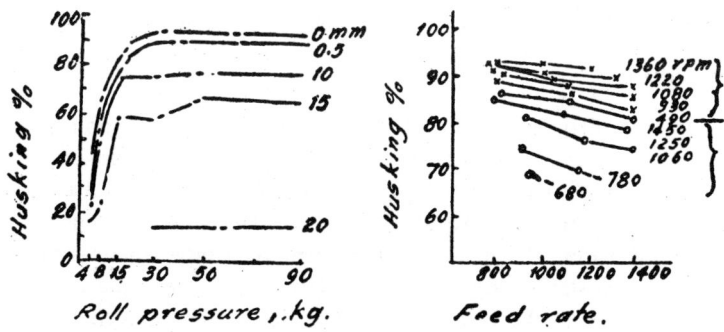

FIG. 12.12a Relation between husk-ing% and roll pressure (Source : Ezaki 1973)

FIG. 12.12b Relation between husking % and feeding quantity of paddy (Source : Ezaki 1973)

Rubber roll husker (European)

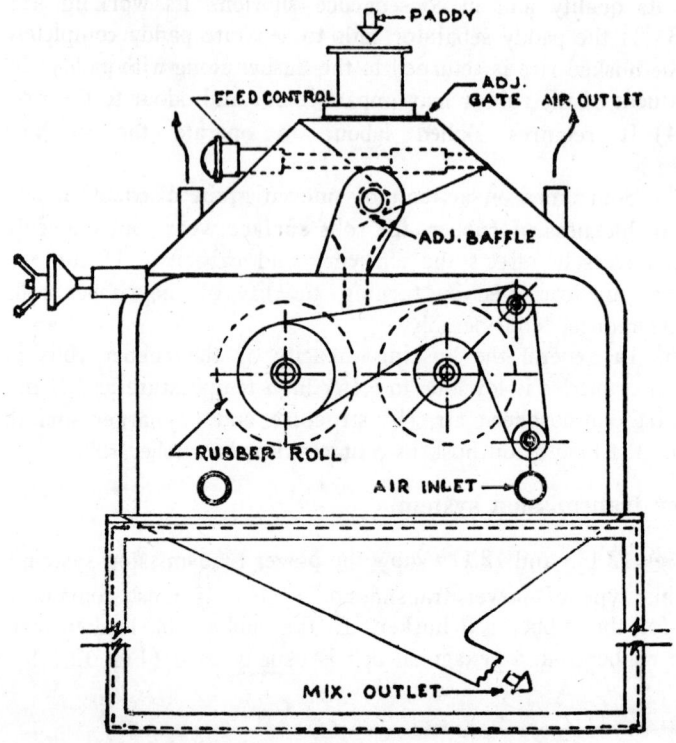

FIG. 12.13   Rubber roll   husker   (European)

It consists of :

(a) a drive pulley ; (b) a box containing wheels and gears etc. ; (c) a special mechanism for adjusting the position of one roller ; (d) a casing containing the two rollers ; (e) a base on which the above parts are fixed ; and (f) steel underframe.

Paddy enters through the transparent feed pipe which is fitted with an adjustable gate to stop the flow. The one baffle is fixed while another baffle is movable. The feed roller driven by the pulley ensures even feeding. To adjust feeding, the hand wheel is turned and this moves the movable roll, the position of which can be seen on the graduated scale. The door is used to see the inside of the chamber (Gariboldi, 1974).

There is also an arrangement for air cooling the rubber rolls and removing the dust as well. In this type of husker the husk aspiration system is installed separately. Usually the husk separator is placed between the husker and paddy separator.

SEPARATION

The husked rice is separated from the mixture of paddy and husked rice by the paddy separator.

Paddy Separator (Japan)

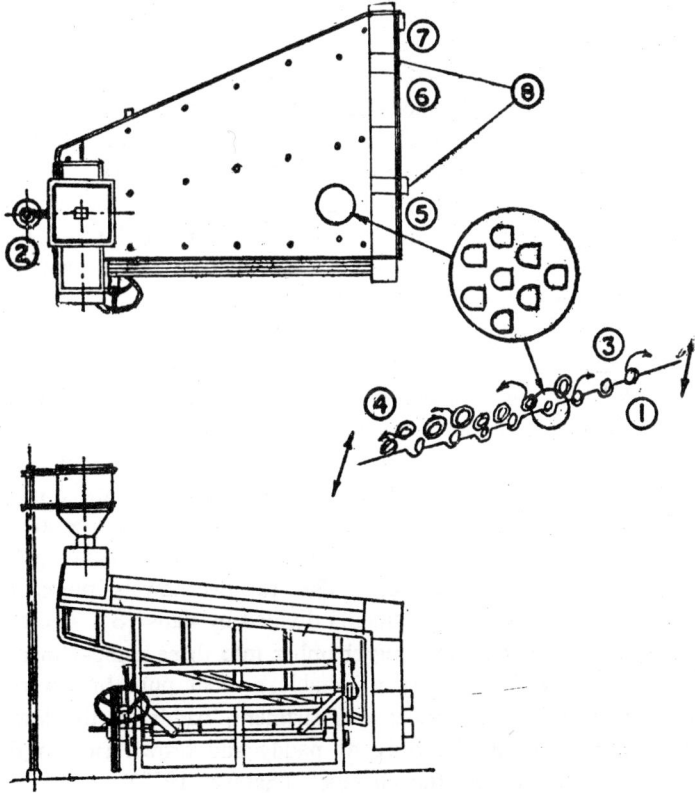

FIG. 12.14 Construction of Indented tray type
Paddy Separator (Japan)

Principle

   The paddy separator (shown in Figs. 12.14 and 12.15) consists of a number of identical inclined trays with dimples (1) over

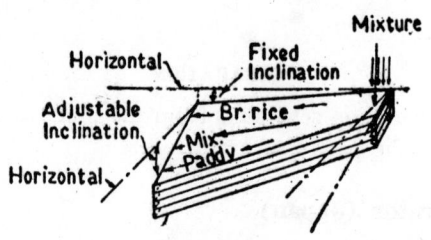

FIG. 12.15   Inclination of the Indented tray type
Separator (Japan)

the surface. These dimpled trays are in reciprocating motion. When a mixture of husked rice and paddy is delivered at the upper corner (2) of the tray, the husked rice being heavier occupies the bottom layer and comes in contact with the dimpled tray, while the paddy being lighter floats on the husked rice. The size of the dimples is slightly bigger than the brown rice but smaller than the paddy. The downward movement of brown rice is thus partially restricted by the dimples while the paddy is free to move downward. With the reciprocating movement of the tray, the husked rice, in contact with the tray picks up the movement and moves to the side (3), while the paddy flows downward fast by gravity (4). At the same time, paddy and husked rice gradually move to the right side of the tray separating the husked rice at the upper part (5) and the paddy at lower part (7) and leaving the mixture at the central part (6). The tray overflow is, therefore, received by the three compartments divided by flaps (8). The two flaps divide the whole receiving chamber into three compartments. The position of the flaps is adjustable so that pure brown rice can be received in the upper compartment, paddy in the lower compartment, and the mixture of paddy and brown rice in the middle compartment of the chamber (Satake, 1973).

Construction

The machine is made of steel. It consists of three to seven identical indented/dimpled trays, mounted one above the other with a spacing of about 5 cm. The whole tray assembly moves up and forward making a typical reciprocating motion during operation. The dimples on the whole surface of the trays provide necessary frictional coefficients for separation of the mixture. The amount of mixture, fed from the distribution box placed on the left top side of the machine, is adjustable. Each tray receives an equal amount of the mixture. The trays are inclined in both latitudinal and longitudinal directions. The latitudinal inclination is fixed at about 5° while longitudinal inclination can be varied within 20°+6°. The inclination adjustment handle located on the frame is used to adjust the longitudinal inclination according to variety, moisture content and other conditions of paddy.

Operation

When the amount of mixture to be delivered becomes small, the grain should be distributed only to the upper plate. At the beginning of separation, paddy is likely to be mixed up with the husked rice outlet(5) until all the separating plates are covered with grain. In this case all grains should be circulated in the machine until enough grain flows through the machine. Similarly too much grain flow causes mixing of husked rice in the paddy outlet (7).

When the machine is not used, the separating trays should be coated with rustproof grease.

Advantages

(1) Perfect separation can be achieved if different varieties are not mixed up.

(2) Separating condition of the mixture on the dimpled tray is always visible and can be adjusted accordingly.

(3) Operation is very simple.

(4) The unit is very compact and requires minimum space.

(5) Power requirement is also small.

14

Disadvantages

(1) It is difficult to manufacture the dimpled trays locally.

(2) Difficulties in perfect separation are encountered when the size and shape of the dimples do not correspond to the length of paddy and brown rice and when moist or dirty grains are separated and when a mixture of different varieties of grain are separated.

Paddy separator (Japan)

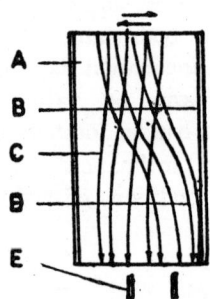

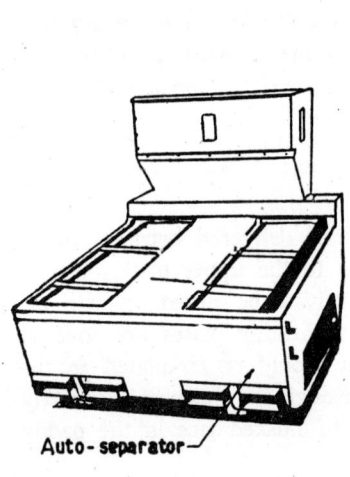

Auto-separator

A - Separating table
B - Plank of separating table
C - Paddy flow
D - Brown rice flow
E - Adjustable panel

FIG. 12.16 Paddy Separator   FIG. 12.17 Separating
(Japan)   conditions

Principle

The paddy separator (shown in Fig. 12.16) consists of vibrating specific gravity table (made of special screen) sloping in the longitudinal direction. When the mixture of paddy and brown rice passes on to the separating table, they are given a special side way motion as they gravitate towards the lower end. At first, paddy being lighter, it starts floating above the heavier and smoother brown rice. Then by the repeated effects of knockings at the bank of separating table, the paddy and brown

rice are drifted to different sides and separated from each other.
Paddy and brown rice are then separately received into each
hopper provided with an adjust-
able panel which can be shifted
by turning the handle. The
movement of the grain on the
separating table is shown in
Fig. 12.17. To increase the capacity, a number of separating
tables are set one above the other
in each block. Two similar blocks
of separating tables are connected together for combined
oscillation (Fig. 12.18).

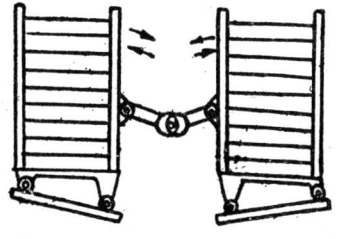

Symmetric drive motion

FIG. 12.18 Connection
between two tables

Advantages

    (1) The unit is compact and simple.
    (2) Power requirement is less.
    (3) The separating condition is visible.

Disadvantages

    (1) The separating table is subject to wear and has to be
replaced.
    (2) After using the table for sometime, the uniformity of
mesh may be lost.
    (3) For efficient separation of different sizes of grain, screens
of different mesh should be used.

Paddy separator (European)

COMPARTMENT SEPARATOR

Principle

    When apparently similar grains move over an inclined plane,
the downward movement of the different grains by gravity is
related to the specific gravity, shape, contact area and coefficient
of sliding friction. The husked rice being small, heavy and
smooth slides down faster than bigger but light, flat and rough
paddy.

The mixture to be separated is distributed over an inclined surface of the machine and given each single component equal and intermittent, obliquely upward thrusts. The thrust is so regulated that it cannot push up the husked rice, thus it acts as a brake, causing them to slide down slowly. On the other hand flatter and rougher paddy grains of lower specific gravity can, however, overcome the upward thrust and move up the inclined surface and fall off at the opposite sides.

Construction and operation

The machine is usually made of wood. It consists of the following main parts : (a) the feed box ; (b) the table enclosing the compartments, the collecting troughs for the separated products and their discharge outlets, and (c) the framework carrying the table, the reciprocating movement drive mechanisms and speed variator.

The main part of the separator is the oscillating compartment assembly where the separation of paddy and husked rice takes place.

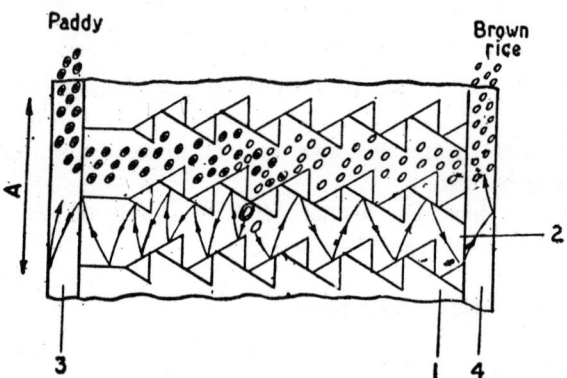

FIG. 12.19 Internal construction of the compartments and
Operational principle of a compartment separator

Figure 12.19 shows how the compartment separator works. The table (1) is divided cross-wise into several compartments (2) the shapes of which form a zigzag. The number of compartments varies from 5 to 8 depending on the capacity. The bottom of these compartments is slightly inclined. The whole assembly consists of one, two, three or four decks.

The mixture of husked and unhusked grains is fed to the compartments in equal quantities, through the hopper. The table (1) moves forward and backward horizontally along the direction of line A. The movement for thrusting the grains towards the upper edge of the slant table is obtained by means of eccentric motion. Normally, the stroke length is about 20 cm and not adjustable. The grains move cross-wise inside the compartment and alternatively hit the zigzag walls. These walls are oblique and the grains rebound obliquely.

The grains receive the oblique upward thrust. The husked paddy moves down slowly whereas the unhusked paddy moves up the inclined plane. The two components are thus separated and discharged from the two opposite sides (Gariboldi, 1974).

Advantages

(1) Running cost is minimum as there is no part to be changed or subject to serious wear.

(2) Life of the machine is very long due to its sturdy construction.

(3) If it is operated properly the separation is perfect.

Disadvantages

(1) The machine is expensive to buy and transport.

(2) It needs strong foundation at the ground level.

(3) It requires skilled labour

(4) The wooden parts of the machine are subject to termite attacks.

WHITENING

The term whitening refers to the operation of removal of germ, pericarp, tegmen and aleurone layers from husked rice kernels. It is also called 'polishing' or 'pearling' or 'scouring'.

There are three major kinds of whitening machines used in the modern rice processing industry. They are : (1) vertical abrasive whitening cone, (2) the horizonontal abrasive whitening roll, and (3) the horizontal metallic friction type roll.

Vertical whitening or Pearling Cone (European)

Principle

Basically, the machine consists of an inverted cast iron frusto-conical rotor covered with abrasive material mounted on a vertical spindle, revolving inside a crib. The crib is lined with steel wire cloth or perforated metal sheets and it is equipped with rubber brakes which are placed vertically and spaced equally and protruded into the gap between cone and crib. The pressure inside the machine can be adjusted by pushing in or pulling out the rubber brakes. The number of brakes to be used depends on diameter and is determined by the formula : $n = (D/100) - 2$ where $D = $ cone diameter, mm. The peripheral speed of the cone should be 13 m/sec. The husked rice enters the gap and is dragged along by the rough surface of the rotating cone. The rubber brakes tend to stop it and cause it to pile up against their side. While pressed up against the brakes, the grains undergo a strong swirling and revolving movement because of their oval shape and smooth surface (Gariboldi, 1974).

Each grain is scoured by the abrasive surface of the cone. It also rubs against the surrounding grains and the rough lining of the crib as well.

The grains meet almost same conditions all the way round the cone until they sink lower and lower by gravity and are finally discharged at the bottom of the cone.

The bran is finally ground due to scouring and rubbing and escapes through the lining of the crib and regularly removed.

As the vertical abrasive roll is an inverted truncated cone, the peripheral speed at the upper part is higher than the lower part. But the density and pressure at the lower part are higher than at the upper part. As a result, the grinding action is predominating at the upper part while frictional force is stronger at the lower part. In the strict sense this machine is a combination of abrasive and friction types of machines.

Generally, a series of two to four whitening cones are used to whiten rice successively in two to four passes.

Construction

The machine consists of a rotating vertical conical cast iron

cylinder covered with an abrasive material. The entire rotating
cone is encased within a fixed perforated metal sheet known as
crib. The gap between the abrasive surface and the crib is about
10 mm. It is provided with rubber brakes, placed vertically
and spaced equally which protrude into the gap between the
abrasive cone and the crib. The clearance between the rubber
brake and crib is about 2-3 mm. The pressure inside the whitening chamber can be adjusted by pushing in or pulling out
the rubber brakes.

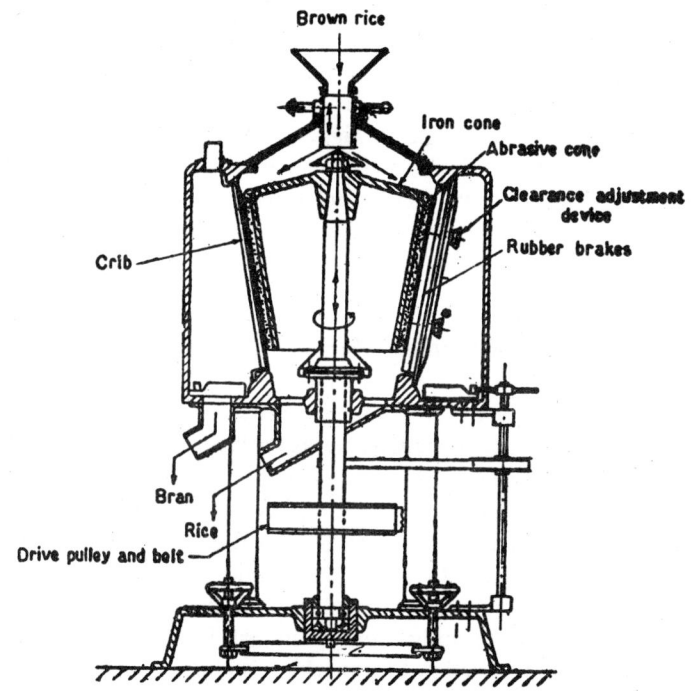

FIG. 12.20   The vertical abrasive whitening cone

The construction of the machine is shown in Fig. 12.20. The
whole abrasive cone can be lifted up or down to adjust the
clearance between the cone and the rubber brake as and when
rubber brakes are worn out a little.

Advantages

(1) The parts of the machine subject to wear are the abrasive surface, the crib lining and the rubber brakes, these can be made and replaced locally.

(2) It can deal with any variety of rice. Its performance is excellent with parboiled rice.

(3) The degree of whitening is adjustable.

(4) Life of the machine is very long.

(5) The operational cost is low.

Disadvantages

(1) The machine is big and heavy.

(2) The machine requires skilled operators and attention.

(3) Power requirement is high.

(4) Power transmission system is troublesome.

(5) As the abrasive roll is not vitrified (i.e., not treated at high temperature) sharpness of the abrasive particles is not much.

(6) Pressure distribution along the vertical line is not uniform.

Horizontal Rice Whitening Machine (Japan)

To remove bran layers from the husked rice, a combination of two different types of whitening machines, namely grinding type (speedo type or horizontal abrasive type) and friction type (or pressure type) are employed by Satake Engg. Co., (Satake, 1973). As the surface of husked rice is smooth and slippery, the grinding type of machine is used at the initial stage of whitening in order to shave and grind the bran layer into smaller particles and impart roughness to the grain surface as well by the thrust (mainly) and frictional force of a revolving abrasive roll. The friction type machine is employed subsequently to peel off the remaining bran layer (in flakes) easily by the friction between rice and rice by the high pressure created by a rotating ribbed steel roll. Functions of these machines are shown in Fig. 12.21a and 12.22b.

If the smooth husked rice kernels were directly whitened by the friction type machine only, it would require much higher pressure and power for whitening. The yield of brokens would also be more.

Grinding type machine is characterised by : the increase of milling efficiency with the increase of speed of abrasive roll and decrease of milling efficiency with the increase of pressure.

The differences in principle and action between the two types of machines are further illustrated in the following tables :

	Grinding type	Friction type
Peripheral speed	Over 600 m/min	Below 300 m/min
Pressure	Below 50 gm/cm²	Over 200 gm/cm²

System/Item	Grinding type		Friction type	
	Initial stage	Middle stage	Initial stage	Middle stage
Efficiency	high	low	low	high
Breakage	small	small	much	small
Whitening degree	high	high	low	low
Glossiness (shine)	low	low	high	high
Moisture absorption	fast	fast	slow	slow
Deformation	partially deformed	partially deformed	full	full
Embryo removal	easy	easy	easy	difficult

In general, the first and second stage of whitening operations are done by the grinding type machines and the last stage of whitening is done by the frictional type machine. Therefore, the friction type machine is used for giving uniform polish and surface finish to the rice. These machines are arranged in series so that the rice is whitened successively. The following combination can be used for *Indica* varieties of paddy : two to three grinding type machines and one friction type machine.

Grinding is caused mainly by impact and partly by friction with the abrasive surface. Grinding type machine is characterised by the following :

(1) Impact should be high and friction should be less.

(2) Milling efficiency decreases with the increase of pressure or friction.

(3) Milling efficiency increases with the increase of speed of the abrasive roll.

Construction

The horizontal abrasive roll type whitening machine is shown in Fig. 12.21. The machine consists of an abrasive roll (1) fitted

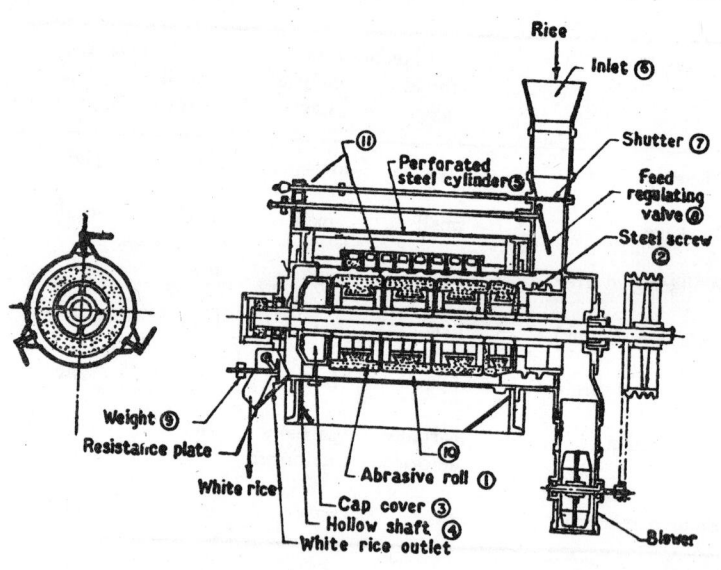

FIG. 12.21 Horizontal abrasive type Whitening
Machine (Japan)

with steel screw (2) and cap cover (3) clamped on a horizontal hollow shaft (4) rotating at a high speed (1000 rpm) in a slotted steel cylinder (5). An inlet hopper (6), shutter (7) and feed control gate (8) are provided above the feeding screw. An adjustable steel plate with weights (9) is fitted to the rice outlet spout. This plate with weight acts as a valve. The counter pressure of this valve which is adjusted by the weight, controls grain flow rate mainly and milling pressure partially.

The outer cylinder, i.e. housing, can be separated into two halves. The bottom half is slotted with rectangular slots. The slots are inclined at an angle of 80° to the rotating direction of the roll so that grains move slowly towards the outlet. Over

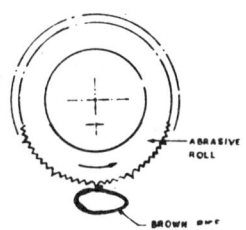

FIG. 12.21a Function of grinding
type machine

the full length of the cylindrical housing two to three rows of adjustable steel resistance pieces are protruded into the annular space between the roll and the cylindrical housing. The

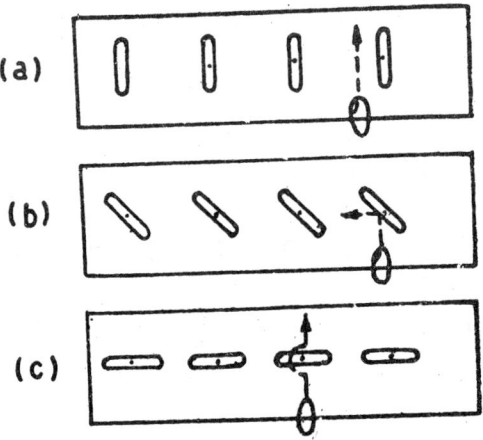

FIG. 12.21b Adjustable steel bar
(resistance pieces)

resistance pieces can be turned from 0° (axial) to 90° (radial) (Fig. 12.21b).

After feeding through the steel screw, the grain passes through the space (10) between the rotating roll and the slotted steel cylinder. The bran layer of the grain is shaved, cut and ground into small particles by the fine and sharp edges of the abrasive roll. The bran passes out through the slots of the steel cylinder. An air current from the hollow shaft flowing through the gaps of the abrasive roll accelerates the separation of bran and cools the grain. The whitened rice is discharged through the outlet (Satake, 1973).

The abrasive roll is made of carborundum (SiC) particles bound by some ceramic substances.

Operation

(a) Pheripheral speed should be more than 600 m/min.

(b) Resistance is slightly varied by weight. Pressure should be less than 50 gm/cm².

(c) Flowing quantity : The progress of whitening action in the abrasive roll type machine is in inverse proportion to the flowing quantity.

(d) Function of resistance pieces (Shibano, 1973) : As the abrasive roll is horizontal rice grain tends to stay in the lower part of the whitening cylinder. In order to overcome this problem, the resistance pieces should be set properly so that the grains are rebound by them.

When the resistance pieces are set at 0°, they give minimum resistance and minimum thrust to the moving grain so that the grain moves along the direction of the slots. When the resistance pieces are set at 45°, they give maximum thrust and medium resistance and when they are set at 90°, they give maximum resistance but no thrust to the moving grain.

If the resistance pieces are set at correct position, the grain density and the pressure will be uniform in the whitening chamber and bran will be dropped equally from all slots of the cylinder. This ensures perfect and effective whitening operation.

By adjusting their inclination, the residence time of the grain inside the whitening chamber can also be adjusted. Thus it helps in controlling the degree of whitening also.

(e) By proper selection of pressure, mesh of the abrasive roll, peripheral speed/rpm of the abrasive roll, this type of machine can produce whitened rice of any desired shape. This is illustrated as follows :

Parameters	Round	Shape of the whitened rice bar like	flat
Peripheral speed	large	medium	small
Mesh	large	medium	small
Pressure	small	medium	large

Renewal of different parts

The various components are replaced under the following circumstances :

(a) When the diameter of abrasive roll is reduced by 15 mm,

(b) When the lower half of the outer cylinder is broken, and

(c) When the resistance pieces are worn out by one-third of their original size.

Advantages

(1) Total and head yields are high.

(2) Bran removal is easier and uniform due to jet air system introduced in the machine.

(3) The edges of the heat treated carborundum roll is very sharp and hard.

(4) The degree of whitening can be adjusted.

Disadvantages

(1) Since the machine is placed horizontally, the rice would tend to settle at the bottom part of the machine, if the angle of inclination of the resistance pieces is not adjusted correctly according to variety and condition of rice resulting in non-uniform whitening of rice.

(2) The machine needs careful attention.

(3) Clearance between the screen and abrasive roll cannot be adjusted.

(4) Once the diameter of the abrasive roll is reduced by about 1.5 cm it has to be replaced. It is difficult to ma ufacture carborundum roll (32 grits) of high quality locally.

Friction Type Whitening Machine (Japan)

Principles

The purpose of the friction type whitener (Fig. 12.22) is to remove remaining bran easily and uniformly from partially whitened rice produced by the horizontal abrasive whiteners. When rice is allowed to enter into the space between the rotating steel roller and the hexagonal screen of the whitener, mutual rubbing of the rice kernels takes place under pressure. Figure 12.22a illustrates the space variation between the rotating roll and the hexagonal screen.

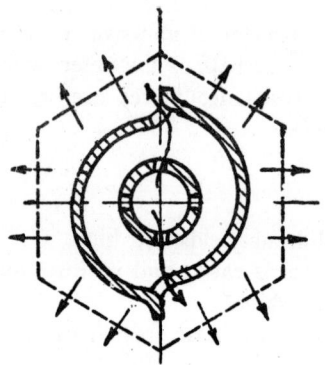

FIG. 12.22a Slotted hexagonal cover
and hollow shaft

The peripheral speed of the steel roller is below 300 m/min. The space between the hexagonal screen and steel roller is different at different points. Mutual rubbing of grain occurs (Fig. 12.22b) at a position where the annular space is narrow, and bran is removed from the rice kernel. After passing through the narrow gap between extruding part of the roller and screen, the grain enters into the wider space where it receives a strong

ai r stream which facilitates the separation of bran from the grain.
It also helps in discharging bran through the slots of the hexagonal

FIG. 12.22b Function of friction
type machine

screen. The whitened rice produced by this machine is free
from bran, slightly shining and cool.

The inner surface of the slotted hexagonal screen has a number
of small projections which enhance rubbing action. Pressure is
applied by the resistance plate with weight. Whitening is mainly
performed by mutual rubbing of grains and partly by rubbing of
grain with the screen. Higher pressure is necessary to accelerate
the whitening.

Construction

The machine (Fig. 12.22) consists of rotating steel cylinder
having two friction ridges (milling roll) (1) and feeding screw
(2) and a lock nut (3) mounted on a horizontal, partly hollow,
perforated shaft (4) encaged in a hexagonal chamber (5). There
are two length-wise openings behind the ridges for the passage
of air. The hexagonal chamber is made of slotted screen and has
small projections on the inner surface. The inlet (6) is located
above the feeding screw. An adjustable steel plate (7) with
weights (8) is fitted at the rice outlet spout (9) to adjust the
variable pressure. This pressure can be varied by adjustment of
the counter weight. Strong air stream is blown by a centrifugal
blower through the long slots of the cylinder and holes of the

shaft to help in separating the bran and dissipating the heat generated by the friction between rice and rice (Satake, 1973).

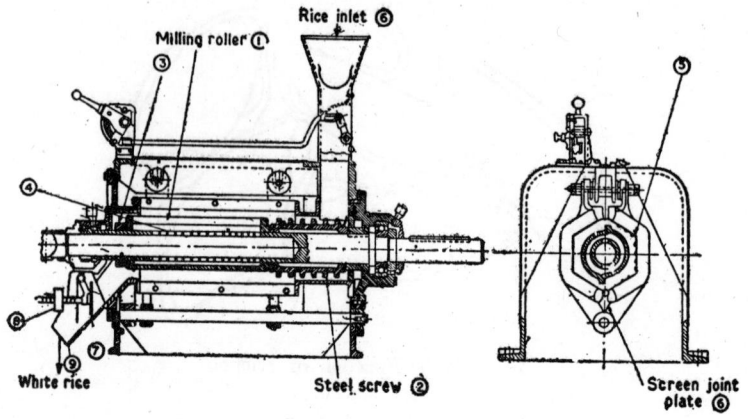

FIG. 12.22 Friction type Whitening machine

Operation (Shibano, 1973)

(1) The rpm of the steel roller should be about 700 (standard). In order to generate effective frictional pressure on the grain, rpm should be so adjusted that the peripheral speed of roller is less than 300 m/min. The peripheral speed varies with the diameter of milling roller.

Whitening efficiency increases as pressure increases. But the milling pressure decreases as the rpm of the roller increases.

(2) Flowing quantity : In order to increase the milling efficiency, it is necessary to keep the pressure on the grain in the whitening chamber sufficiently high and density of grain even.

Adjustment of milling pressure should be made mainly by the flowing quantity and partly by the weight at the outlet. The milling pressure above 200 gm/cm² is effective.

(3) Jet air : Proper quantity of air should be supplied otherwise germ separation may be difficult.

(4) Resistance by weight : Generally, resistance to the rice can be divided into fixed resistance and variable resistance. A friction type machine is characterised by the proportion of the two kinds of resistance.

Renewal of different parts

Due to high pressure, the rate of wear of different components of the machine is much more compared to the abrasive roll type machine. The following components are to be replaced at proper time to maintain the whitening efficiency of the machine.

(a) When diameter of the screw of the roller is reduced by 2 mm.

(b) When height of the ridges of the milling roller is reduced by 3 mm.

(c) When the size of the projection on the screen is reduced to half of its original size or when new holes are developed on the screen and when the screen joint is broken.

Advantages

(1) Production of uniformly whitened rice with shining appearance is the main feature of this machine.

(2) Strong air current helps in lowering rice temperature, generated by friction and removing from the whitened rice.

(3) Pressure is adjustable.

(4) It can produce uniformly whitened parboiled rice without increase of brokens.

Disadvantages

(1) Broken percentage may be increased if the machine is not operated properly. However, its performance is excellent with bold/short *Japonica* varieties of rice.

(2) In case of parboiled paddy, the screen may be choked with the oily bran if higher percentage of polish, is given particularly in the humid atmosphere.

(3) The slotted screen and the steel cylinder are subjected to wear and are replaceable.

15

CHAPTER 13

Milling of Corn, Wheat and Pulses

Corn milling

Introduction

Corn is one of the world's most versatile seed crops. Its botanical name is *Zea mays*. Corn is used as food and feed. Corn can be processed into various food and feed ingredients, industrial products and alcoholic beverages. But the modern corn milling technology developed for the above products is mostly confined to some of the developed countries only. However, modern corn milling technology is to be suitably adopted for producing the types of products required for other countries. At present, there are two modern methods of milling of corns, dry milling and wet milling. Besides germ for corn oil extraction and husk and deoiled germ, etc., for feed, grits (mainly used for the breakfast cereals) are the main products of corn dry milling whereas pure starch, germ and feed are the major products of wet milling.

Composition and structure

The mature corn kernel is composed of four major parts : (a) endosperm (82 per cent), (b) germ (12 per cent), (c) pericarp (5 per cent) and (d) tip cap (1 per cent).

Average composition of the whole corn (Dry basis)

Fraction	Percentage of					
	Kernel	Starch	Protein	Lipid	Ash	Sugar
Whole grain	—	71.5	10.3	4.8	2.0	1.4
Endospern	82.3	86.4	9.4	0.8	0.6	0.3
Germ	11.5	8.2	18.8	34.5	10.8	10.1
Bran	5.3	7.3	3.7	1.0	0.3	0.8

Pericarp : The pericarp is mainly composed of four successive layers, namely, outermost thick layer of tough cells, spongy layer of cells, seed coat or testa layer and aleurone layer. The spongy layer is continuous with spongy cells of tip cap.

Germ : The germ is mainly composed of scutellum and embryonic axis. The major parts of lipids and proteins are reserved in the scutellum.

Endosperm : The endosperm of corn is composed of floury and horny parts. The proportion of horny to floury parts varies widely from dent corn to floury corn variety. The ratio of horny to floury endosperm is about 2 : 1 in dent whereas the floury corn contains little horny part. The horny parts being hard and floury parts being soft, the latter is milled into flour easily during rolling. The horny regions have 1.5 to 2 per cent higher protein content than the floury regions.

Corn Dry Milling

Corn dry milling system can be divided into two groups : the traditional non degerming system and modern degerming system. In the non degerming system, the whole corn is ground into meal of high fibre as well as high protein contents by a stone grinder without removing germ. After grinding certain amount of germ and hull can be removed from the meal by sifting.

In the degerming system the corn is moistened with a little amount of water and tempered for moisture equilibration. After degerming the stock is dried, milled and classified into different products. The purpose of all dry degerming corn milling methods is to remove hull, germ and tip cap from the corn kernel as far as practicable and primarily produce corn grits with some meals and flours. The germ is then used for oil extraction and deoiled germ, hull, etc., are used as feed which is known as hominy feed. The yield of endosperm products and hominy feed are about 70 per cent and 30 per cent respectively.

Temperering-Degerming (T.D.) Method of Dry Milling

The major objectives of this method are : (a) to remove essentially all germ and hull so that endosperm contains as low fat and fibre as possible, (b) to recover a maximum amount of the endosperm as large clean grits without any dark speck, and

(c) to recover a maximum amount of germ as large and pure particles.

Description of the T.D. system

The basic operations/processes involved in the T.D. method are as follows :

(1) Cleaning of the corn.

(2) Conditioning of the corn by addition of control amount of moisture either at ordinary temperature or at an elevated temperature to toughen the germ and husk and facilitate their removal from the endosperm.

(3) Releasing hull, germ, and tip cap from the endosperm in a degermer.

(4) Drying and cooling the degermer products obtained from the degermer.

(5) Fractionating degermer stock by multistep milling through a series of machines namely roller mills, sifters, aspirators, gravity table separators, and purifiers to separate and recover the various products.

(6) Further drying of the products is done as and when necessary.

(7) Blending and packaging of products.

The flow diagram of the system is shown in Fig. 13.1.

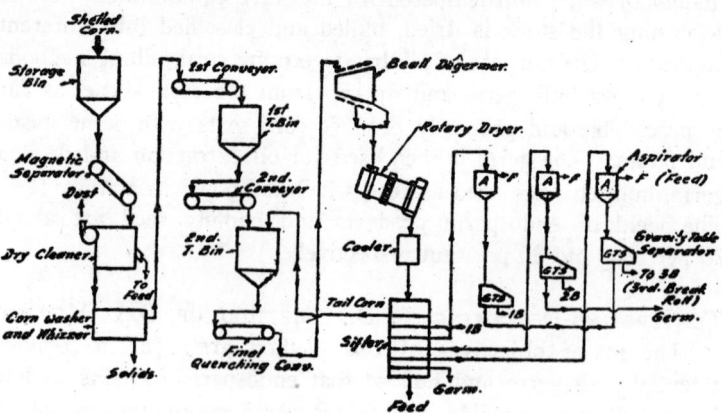

Fig. 13.1. Flow Diagram for T. D. Type Corn Mill

Cleaning of corn
Thorough cleaning of corn is essential for the subsequent milling operations.

Pieces of iron, etc., are removed by magnetic separators. Dry cleaners consisting of sieves and aspirators and sometimes a wet cleaner consisting of a washing destoning unit and a mechanical type dewatering unit, known as whizzer, are used for cleaning of corn.

Hydrothermal treatment/conditioning
Predetermined amount of moisture is added to the corn in the form of cold or hot water or steam in one, two or three stages with appropriate tempering times after each stage. The tempering times (rest periods) vary according to the hydration methods. So also tempering temperatures vary from room temperature to about 50° C accordingly.

The optimum moisture content for degerming in the Beall Degermer is 21-25 per cent. Either cold or hot water is used for the addition of moisture. A little heat in the form of open steam is added as and when necessary.

Degerming
The purpose of degerming is to remove hull, tip cap, and germ as far as practicable and leave the endosperm into large grits. However, the products from degermer consists of a mixture of kernel components. freed from each other to varying degrees, with the endosperm particles varying in sizes from grits to flour.

The Beall Degermer consists of a rotating cast iron conical roller mounted on a horizontal shaft in a conical cage.

Part of the cage is fitted with perforated screens and the remainder with plates having conical projections on its inner surface The rotating cone has similar projections over most of its surface. The feed end of the cone has spiral corrugations to move the corn forward whereas the large end has corrugations in an opposite direction to retard the flow. The product leaves the unit in two streams.

The major portions of the released germ, husk and fines as well as some of the grits are discharged through the perforated screens. Tail stock containing large amount of grits, escapes through an opening fitted with the large end of the cone. A hinged gate with an adjustable weight adjusts pressure inside the chamber and controls the flow of the stock.

Drying and cooling of degermer stock

The degermer products are to be dried to 15 to 18 per cent moisture content for proper grinding and sifting.

Generally rotary steam tube dryers are used for drying the product. Rotary Louver type dryer can also be employed. The stock is heated to about 50° C.

Counter-flow or cross-flow rotary, vertical gravity or fluidised bed types of cooler can be used for cooling the dried products.

Rolling and Grading

Recovery of various primary products is the next step. Further release of germ and husk from the endosperm products occurs during their gradual size reduction roller mills.

The germ, husk and endosperm fragments are then separated by means of sifters, aspirators, specific gravity table separators or purifiers.

Sifting is an important operation and is variously referred to

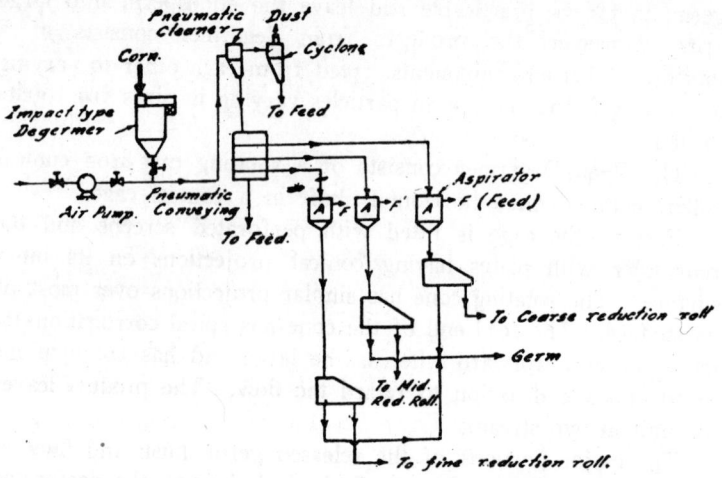

FIG. 13.2. Flow Diagram For Miag Process

as scalping, grading, classifying, or bolting depending upon the means used and purpose. Sifting is actually a size separation operation on sieves. Scalping is the coarse separation made on the product leaving a roller mill or degermer. Grading or classifying is the separation of a single stock (usually endosperm particles) into two or more groups according to particle size. Bolting is the removal of hull fragments from a corn meal or flour.

Another modern Corn dry milling method, known as Miag process is shown in Fig. 13.2. Only the flow diagram of the Miag process is given in the figure but detailed process has not been described here.

Corn Wet Milling

It has been discussed earlier that pure starch, pure germ and feed are the basic products of corn wet milling. But a few hundreds of byproducts can be produced from these three main products. A list of these byproducts with their uses is given in Table. 13.1.

The raw corn for wet milling should contain 15-16 per cent moisture and it should be physically sound. Insect and pest infested, cracked and heat damaged corns (treated at temperature around 75° C during drying) are unsuitable for wet milling. The heat damaged corn affects the quality of oil extracted from its germ.

Sufficient amount of moisture is added to the corn during steeping in the wet milling process in order to prepare the corn for subsequent degerming, grinding and separation operations.

The wet milling process consists of the following steps : (a) cleaning, (b) soaking, (c) germ separation and recovery, (d) grinding and hull recovery, and (e) separation of starch and gluten.

Cleaning

All impurities such as dust, chaff, cobs, stones, insect-infested grain and broken grain, and other foreign materials are removed from corn by screening and aspirating. The clean grains are conveyed to the storage bins.

Table 13.1 : Corn wet milling products

Product	Feed/food uses	Industrial uses
Germ oil and meal foots	Livestock	Soap, glycerine, leather dressing, etc.
Refined oil	Salad and table oils, cooking oils, margarine	Pharmaceuticals
Steep water	Yeast-food	Phytic acid, inositol
Gluten and hulls	Livestock and Poultry feed	
Starch	Corn starch, chewing gum, bakeries, baking powder, brewing confectionery	Textiles, laundry, paper and paper boxes, explosives, cosmetics, adhesives.
Syrup	Bakery products, canned fruits, ice cream, confectionery, soft drinks, chewing gums, mixed syrups, and jellies.	Textiles, leather tanning, pharmaceuticals, tobacco.
Sugar	Bakery products, pharmaceuticals, jams and jellies, ice cream, canned foods, confectionery.	Rayon, tanning, fermentation, brewing, vinegar, caramel colour, fermentation products, tobacco.

Steeping

The major objectives of steeping are (1) to soften the kernel for grinding, (2) to facilitate separation of germ, (3) to facilitate separation of gluten from the starch granules, and (4) to remove solubles, mainly from the germ.

Water impregnated with SO_2 (i.e., acidulated water with H_2SO_3) is used for steeping. It helps in arresting certain fermentation during long steeping process.

The steeping is carried out at about 50° C for a period

varying from 28 to 48 hours in different plants. The steeped corn attains a moisture content of about 45 per cent.

The flow diagram of corn wet milling process is shown in Fig. 13.3.

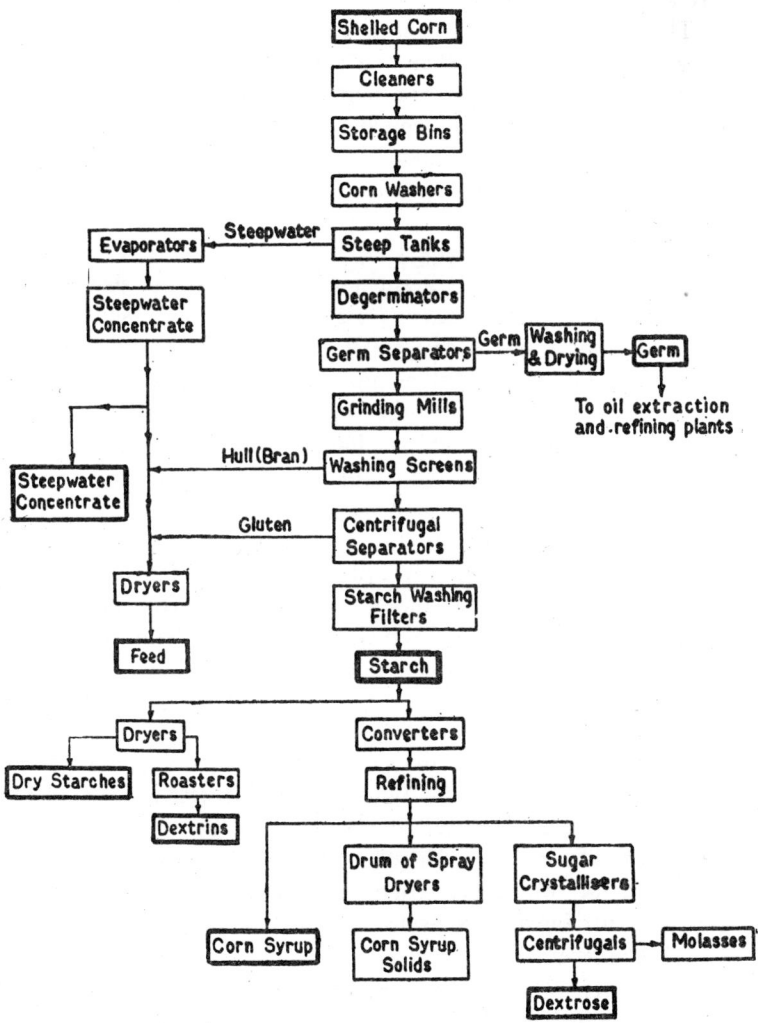

FIG. 13.3. Flow Diagram of Corn wet Milling and Refining Processes

Germ Recovery

The wet and softened corn kernels containing about 45 per cent moisture are conveyed to the degerminating unit. This machine consisting of a metallic stationary plate and a rotating plate with projecting teeth is employed only for tearing the soft kernels apart and freeing the germs without grinding them.

The pulpy mixture containing germs, husk, starch and gluten is passed through hydroclones, where the germ being lighter is separated from other heavier ingredients, by centrifugal force. Only modern starch plants employ hydroclones for germ separation. Oherwise the floatation method of germ separation is still in use in old types of mills.

Milling and Fibre Recovery

After separation of germ and screening of the coarse particles, the mixture contains starch, gluten and hulls.

Mainly horny endosperm and hull are then generally ground by either traditional Burstone mill or modern entoletor impact mills to release the rest of the starch. Material to be ground enters the machine through a spinning rotor and is thrown out with great force against the impactors at the periphery of the rotor and also against a stationary impactor resulting in considerable reduction in particle size. Here only the starch is readily released, with a very little size reduction of hulls.

The milled slurry, containing the ground starch, gluten, and hulls, is passed through a series of hexagonal reels where the coarser hulls and fibres are removed.

Starch-Gluten separation

In the modern process, the slurry containing starch and gluten is concentrated and then the lighter gluten particles are separated from the relatively heavier starch particles by the centrifugal force in high speed centrifuges. The centrifuging of starch is carried out in two stages. In many modern plants, the second stage of centrifugation is performed by a number of hydroclone type of equipments.

The starch obtained from the second stage of separation is filtered and then dried to produce dry starches.

Wheat milling

Introduction

Wheat is the principal food grain in many countries of the world. It is one of the most important cereals and is used as staple food in the form of flour. In India, a large proportion of wheat is used as the familiar *atta* and *maida* (white flour). The hard wheats are also ground into *suji* (semolina). Whole wheat is ground into atta by the traditional stone grinder without prior separation of bran and germ from it.

Flour Milling

The objective of modern flour milling is to obtain the maximum amount of white flour from the wheat endosperm without any bran or germ content. Conditioning of wheat by hydrothermal treatment prior to milling helps in the separation of barn and germ from the endosperm. If wheat is conditioned by hydrothermal treatment, bran and germ become rubber-like while the endosperm becomes soft. It also eliminates the difference in grinding characteristics between soft and hard wheat. When the conditioned wheat is sheared by the corrugations of first break roll during the milling operation, it splits open releasing small endosperm pieces and thus exposing the remaining endosperm which could be carefully scraped off the bran in successive break rolls.

The yields of white flour and byproducts (called mill feed) from white flour milling are about 70 per cent and 30 per cent by weight, respectively. The mill feed is composed of 12 per cent bran, 3 per cent germ and 15 per cent shorts.

Wheat consists of bran (12 per cent), germ (3 per cent) and endosperm (85 per cent).

Modern flour milling consists of six steps : (1) receiving, drying and storage of wheat, (2) cleaning, (3) conditioning, (4) milling into flour and byproducts, (5) packaging and storage of finished products, and (6) blending. Of them the most important operations namely, cleaning, conditioning and milling have been discussed here.

Cleaning

Wheat is thoroughly cleaned to remove all fine impurities

and the dirt sticking to the surface of the grain. To remove loose fine impurities a set of cleaners is employed. Small pieces of sticks, stones, sand, etc., are removed by sieving and the light impurities like chaff, etc., are removed by aspirations. Then the wheat is allowed to pass over powerful magnetic separators to remove pieces of ferromagnetic materials. The seeds of other food grains, defective grains and weed are removed by disc separators.

The next step in the cleaning operation is the removal of dirt sticking to the surface by scouring. Usually, wheat is moved by paddles against stationary emery-coated surface. Then the dirt and loose outer coating are aspirated off. The scratches and cracks formed in wheat during scouring help in increasing the rate of moisture absorption at the time of washing and conditioning.

The final cleaning step is washing by water which allows the dirt and bits of metal to sink. The moisture content of wheat is increased by about one per cent during washing.

Conditioning/hydrothermal treatment

The conditioning of wheat can be done either at room temperature, elevated temperature or at high temperature. But the temperature of wheat grain should not be raised above 47° C otherwise the gluten quality will be affected which deteriorates the baking quality of the flour.

Generally the moisture contents of soft and hard wheats are increased to 15 to 17 per cent and 16 to 19 per cent respectively by soaking and then the moisture of the grain is equilibrated by tempering for 18 to 72 hours in the tempering bin.

In a modern system conditioning of wheat is performed in four stages. The conditioner mainly consists of three sections, namely, preheating section, moistening section, and cooling section. In the first section wheat is preheated to the proper temperature, in the second section wheat is moistened to the desired moisture level and in the third section soaked wheat is cooled to the room temperature. Finally the treated wheat is kept in a separate tempering bin for 18 to 72 hours.

Hydrothermal treatment of grain by direct steaming has been popular for the last few years. It has many advantages over heating by air because both moistening and heating are carried out simultaneously in a single operation. Moreover, the grain is heated within 20 to 30 seconds to about 47° C. But the grain temperature above 47° C may adversely affect the quality of the flour. The rapid rate of heating weakens the intermolecular bonds in various parts of the grain to a considerable extent resulting in easier separation of bran, more effective grinding of endosperm and stronger action on proteins and enzymes.

Grinding (milling)

Milling of wheat is carried out by roller mills. The roller milling system is mainly divided into the break roll and reduction roll systems. In addition most of the flour mills keep a stand-by system known as scratch system. The scratch system is nothing but an extension of the break roll system. The break rolls and the reduction rolls are differentiated with the variation in their surface conditions. The surface of the reduction roll is smooth whereas the surface of break roll is corrugated. In the break rolls, the bran is cracked, the kernel is broken open. The endosperm adhering to bran is milled away successively in a few steps. Generally a series of four sets of break rolls are used. Each set of rolls takes stock from the preceding one. After each break, the mixture of free bran, free endosperm, free germ and endosperm still adhering to the bran is sifted and separated. The endosperm adhering to bran is passed through the next break roll while the middle size endosperms called middlings are sent to the reduction rolls for proper size reduction to flours. Therefore, the break rolls are mainly used for the production of middlings and the reduction rolls are used for grinding of free middlings into proper flour size. After each reduction of endosperm (middlings) the flour is sifted away from the bigger size middlings and the remaining middlings are passed to the next reduction rolls. The above operations are continued until the desired products are obtained. As many as 12 to 14 reduction rolls are used in most flour mills. But all reduction rolls are not used for all break products (Matz, 1959). The flow diagram of the flour milling system is shown in Appendix.

Storage of Finished Products

The flour and the mill feed (bran, germ and shorts) are

bagged in waterproof bags, stitched and stored in cold dry condition in flat godowns.

COMPONENTS OF A WHEAT MILL

(1) *Break roll*

Break roll consists of twin pairs of corrugated steel rolls. One roll of a pair revolves faster than the other, differential speed being in the proportion of 2.5 to 1.

(2) *Break sifting system*

This can be divided into two parts—plan sifters and purifiers.

(a) *Plan sifter.* Plan sifter is a scalping system removing large bran pieces adhering with endosperm at the top. The next series, which are finer, remove the bran and germ. The next layer of still finer sieve removes the endosperm middling and the bottom rough flow.

(b) *Purifier.* The middling containing finer bran particles are removed by purifer before they move to reducton roll.

(3) *Reduction roll.*

The reduction roll comprises of two smooth rolls. The rolls in the reduction system are further divided into coarse rolls and fine rolls depending on the clearance between the rollers.

It is possible to grind flour into very fine particles by gradual grinding. But under high grinding pressure the starch is ruptured and this should be avoided.

(4) *Reduction sifting system*

The same plan sifting system is used here.

After each reduction the product is separated by plan sifters where the finished flour is sifted by 120 mesh sieve (silk) and removed and oversized material is sent back to the reduction rolls for further processing.

(5) *Scratch system*

If the mill is functioning properly, i.e., good release of endosperm is obtained on the break rolls, the scratch system can be bypassed, if not, the scratch system is employed to maintain proper release of endosperm from bran. The scratch system is an extension of the break system and thus used as stand-by system only.

Milling of pulses

Introduction

Pulses are rich in proteins and are mainly consumed in the form of dehusked split pulses. Pulses are the main source of protein in vegetarian diet. There are about 4000 pulses mills (*Dhal mills*) in India. The average processing capacities of pulses mills in India vary from 10 to 20 tonnes/day. Milling of pulses means removal of the outer husk and splitting the grain into two equal halves. Generally, the husk is much more tightly held by the kernel of some pulses than most cereals Therefore, dehusking of some pulses poses a problem. The method of atlernate wetting and drying is used to facilitate dehusking and splitting of pulses. In India the dehusked split pulses are produced by traditional methods of milling. In traditional pulses milling methods, the loosening of husk by conditioning is insufficient. Therefore, a large amount of abraisive force is applied for the complete dehusking of the grains which results in high losses in the form of brokens and powder. Consequently, the yield of split pulses in traditional mills is only 65 to 70 per cent in comparison to 82 to 85 per cent potential yield.

It is, therefore, necessary to improve the traditional methods of pulses milling to increase the total yield of dehusked and split pulses and reduce the losses.

Varieties, Composition and structure

Green gram, red gram, bengal gram, horse gram, cluster bean, field pea, *arhar* are some of the common types of pulses.

The botanical name of *Arhar* is *Cajanas cajan..* Its chemical composition and structure are :

Moisture	—	10.35 per cent
Protein (N×6.25)	—	24.19 per cent
Ether extract	—	1.89 per cent
Ash	—	3.55 per cent
Crude fibre	—	1.01 per cent
Carbohydrate	—	59.21 per cent

The average percentage of husk and endosperm in *arhar* is 15 per cent and 85 per cent respectively. The structure is shown in Fig. 1.4.

Milling of pulses

In India there are two conventional pulses milling methods : wet milling method and dry milling method. The latter is more popular and used in commercial mills.

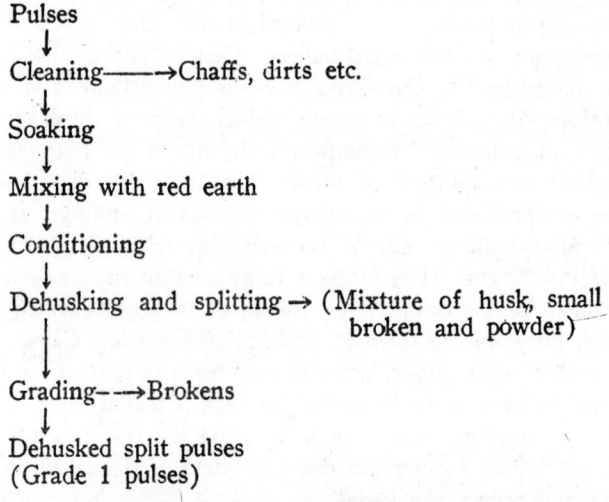

Pulses
↓
Cleaning———→Chaffs, dirts etc.
↓
Soaking
↓
Mixing with red earth
↓
Conditioning
↓
Dehusking and splitting → (Mixture of husk, small broken and powder)
↓
Grading-—→Brokens
↓
Dehusked split pulses
(Grade 1 pulses)

Flow diagram of wet milling

TRADITIONAL DRY MILLING METHOD ('DHAL' MILLING)

There is no common processing method for all types of pulses. However, some general operations of dry milling method such as cleaning and grading, rolling or pitting, oiling, moistening, drying and milling have been described in subsequent paragraphs.

Cleaning and grading

Pulses are cleaned from dust, chaff, grits, etc., and graded according to size by a reel type or rotating sieve type cleaner.

Pitting

The clean pulses are passed through an emery roller machine.

In this unit, husk is cracked and scratched. This is to facilitate the subsequent oil penetration process for the loosening of husk. The clearance between the emery roller and cage (housing) gradually narrows from inlet to outlet. As the material is passed through the narrowing clearance, mainly cracking and scratching of husk takes place by friction between pulses and emery. Some of the pulses are dehusked and split during this operation which are then separated by sieving.

Pretreatment with oil
The scratched or pitted pulses are passed through a screw conveyor and mixed with some edible oil like linseed oil (1.5 to 2.5 kg/tonne of pulses). Then they are kept on the floor for about 12 hours for diffusion of the oil.

Conditioning
Conditioning of pulses is done by alternate wetting and drying. After sun drying for a certain period, 3-5 per cent moisture is added to the pulses and tempered for about eight hours and again dried in the sun. Addition of moisture to the pulses can be accomplished by allowing water to drop from an overhead tank on the pulses being passed through a screw conveyor. The whole process of alternate wetting and drying is continued for two to four days until all pulses are sufficiently conditioned. Pulses are finally dried to about 10 to 12 per cent moisture content.

Dehusking and splitting
Emery rollers, known as Gota machine are used for the dehusking of conditioned pulses. About 50 per cent pulses are dehusked in a single operation (in one pass). Dehusked pulses are split into two parts also. The husk is aspirated off and dehusked, split pulses are separated by sieving. The tail pulses and unsplit dehusked pulses are again conditioned and milled as above. The whole process is repeated two to three times until the remaining pulses are dehusked and split.

Polishing
Polish is given to the dehusked and split pulses by treating them with a small quantity of oil and/or water.

16

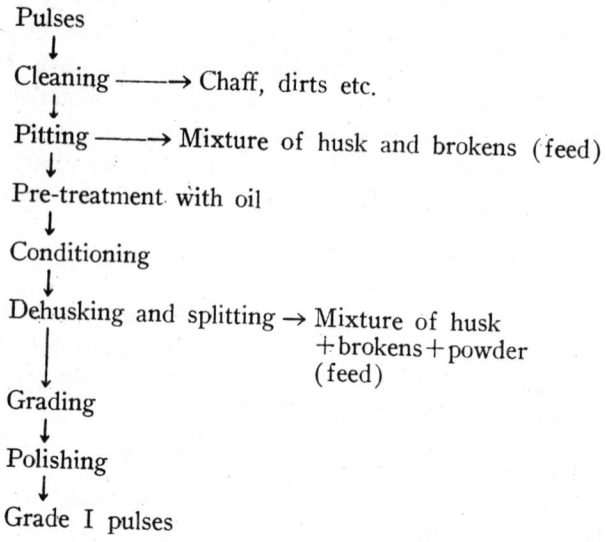

Flow diagram of dry milling of pulses

Commercial Milling of Pulses by Traditional Methods

It is discussed earlier that the traditional milling of pulses are divided into two heads, namely, dry milling and wet milling. But both the processes involved two basic steps : (i) Preconditioning of pulses by alternate wetting and sundrying for loosening husk and (ii) subsequent milling by dehusking and splitting of the grains into two cotyledons followed by aspiration and size separation using suitable machines. 100 per cent dehusking and splitting of pulses are seldom achieved particularly in cases of certain pulses like tur, black gram and green gram. Of them tur is the most difficult pulses to dehusk and split. Only about 40 to 50 per cent tur grains are dehusked and split in the first pass of preconditioning and milling. As sundrying is practised the traditional method is not only weather dependent but also it requires a large drying yard to match with the milling capacity. As a result it takes 3 to 7 days for complete processing of a batch of 20 to 30 tonnes of pulses into dhals. Moreover milling losses are also quite high in the traditional method of milling of pulses.

In general, simple reciprocating or rotary sieve cleaners are used for cleaning while bucket elevators are used for elevating pulses.

Pitting or scratching of pulses is done in a roller machine. A worm mixer is used for oiling as well as watering of the pitted pulses.

The machines used for dehusking are either power driven disc type sheller 'chakki' or emery-coated roller machine, which is commonly known as 'gota' machine. The emery roller is encaged in a perforated cylinder. The whole assembly is normally fixed at a horizontal position. The Engelberg type rice hullers are also used for dehusking of return unhusked black gram and green gram pulses in some parts of south India, where coarse stone powder at 0.5 to 0.75 per cent level is mixed with the grains as a abrasive material.

Sometimes either a cone type polisher or a buffing machine is employed for removal of the remaining last patches of husk and for giving a fine polisher to the finished dhal The cone polisher is similar to the polishing machine used for polishing of rice (i.e. for removal of bran from brown rice). The buffing machine is equipped with a rotating paddle having leather straps which can remove the last patch of husk and can give a fine polish to the dehusked pulses.

Blowers are used for aspiration of husk and powder from the products of the Disc sheller or Roller machine. Split dhals are separated from the unhusked and husked whole pulses with the help of sieve type separators.

Sieves are also employed for grading of dhals.

In general, the raw pulses may contain 2 to 5 per cent impurities (foreign materials), some insect infested grains and some extra moisture. Though the clean pulses contain about 10-15 per cent husk and 2-5 per cent germs, the yield of dhals from commercial dhal mills varies from 68-75 per cent. It may be noted that the average potential yields of common dhals vary from 85 to 89 per cent. (Kurien, 1979). These milling losses in the commercial pulses mills can be attributed to small brokens and fine powders formed during scouring and simultaneous dehusking and splitting operations.

Some of the commercial milling methods commonly followed for different pulses are briefly described in the subsequent paragraphs.

Dry milling of Tur

The dry milling of tur is generally practised in M.P. and

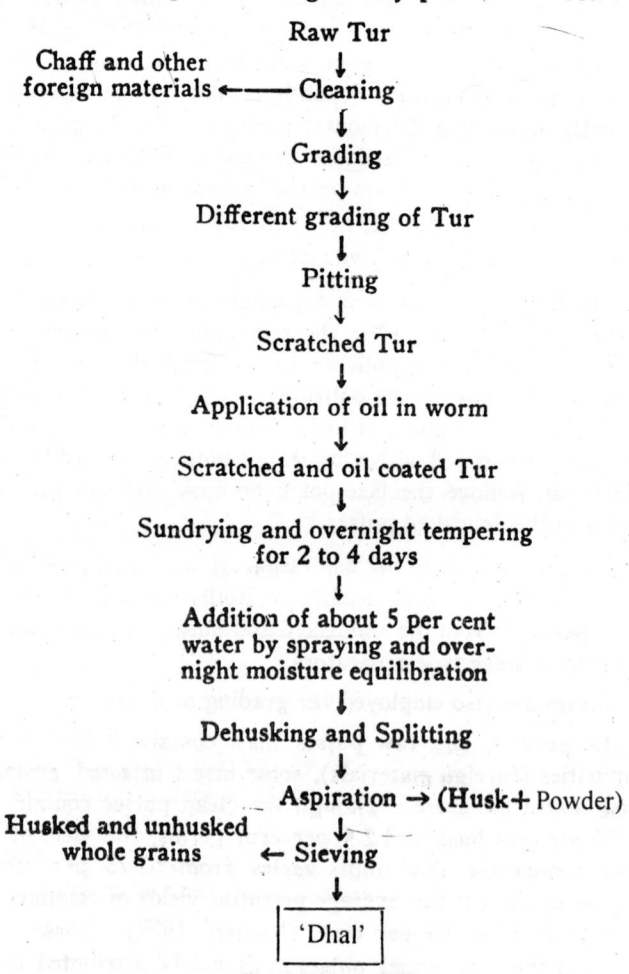

Dry Milling of Tur

U.P. as it can give higher turnover in terms of capacity of a mill having the same area of drying facilities. In this method the pulses are subjected to pitting in a roller and then they were subjected to oil treatment by applying 0.5 to 2 per cent linseed or any other edible oil in worm mixers. The pulses are then spread in the drying yard for sundrying for 2 to 4 days. The pulses are tempered by heaping and covering during the nights in between these days. After thorough sundrying the pulses are once again moistened uniformly with about 5 per cent water and kept as such on heaps overnight for uniform moisture equilibration. Then these graing are passed through the rollers for dehusking and splitting. About 50 per cent grains are dehusked and split in first operation.

After removal of the husk by aspiration the split dhal is separated from a mixture of husked and unhusked whole pulses. The mixture is once again moistened by spraying water and dried in the sun and then dehusked and split as before either in roller or in an under runner disc sheller, where around 30 per cent of the grains are dehusked and split. The above process of alternate wetting and drying is repeated until almost all the remaining pulses are converted into split dhal. The average yield of dhal ranges from 68 to 75 per cent.

Dry milling of black gram

After cleaning the black grams are subjected to pricking in a rough roller mill for some scratching as well as partial removal of the waxy coating on the black grams. The scratched grains are then coated with 1 to 2 per cent oil in a worm mixer and then heaped over night for diffusion of the oil in the grains. The scratched and oil coated pulses are sprayed in drying yards for sundrying for 4 to 6 hours. The partially dried grains are moistened with a spray of 4 to 5 per cent water and kept over night for moisture equilibration. The wetted pulses are then dried for 3 to 4 days in the sun and tempered over nights in between these drying periods. The thoroughly dried pulses are dehusked in a roller. About 40 to 50 per cent pulses are dehusked and split in first milling operation. The husk and powder are then aspirated off. Then the split 'dhal' is separated from the dehusked whole dhal and unhusked pulses by sieving. Both husked and unhusked whole grains are again dried in the sun and milled as above and the same process is repeated until the desired milling of pulses is achieved. The average yield of dhal is 70-71 per cent. Sometimes the last part of the unsplit grains and partially husked grains are allowed to pass through sheller and polisher machines for splitting and removal of the husk, which result in a large amount of losses due to formation of powder and brokens.

In some cases polishing is done in a buffing machine. In order to give a white finish and to protect from insect attack a coating of soapstone powder is generally given to these 'dhals'

Dry milling of Bengal gram, Lentil and peas

It is comparatively easy to dehusk and split Bengal gram, Lentil and Peas as their husks are loosely attached to the cotyledons. It requires shorter period of preconditioning prior to milling these pulses.

After cleaning, the pulses are pitted in a roller machine. The pitted grains are then wetted with water (5 to 10 per cent) in a worm mixer and then these are kept in heaps for a few hours for diffusion of water into the grains. These grains are dried in the sun for a day or two, with overnight tempering in between these days. About 60 to 70 per cent dried pulses are then dehusked and split in the first pass of a roller machine. The husk and powder are aspirated off. The split pulses are separated from the unhusked and husked whole grains by sieving. The alternate wetting with 5 per cent water and sun-drying and subsequent milling operations are repeated till the most of the pulses are converted to 'dhal' (Kurien, 1979).

The preconditioning and milling of Lentils and Peas are comparable with bengal gram. The same initial pitting, wetting, conditioning, sundrying and subsequent milling by dehusking and splitting in a roller and aspiration of husk with a blower and separation of split dhal from the mixture of unhusked and husked whole grains with a sieve, are being followed. The whole process of preconditioning and milling are repeated till most of the pulses are converted into dhal. However, the conversion of these pulses into dhals are easy compared to tur. It takes about 3 to 5 days for complete processing of a batch of pulses.

Dry milling of Green Gram

In dry milling of green gram, both oil and water treatments are given to the grains. The wetted grains are dried in the sun. Then the dried pulses are simultaneously dehusked and split using a dehusking machine. After removal of husk split dhal is separated from the mixture as usual. The yield of dhal is poor which varies from 62 to 65 per cent only (Kurien, 1979).

Wet milling of Tur

The flow diagram of the wet milling of Tur is given below.

<pre>
                    Raw Tur
                       ↓
               Soaking in water
                 for 3—12 hours
                       ↓
             Mixing of soaked pulses
             with wet earth (5 per cent)
                       ↓
             Conditioning overnight for
               moisture diffusion and
                  equilibration
                       ↓
             Alternate sundrying and
             tempering for 2—4 days
                       ↓
                Separation of red earth
  Red earth ←— from the mixture by sieving
                       ↓
             Dehusking and splitting of
                dried pulses by a disc
  Husk and ←—   sheller 'chakki'
  powder
                       ↓
             Size separation by   Unhusked and
                  seiving   —→   husked whole
                       ↓   grains
                   | 'Dhal' |
                Wet milling of Tur
</pre>

In wet milling of tur the grains are soaked in water for a period of 3 to 12 hours. The soaked pulses are thoroughly mixed with wet red earth at about 5 per cent level. The mixture is kept in heaps overnight. The whole mixture is then dried in the sun for 2 to 4 days until the husk of all grains are loosened. The pulses are tempered overnight in between these days. The red earth is then separated from the pulses by sieving. The sundried grains are dehusked and split in a disc sheller (chakki). Dhal and other fractions are separated as usual. It is claimed that about 95 per cent of the grains can be dehusked and split in a single milling operation. The split dhal is separated from the mixture usually. The rest of the unhusked and husked whole grains are preconditioned and milled as above for conversion of these grains into dhal. Though the above wet milling of tur is popular in South India, the purpose of using earth is not well understood. However, it is believed that the red earth facilitates in increasing the rate of drying and in consequence in loosening the husk. So also the earth may act as a milling aid on account of its abrasive nature. It is also considered that dhals produced by following wet method are attractive in colour and good taste. The wet method requires 5 to 7 days for complete processing of a batch of grains (Kurien, 1979)

MODERN CFTRI METHOD OF PULSES MILLING (UNDER STUDY)

CFTRI method of *dhal* milling is described as follows :

Cleaning

Cleaning is done in rotary reel cleaners to remove all impurities from pulses and separate them according to size.

Preconditioning

The cleaned pulses are conditioned in two passes in a dryer (LSU type) using hot air at about 120° C for a certain period of time. After each pass, the hot pulses are tempered in the tempering bins for about six hours. The preconditioning of pulses helps in loosening husk significantly.

Dehusking

The preconditioned pulses are conveyed to the Pearler or

Dehusker where almost all pulses are dehusked in a single operation. The dehusked whole pulses (*gota*) are separated from split pulses and mixture of husk, brokens, etc. (*chuni-bhusi*) and are received in a screw conveyor where water is added at a controlled rate. The moistened *gota* is then collected on the floor and allowed to remain as such for about an hour.

The flow diagram of the modern milling of pulses by CFTRI Method as given below is self-explanatory.

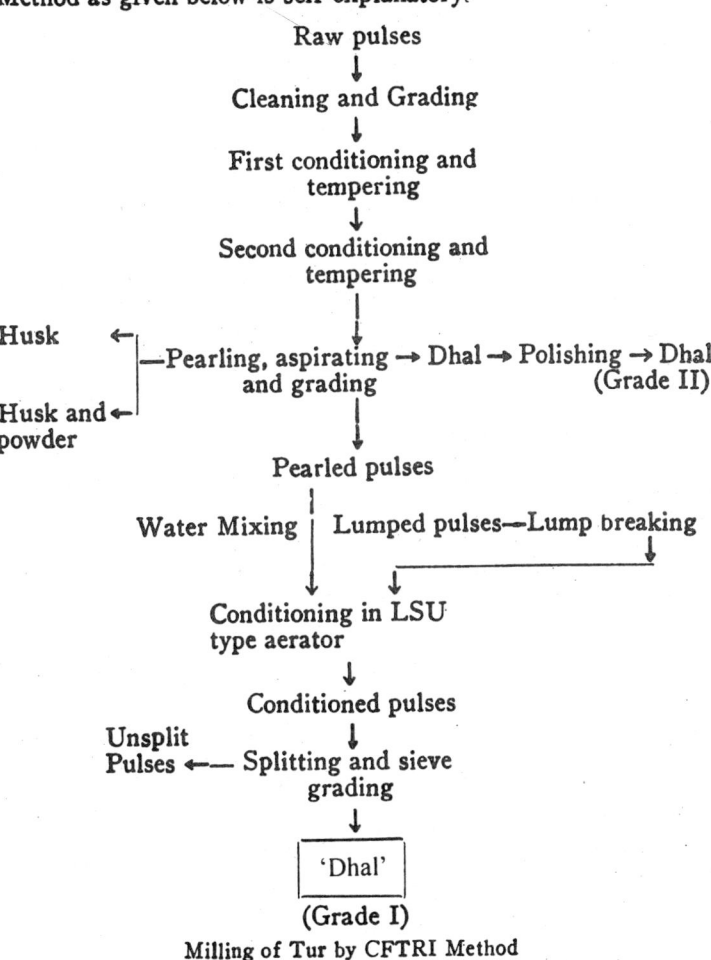

Raw pulses
↓
Cleaning and Grading
↓
First conditioning and tempering
↓
Second conditioning and tempering
↓

Husk ←
Husk and ← —Pearling, aspirating → Dhal → Polishing → Dhal
powder   and grading   (Grade II)
↓
Pearled pulses

Water Mixing | Lumped pulses—Lump breaking
↓   ↓
Conditioning in LSU type aerator
↓
Conditioned pulses

Unsplit   ↓
Pulses ←— Splitting and sieve grading
↓
'Dhal'
(Grade I)

Milling of Tur by CFTRI Method
(Under development)

Lump Breaking

Some of the moistened *gota* form into lumps of varying sizes. These lumps are fed to the lump breaker to break them.

Conditioning and Splitting

After lump breaking the *gota* is conveyed to LSU type of dryer where it is exposed to hot air for a few hours. The *gota* is thus dried to the proper moisture level for splitting. The hot conditioned and dried dehusked whole pulses are split in the emery roller. All of them are not split in one pass. The mixture is graded into Grade 1 pulses, dehusked whole pulses and small brokens. The unsplit dehusked pulses are again fed to the conditioner for subsequent splitting.

BIBLIOGRAPHY ON SECTION III

1. Anderson, R. A., 1962, A note on wet-milling of high amylose corn containing 75 per cent—amylose starch, *Cereal Chem.*, 39, 406-408.

2. Anderson, R. A., 1963, Wet-milling Properties of grains : Bench-Scale Study, *Cereal Sci. Today*, 8, No. 6, 190-92, 195, 221.

3. Anon, 1964, Joint United States—Canadian tables of feed composition, *Natl. Acad. Sci.*, Nath. Res. Council Publication 1232.

4. Atkins, T. A., and Geddes, W. F., 1939, The relationship between protein content and strength of flours in gluten enriched flours, *Cereal Chem.*, 16, 223-31.

5. Autrey, H. S., 1953, Effect of variables upon milling yields, *Rice J. Annual.*

6. Autrey, H. S., Grigorieff, W. W., Attschul, A. M., and Freeman, E. E., 1955, Effect of milling conditions on breakage of rice grains, *J. Agr. Food Chem.*, 3(7), 593.

7. Baird, P. D., Mac Masters, M. M., and Rist, C. E., 1950, Studies on a rapid test for the viability of corn for industrial use, *Cereal Chem.*, 27, 508-13.

8. Banerjee, S. N., 1975, Report on the evaluation of the modern dal mill, Department of Food, Govt. of India.

9. Bishop, W., and Dustin, J., 1951, Topnotch wet corn mill house, *Food Ind.*, 23, No. 3, 121-24, 211-12.

10. Borasio, L., and Gariboldi, F., 1957, Illustrated glossary of rice processing machines, Food and Agricultural Organization of the United Nations, Rome.

11. Boundy, J. A., Woychik, J. H., Dimler, R. J., and Wall, J. S., 1967, Protein composition of dent, waxy, and high-amylose corns, *Cereal Chem.*, 44, 160-169.

12. Bradbury, D., Wolf, M. J., and Dimler, R. J., 1962, The hilar layer of white corn, *Cereal Chem.*, 39, 72-78.

13. Brautlecht, C. A., 1953, *Starch, Its sources, Production and Uses*, Reinhold Publishing Corp., New York.

14. Brekke, O. L., Weinecke, L. A., Boyd, J. N., and Griffin, E. L., Jr., 1963, Corn dry milling : Effects of first-temper moisture, Screen perforations, and rotor speed on Beall degerminator throughput and products, *Cereal Chem.*, 40, 423-29.

15. Brekke, O. L., and Weinecke, L. A., 1964, Corn dry-milling, A comparative evaluation of commercial degermer samples, *Cereal Chem.*, 41, 321-28.

16. Brekke, O. L., 1967, Corn dry milling : Pretempering low-moisture corn, *Cereal Chem.*, 44, 521-31.

17. Brekke, O. L., 1968, Corn dry-milling : Stress crack formation in tempering low-moisture corn, and effect on degerminator performance, *Cereal Chem.*, 45, 291-303.

18. Brekke, O L., and Kwolek, W. F., 1969, Corn dry milling : Cold tempering and degermination of corn of various initial moisture contents, *Cereal Chem.*, 46, 545-49.

19. Brekke, O. L., 1970, Dry milling artificially dried corn : Roller milling of degerminator stock at various moistures, *Cereal Science Today*, 15, 37-42.

20. Chandra, P. K., 1972, Methodology and Procedures for evaluating performance of commercial rice mills, Unpublished M. Tech. Thesis, I. I. T., Kharagpur.

21. Dandekar Machinery Works, Catalogue for rice and pulse milling machinery, M/s. G. G. Dandekar Machine Works Ltd., Bhiwandi, Thana, Maharashtra, India.

22. Earle, F. R., Curtis, J. J., and Hubbard, J. E., 1946, Composition of the component parts of the corn kernel, *Cereal*

Chem., 23, 504-11.

23. Elias, D. G., and Scott, R. A., 1957, British flour milling technology, *Cereal Sci. Today*, 7, 180-84.

24. Ezaki, H., 1973, Paddy husker, Group training course— Fiscal, Institute of Agricultural Machinery, Japan.

25. Finney, K. F., and Barmore, M. A., 1948. Loaf volume and protein content of hard winter and spring wheats, *Cereal Chem.*, 25, 291-311.

26. Gariboldi, F., 1974, Rice Milling Equipment Operation and Maintenance, Agricultural Services Bulletin No. 22, FAO, Rome.

27. Grist, D. H., 1959, Rice (3rd ed), Longmans Green and Co. Ltd., London.

28. Hogan, J. T., and Deobald, H. J., 1965, Measurement of the degree of milling of rice, *Rice J.*, 68 (10), 10.

29. Houston, D. F., Western Marketing and Nutrition Research Division, Agricultural Research Service, U. S. Department of Agriculture, Berkeley, California.

30. I.C.A.R., 1970, Pulse Crops of India, I.C.A.R. Publication, New Delhi.

31. Jones, C. R., 1940, The production of mechanically damaged starch in milling as a governing factor in the diastatic activity of flour, *Cereal Chem.*, 17, 133-69.

32. Kent-Jones, D. W., and Amos, A. J., 1957, Modern Cereal Chemistry, Fifth Ed., Northern Publishing Co. Ltd., Liverpool.

33. Kerr, R. W., 1950, Chemistry and Industry of starch, 2nd Edition, Academic Press, New York.

34. Kester, E. B., and Matz, S. A., 1970, Rice Processing, In : Cereal Technology, ed. by S. A. Matz. Avi Pub. Co., Westport, Conn.

35. Koga, Y., 1969, Drying, husking and milling in Japan IV and V., *Farming*, Japan.

36. Kuprits, Y., ed., Technology of grain processing and provender milling, Tekhnologiya perer atbotki zernai Kombikormovoe, Izd. 'Kolos' : Moscow (1965). (Translation by Israel Program for Scientific Translation, Jerusalem, Israel, 1967.)

37. Kurien, P. P., and Parpia, H. A. B., 1968, Pulse milling in India, I, Processing and milling of tur and arhar (*Caianas cajan*), .*Food Sc. and Tech.*, 5(6) : 203-207.

38. Kurien, P. P. 1979   Pulses Milling in Food Industries, C. F. T. R. I., Mysore pp 3.1-3.20.

39. Lockwood, J. F., 1952., *Flour Milling*, Third ed., Northern Publishing Co. Ltd., Liverpool.

40. Lockwood, J. F., 1960, *Flour Milling*, The Northern Publishing Co., Liverpool.

41. Matz, S. A., 1959, The Chemistry and Technology of Cereals as Food and Feed, Avi Publishing Co., Westport, Conn.

42. Modi B. S., 1972, Factors affecting the performance of paddy separator, Unpublished M. Tech. Thesis, I. I. T. Kharagpur.

43. Peplinski, A. J., and Pfeifer, V. F., 1970, Gelatinization of corn and sorghum grits by steam-cooking, *Cereal Science Today*, 15, 144, 149-51.

44. Primo, E., Barber, S., Tortosa, E., Camacho, J., Ulldemolins, J., Jimenez, A., and Vega, R., 1970. Chemical composition of the byproducts obtained in the different steps of the rice milling process (In Spanish), Rev. Agroquim Tecnol, Alimentos 10 : 244.

45. Schoch, T. J., 1941, Physical aspects of starch behavior, *Cereal Chem.*, 18, 121-28.

46. Scott, J. H., 1951, *Flour Milling Processes*, Second ed., Chapman and Hall, London.

47. Smith, L., 1944, *Flour Milling Technology*, Third ed., Northern Publishing Co., Liverpool.

48. Stivers, T. E., Jr., 1955, American corn milling systems for degermed products, *Assoc. Operators Millers Bull.*, 2168-79.

49. Sugden, G. H., 1956, Various aspects of wheat conditioning, *Cereal Science Today*, I, 136-42.

50. Satake Owner Manual, Type-03, Satake Engg. Co., Ltd., Japan.

51. Stermer, R. A., 1968, Environmental conditions and stress cracks in milled rice, *Cereal Chem.*, 45, 365.

52. Satake Engineering Co. Ltd., 1973, Rice Milling Machinery,

Technical Note No. 601, Extension and Training Institute, Satake Engineering Co. Ltd., Tokyo, Japan.

53. Shibano, M., 1973, Construction and Function of Abrasive Roll Type Rice Whitening Machine, Technical note, JRMA, Japan.

54. Shibano, M., 1973, Construction and Function of Friction Type Rice Whitening Machine, Technical note, JRMA, Japan.

55. Thompson, R. A., and Foster, G. H., 1963, Stress cracks and breakage in artificially dried corn, U. S. Dept. Agr., AMS, 631.

56. Tuite, J., and Foster, G. H., 1963, Effect of artificial drying on the hygroscopic properties of corn, *Cereal Chem.*, 40, 630-37.

57. Watson, S. A., Sanders, E. W., Wakely, R. D., and Williams, C. B., 1955, Peripheral cells of the endosperms of grain sorghum and corn and their influence on starch purification, *Cereal Chem.*, 32, 165-82.

58. Watson, S. A., Hirata, Y., 1962, Some wet-milling properties of artificially dried corn, *Cereal Chem.*, 39, 35-43.

59. Watson, S. A., 1976a, Manufacture of corn and milo starches, In : *Starch : Chemistry and Technology*, Vol. II, R. L. Whistler, and E. F. Paschall (Editors), Academic Press, New York.

60. Watson, S. A., and Yahl, K. R., 1976b, Comparison of wet-milling properties of opaque-2 high-lysine corn and normal corn, *Cereal Chem.*, 44, 488-98.

61. Weinecke, L. A., Brekke, O. L., and Griffin, E. L., Jr., 1963, Corn dry milling : Effect of Beall degerminator tailgate configuration on product streams, *Cereal Chem.*, 40, 575-81.

62. Wolf, M. J., Buzan, C. L., Mac Masters, M. M., and Rist, C. E., 1952a, Structure of the mature Corn Kernel, I, Gross anatomy and structural relationship, *Cereal Chem.*, 29, 321-33.

63. —————————————, 1952b, Structure of the mature Corn Kernel, II, Microscopic structure of pericarp, seed coat, and hilar layer of dent corn, *Cereal Chem.*, 29, 334-48.

64. —————— —————, 1952c, Structure of the mature Corn Kernel, III, Microscopic structure of the endosperm of dent corn, *Cereal Chem.*, 29, 349-61.

65. —————————————, 1952d, Structure of the mature Corn Kernel, IV, Microscopic structure of the germ of dent corn, *Cereal Chem.*, 29, 362-82.

66. Kuprits, Ya. N., 1967, Technology of Grain Processing and Provendor Milling, Israel Program for Scientific translations, Jerusalem.

67 Zipf, R. L., 1951, Wet milling of cereal grains, Yearbook Agr., U. S. Dept. Agr., Washington, D. C.

SECTION IV
PROCESSING OF OILSEEDS
AND RICE BRAN

Processing of Oilseeds

For the last two decades, India is meeting the shortage of oils and fats by importing these commodities at huge costs in foreign exchange. Based on an income elasticity of 1.32 and a national income growth rate of 3.5 per cent, the demand for vegetable oils in 2000 A.D. will be 8.75 million tonnes as against an expected production of 5.15 million tonnes. In order to augment the oils and fat resources in India the following steps should be taken :

To make up the deficit of oil, rice bran oil, corn oil and other non-conventional oils are to be made available to the maximum extent.

High Yielding varieties of plam, sunflower, corn, cotton etc. are to be grown widely.

Collection of forest oilseeds such as 'sal', 'mowrah' etc. needs to be intensified. The potential of these sources is as high as 15 million tonnes which is equivalent to 2 million tonnes of oils and fats.

Improved post harvest technology of oilseeds is to be introduced.

The oils and fats are composed of different mixtures of glycerides of various fatty acids. The waxes are mixtures of higher polyhydric alcohols (other than glycerol) with fatty acids. The fatty acid compositions and their contents of different oils are given in Table 14.1.

It may be noted that the main constituents of the vegetable oils are the 16 and 18 carbon acids. Esters containing more unsaturated acids and having lower melting points are oils. The more saturated Esters constitute fats. All fats and oils are broadly classified into edible and nonedible. Groundnut.

TABLE 14.1 : Percentage Composition of Fatty Acid of different
vegetable oils

No. of C atoms	Fatty acid	Chemical formula	Linseed oil	Cotton-seed oil	Soybean oil	Coconut oil
8	Caprylic	$C_7H_{15}COOH$	—	—	—	87.8
10	Capric	$C_9H_{19}COOH$	—	—	—	7.3
12	Lauric	$C_{11}H_{23}COOH$	—	—	—	48.0
14	Myristic	$C_{13}H_{27}COOH$	—	1.6	0.5	17.5
14	Unsaturated	$C_{13}H_{25}COOH$	—	—	—	—
16	Palmitic	$C_{15}H_{31}COOH$	6.0	23.0	10.2	9.0
16	Unsaturated	—	—	2.0	1.2	—
18	Stearic	$C_{17}H_{35}COOH$	2.9	1.3	2.5	2.2
18	Oleic	$C_{17}H_{33}COOH$	19.0	22.8	23.5	5.7
18	Linoleic	$C_{17}H_{31}COOH$	24.4	47.9	51.0	2.5
18	Linolenic	$C_{17}H_{29}COOH$	47.0	—	8.5	—
20	Arachidic	$C_{19}H_{39}COOH$	0.5	1.4	2.6	—
24	Lignoceric	$C_{23}H_{47}COOH$	0.2	—	—	—

cottonseed, linseed, soybean are some of the sources of the edible oil. The edible oils are mainly used for cooking purposes, table uses and salad dressings. Oils are also used for inedible purposes. These include soap industry, drying oil industries including paints and varnishes, plasticizers. The waxes are used as components in the manufacture of floor and shoe polishes,

TABLE 14.2. World Production of some common vegetable oils

Primarily edible oil	Production, 1000 metric tons 1978/1979
Soybean	12,440
Sunflower	4,335
Groundnut	2,745
Coconut	2,710
Rapeseed	3,225
Cottonseed	2,950
Palm	3,545
Palm kernel	545

(Pryde, 1981)

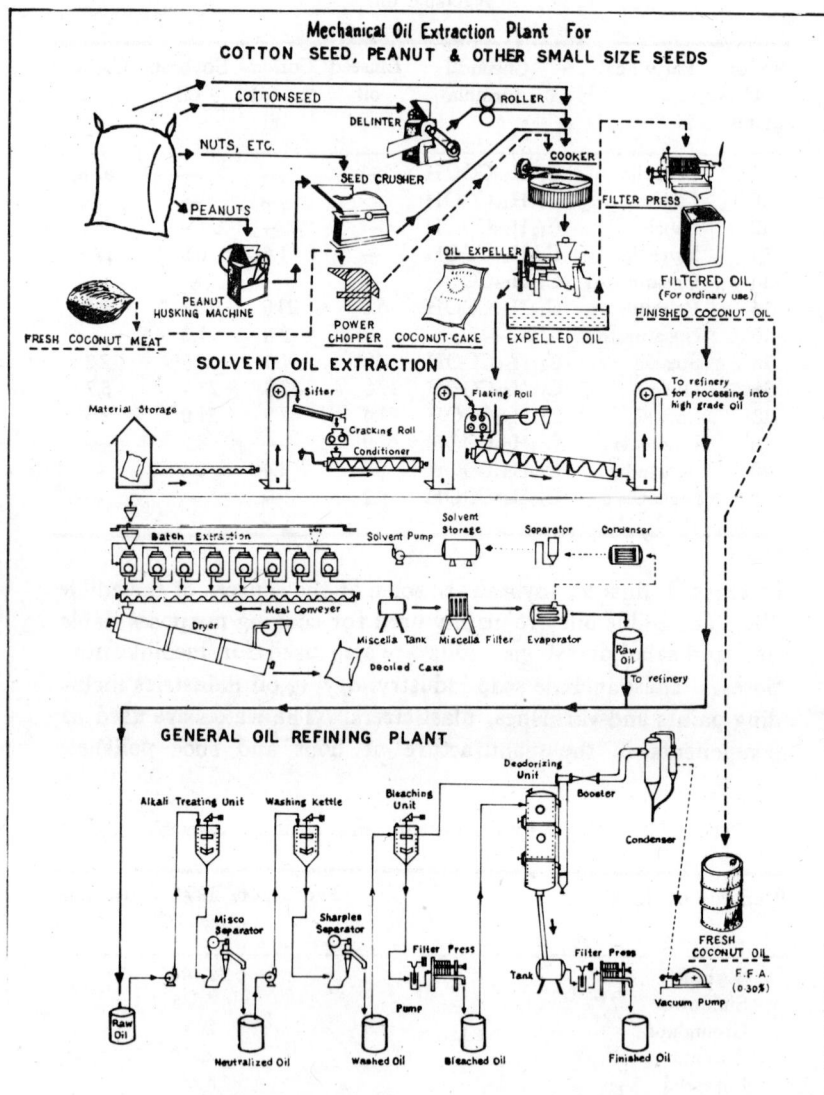

FIG. 14·1 GENERALISED FLOW SHEET FOR MECHANICAL EXPRESSION SOLVENT EXTRACTION AND REFINING OF OIL.

carbon paper, candles etc. The world production and average oil contents and the average yields of some common oilseeds are, indicated in Tables 14.2 and 14.3 respectively.

TABLE 14.3 : Oil content and average yield of some common oilseeds

Oilseed	Oil content, Wt(%)	Average, Yield, kg/ha	
		Oil	Total
Cottonseed	18—20	140	863
Shelled groundnuts	45—50	790	2494
Rapessed	40—45	409	1166
Soyabean	18—20	319	1788
Oil palm kernels	45—50	3895	4455
Safflower	.30—35	762	2119
Seasame	50	260	—
Flaxseed	35—42	230	650
Sunflower	35—45	589	1469

(Pryde, 1981)

The mechanical extraction as well as solvent extraction methods are employed for the manufacture of oil from the oilseeds. Almost all oils contain some free fatty acids, colouring and odouring matters and in some cases gums and waxes (particularly in rice bran oil). The crude vegetable oils are, therefore, to be refined for removal of these undesirable materials prior to their uses for edible purposes. Though steps followed in extraction and refining of oil vary to some extent from one oilseed to other, for convenience a general flow diagram for extraction of oils from some common oilseeds and their refining is outlined in Fig. 14.1.

The specific methods of production of crude and refined oil from different oilseeds are discribed below.

Preduction and Refining of Cottonseed oil

The flow sheet of the method of production of crude cottonseed oil by mechanical expression and its refining process are presented in Fig. 14.2. The processes and operations for the production of crude oil are outlined in the following sequences :

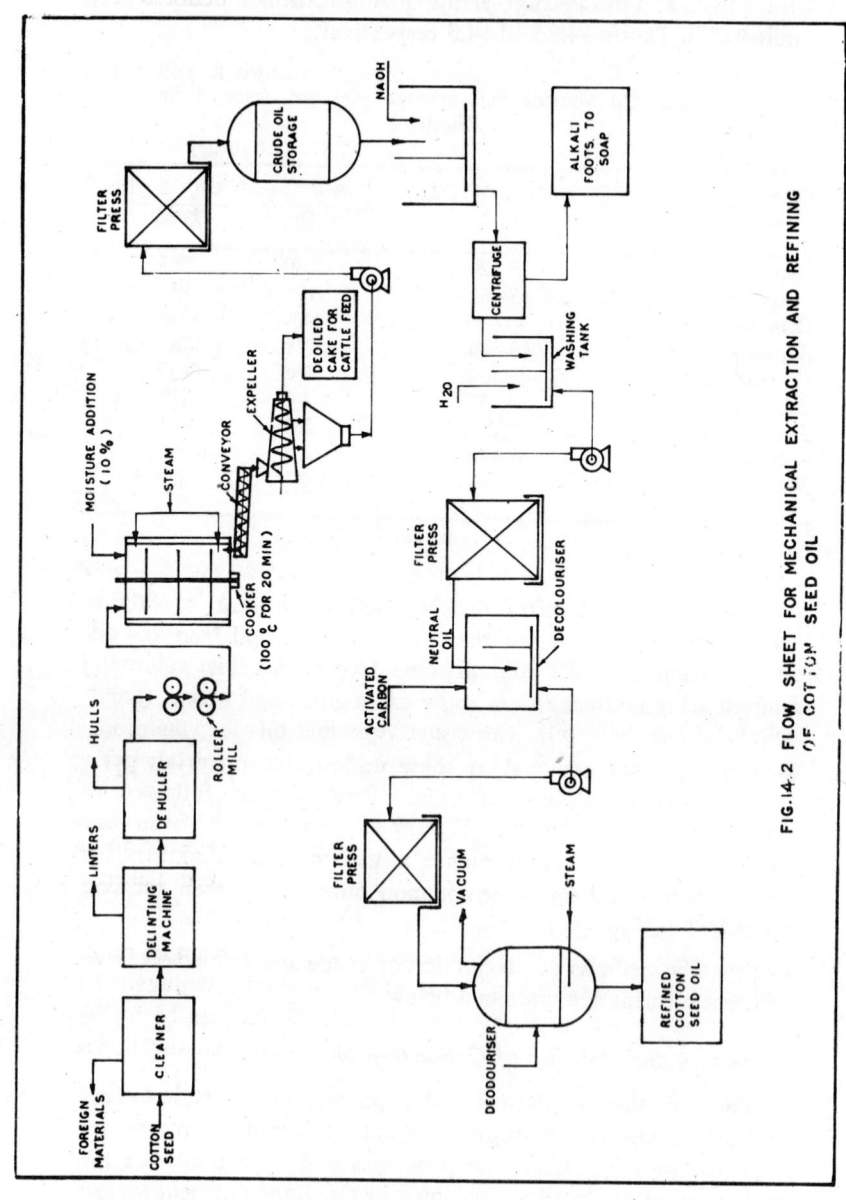

FIG. 14.2 FLOW SHEET FOR MECHANICAL EXTRACTION AND REFINING OF COTTON SEED OIL

Mechanical expression of cottonseed oil

The cottonseeds are thoroughly cleaned, delinted and dehulled.

These materials are allowed to pass through a roller mill to convert them into thin flakes.

The flakes are then cooked to precipitate the phosphatides,to detoxify the gossypol, to coagulate the protein and to bring down the moisture content of the flakes from about 12 to 5%.

Hydraulic press is mostly used for expelling cottonseed oil. However, expeller or screwpress is also employed in smaller proportion for the same operation. The cooked flakes are placed in the hydraulic press and gradually pressure is applied. The pressure is raised to a maximum of 113 to 141 kg/cm^2 till the oil begins to flow. Then the pressure is drained for 30 to 45 min. The cakes are discharged. The capacity of a press may be as high as 7 tonnes of cooked flakes per day. A continuous motor driven screw press consisting of a tapered screw operating inside a perforated barrel can also be employed. It can apply a pressure of 1550 to 1860 kg/cm^2 and can discharge oil through the barrel spacings and deoiled cake through the orfice of the tapered end of the barrel. The residual oil in the deoiled cake is 4 to 5% only, but the power consumption is very high.

The yields of the oil, deoiled cakes, hulls, and linters from 1 tonne of raw cottonseed are 136 kg, 408 kg, 227 kg and 91 kg respectlvely. (Shreve. 1956).

Now-a-days solvent extraction is also practiced for the extraction of oil from either full fatted cottonseed flakes or mechanically deoiled cakes.

The cotton seed oil can be used for the production of refined cooking oil or salad oil, margarine and shortenings. The deoiled cake is used for cattle feed. The linters can be utilised as a source of highly pure cellulose. The hulls can also be used for live stock feeding.

Refining of Crude Cottonseed Oil

The crude oil is refined as follows : Free fatty acids are

neutralised with either caustic soda (NaOH) or soda ash with the formation of soaps commonly known as alkalifoots.

The soaps are removed from the oil by centrifuges and filters.

The neutral oil is washed twice or thrice with water for washing out the remaining soap in the oil. The waste water is separated by filters and centrifuges.

The oils are then decolourised with the help of the adsorbent like activated carbon and or activated clay at a high temperature by a batch process or by a continuous process.

The bleached oil is then deodourised by heating the oil with super heated steam under high vacuum.

For the manufacture of salad oil bleached oil is subjected to winterization which consists of cooling the oil to a low temperature for a long time and filtering the solid materials from the oil.

Solvent Extraction of Soyabean Oil

Soyabeans are subjected to preliminary cleaning and milling operations as usual. The soy meal is then cooked. But the cooking of meal by heat treatment is done under mild conditions. The heat treated meals are then converted into flakes using smooth flaking rolls. Solvent extraction of the cooked flakes can be done batch wise or continuously. In continuous extraction method countercurrent solvent flow is preferred. The oil from the miscella is separated by distillation and stripping under vacuum. The extracted meal is desolventized by heating with live steam in a desolventizer. The solvent from the distillation and stripping columns as well as from the desolventizer is condensed and recovered and stored in the solvent storage tank. The oil, separated from the miscella in the distillation column goes to oil storage tank after cooling. The flow sheet for a continuous solvent ectraction process of soyabean is shown in Fig. 14.3 (Shreve. 1956). The deoiled cake contains about 1% residual oil.

Extraction of sunflower Oil

Both solvent extraction process and mechanical expression methods are in use for the extraction of oil from the sunflower

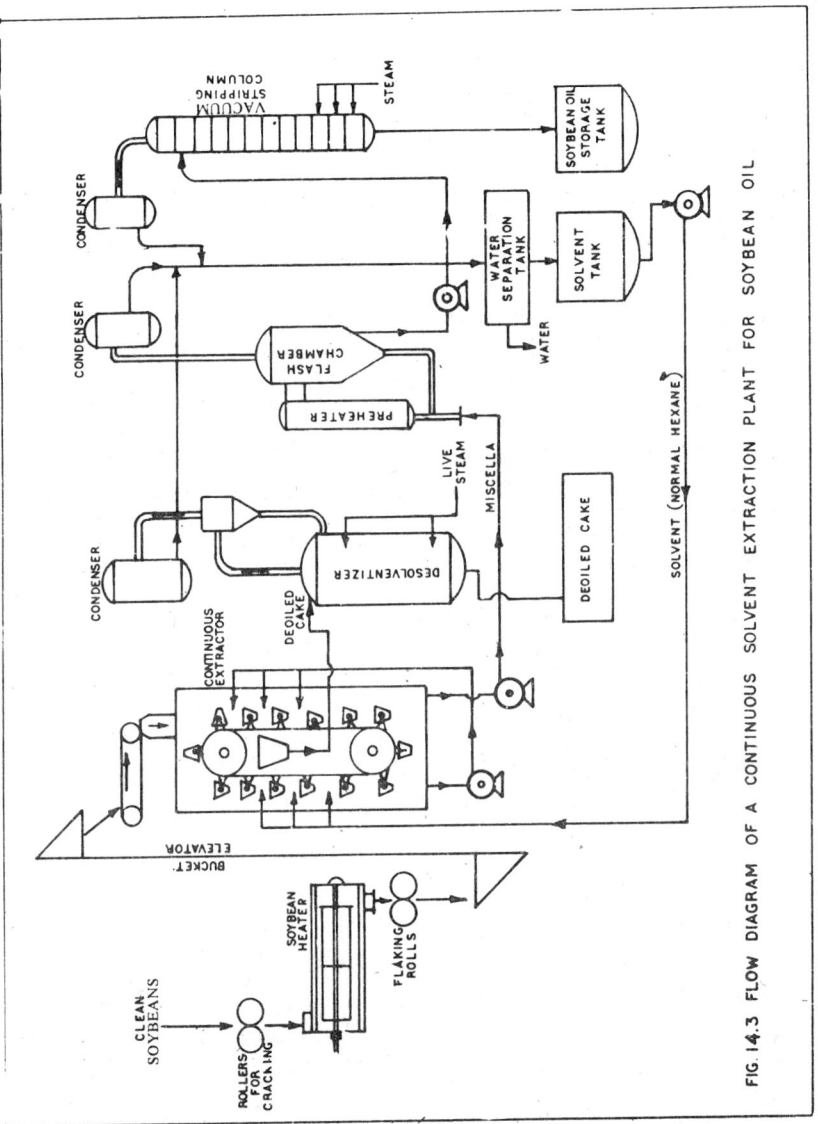

FIG. 14.3 FLOW DIAGRAM OF A CONTINUOUS SOLVENT EXTRACTION PLANT FOR SOYBEAN OIL

oilseeds. In the expression of oil by the screwpress, 60 to 70% of the oil from the meal is recovered. The operations and the processes followed for the mechanical extraction of oil using a screwpress is outlined below.

The oilseeds are cleaned to remove all foreign materials including stones, metals and dust from the seed.

Then dehulling of the clean seed is done to reduce the fibre content and increase the oil and the protein contents in the dehulled kernel.

The kernels are then allowed to pass through the roller mills to rupture the seed and increase the oil recovery efficiency.

The rolled flakes are then cooked by heat treatment for further increase in oil recovery.

The oil from the cooked flakes is extracted by pressing the cooked flakes in the expellers. The oil is then filtered to remove the seed particles.

The sizes of the deoiled cakes are reduced and then these are bagged for storage.

The crude oil is refined for the production of edible grade oil.

Extraction of Palm Oil

The palm oil fruits and bunches are boiled for about an hour to sterilize the fruits.

The fruits are separated from the stalk.

The mesocarp is pulped and separated from the nut by a process known as Maceration.

The oil is expelled from the fibres by pressing.

The fibres and nut are separated. The fibre is dried to about 15% moisture content.

The nut is also dried to a desired moisture level.

The kernel is removed by cracking the nut.

The kernel is crushed. The oil is squeezed out under high pressure and temperature ranging from 70° to 100°C.

The end products namely palm oil and palm kernel oil are stored separately.

The by products of the above process include fibres, nutshell, deoiled palm kernel cake, bunch stalk and palm fronds.

Extraction of Coconut Oil.

The coconut is the most extensively grown and used nut in the world. About 10 million people in India and several millions of people in other tropical regions depend on the coconut plant for their livelihood. India is the third largest coconut producing country of the world with an area of about 1.12 million hectares countributing to 18% of world production. India produces about 6000 million nuts annually. A whole coconut consists of 50% husk, 15% shell, 25% meat and 10% water.

The coconut shells contain 34% cellulose, 36% Lignin, 29% pentosans and 1% Ash.

The percentage composition of coconut kernel and copra is presented in Table 14.4.

TABLE 14.4   Composition of fresh coconut kernel and copra

Product	Moisture %	Fat %	Protein %	Carbohydrate %	Mineral %	Fibre %
Kernel (wet)	40—50	35	4	8—20	1	2
Copra	6—7	62—65	7—8	15	2	3—4

```
Coconut  ( Sun-drying    —3-4 days )                Crusher    Cooker
  Meat → { Smoke-drying—3-4 days } → Copra →    or    → 30 min/
         ( Heat-drying  — ½ day  )                Chopper    charge
                                                               ↓
         ↓
Oil Expeller ──→ Filter Press ──→ Refining ──→ Coconut Oil
                      ↓              (optional)
                 Deoiled cake
```

FIG. 14.4. Flow Diagram of a Traditional Method of expelling Coconut oil.

Traditional method

The coconut oil is traditionally extracted from copra. The copra can be obtained by separating the coconut meat from the whole coconut shell followed by sundrying and smoke drying for about 6 to 8 days. The copra is then chopped to small sizes and cooked by heating the small pieces of copra in a cooker for about 30 mins. The oil is squeezed out from cooked copra by an expeller and then filtered by a filterpress. The flow diagram of this traditional process is shown in Fig. 14.4.

Mechanical Extraction of Coconut Oil from the Fresh Coconut Meat

The processes and operations involved in modern mechanical expression of coconut is given below.

The coconut shells are cracked and the coconut meat is separated.

The fresh coconut meat is chopped and sliced into thin flakes of the desired size.

The thin flakes of coconut meat are cooked in a cooker by heating them at an elevated temperature for 90 mins.

The oil is expelled from the heat treated cooked coconut meat (at a temperature of about 70°C) in an oil expeller.

Clear raw coconut oil with fresh flavour and with very low free fatty acid (0.3 to 0.4) is obtained after filtering the oil with a filterpress.

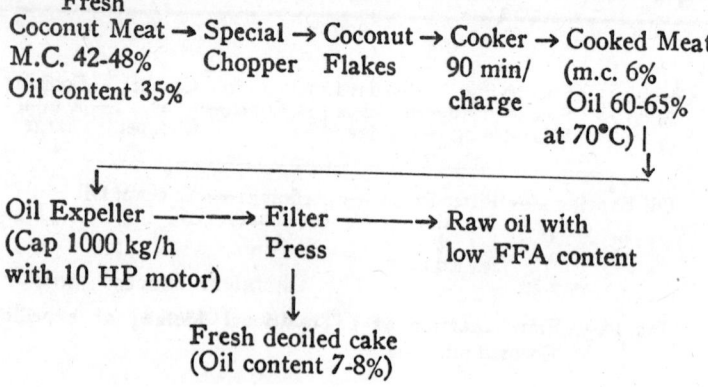

Fresh
Coconut Meat → Special → Coconut → Cooker → Cooked Meat
M.C. 42-48%   Chopper   Flakes   90 min/   (m.c. 6%
Oil content 35%   charge   Oil 60-65%
                                             at 70°C) |

Oil Expeller ———→ Filter ———→ Raw oil with
(Cap 1000 kg/h   Press   low FFA content
with 10 HP motor) |
                    ↓
            Fresh deoiled cake
            (Oil content 7-8%)

FIG. 14.5 A Modern Japanese Method of Production of Coconut Oil from Fresh Coconut Meat

The oil is stored in an air tight container in a dark cool and dry place for a log and safe storage.

The deoiled cakes obtained from this process is suitable for human consumption. Some details of this process are outlined in the flow diagram (Fig. 14.5).

BIBLIOGRAPHY

1. Bailey, A. E. (1951). Oil and Fat Products. Interscience Publishers, Inc., New York.

2. Bailey, A. E. (1948). Cotton Seed and Cotton Products. Interscience Publishers, Inc., New York.

3. Hofman, V., et al. (1979). Sunflower Oil as a Fuel Alternative. North Dakota Ext. Bul. 13 AENG-5. 4 pp.

4. Hofman, V., et al. (1981). Sunflower for Power : North Dakota Ext. Circ. AE-735. 12 pp

5. Markley, K. S. (1950). Soybean and Soybean Products. Interscience Publishers, Inc., New York

6. Pryde, E. H. (1981). Vegetable Oil vs. Diesel Fuel : Chemistry and Availability of Vegetable Oils. Alcohol and Vegetable Oil as Alternative Fuels. Proceedings of Regional Workshop : USDA Peoria, IL.

7. Quick, Graeme R., (1980). An In-depth Look at Farm Fuel Alternatives. Power Farming Magazine, Feb. 10-17 pp.

8. Quick, G. (1980). Developments in use of Vegetable Oils as fuel for Diesel Engines. ASAE Paper 80-1525. 15 pp.

9. Shrivastava, H. C. (1985). Oil Seeds Production Constraints and Opportunities. Oxford & IBH Pub. Co., New Delhi.

10. Shreve, N. R. (1956). The Chemical Process Industries, McGraw-Hill Book Co. Inc., Tokyo.

CHAPTER 15

Utilization of Rice Bran

Rice husk and rice bran are the two main by-products of rice milling industry. Several valuable chemicals and other products have been produced from rice husk (Bibliography), but their commercial success has yet to be established. Commercially rice bran is the most valuable by-product. It is obtained from the outer layers of the brown rice. Generally rice bran consists of pericarp, aleurone layer, germ and a part of endosperm. Bran removal amounts to 4 to 9% of the weight of paddy milled. True bran amounts to 4 to 5% only, rest is polish consisting of inner bran layers and portion of the starchy endosperm. Rice bran is characterised by its high fat and protein contents. It also contains vitamins, minerals and many other useful chemicals.

Bran can be utilised in various ways. It is a potential source of vegetable oil. Because of its nutritional value, it is being used as feed for poultry and livestock. More stable defatted bran containing higher percentage of protein, vitamins and minerals than full fatted bran is an excellent ingredient for both food and feed. Crude bran oil of high FFA content is used for the manufacture of soap and fatty acids. Edible grade oil is produced by refining of the crude bran oil of low FFA content (about 5%). In addition tocoferol, waxes of high melting point suitable for various industrial purposes are the by-products of the bran oil refining industry. Various uses of rice bran have been discussed at the end of this chapter.

Commercial bran is always contaminated with some amount of husk which varies widely with the type of rice mill used. The huller bran contains a very high amount of husk where as sheller-bran contains small amount of husk and the bran, produced by the modern rubber roll type mill, is almost pure containing negligible amount of husk. The characteristics of rice bran obtained from different mills are given in Table 16.1. Therefore,

TABLE 16.1 Characteristics of rice bran from hullers, shellers and modern rice mills

Sl. No.	Variety	Moisture per cent	Oil per cent	Protein per cent	Ash		Crude fibre per cent
					Total per cent	Insoluble per cent	
1. *Raw*							
	Huller	8.0–9.5	5.0-10.0	5.5- 9.5	13.5-22.5	2.2-19.0	5.8-22.7
	Sheller	8.5-11.5	11.5-19.0	9.0-13.0	8.0-22.5	3.5-19.0	6.0-14.5
2. *Parboiled*							
	Huller	4.0- 9.5	6.5-12.5	4.5- 9.5	17.5-20.0	14.5-18.5	20.5-30.0
	Sheller	3.0-11.5	12.0-27.5	10.0-15.5	8.5-22.5	3.0-21.0	6.5-32.0
3.	Modern Rice Mill	8.0- 9.5	15.0-18.5	13.0-14.0	9.0-11.5	2.5-4.5	8.5-10.5

(OTRI, 1974)

complete exploitation of the usage of bran is largely dependent on its purity.

Rice bran can be classified into three groups : (1) full fatted raw bran (raw bran) obtained from milling of raw paddy; (2) full fatted parboiled bran (parboiled bran) obtained from milling of parboiled paddy and (3) defatted/deoiled bran obtained after extraction of oil from either raw or parboiled bran. Raw bran contains 12 to 18% oil whereas parboiled bran contains 20 to 28% oil. After extraction of oil from raw and parboiled bran, the deoiled bran contains about 1 to 3.0% oil only. The chemical compositions of raw, parboiled and deoiled bran are presented in Tables 16.2 and 16.3.

TABLE 16.2. Chemical composition of raw and parboiled rice bran

Constituents %	Raw bran Grade I	Parboiled bran Grade I
Moisture	11.9	89.1
Crude Protein	12.5	12.8
Oil	14.6	20.3
Crude fibre	8.9	10.0
Ash	10.7	10.7
N F E	42.9	36.1

TABLE 16.3 Chemical composition of regular (full fatted) and defatted rice bran

Constituents %	Regular bran	Defatted bran (solvent extracted)	Defatted bran (pressed)
Moisture	12.59	9.31	12.28
Crude Protein	13.31	16.07	17.31
Crude fat	21.21	1.12	1.32
Crude fibre	9.05	10.79	11.59
Ash	9.40	11.41	12.01
N F E	33.44	41.13	45.49

(Yokochi, 1972)

Raw bran is a light colour oily, unstable meal of various particle sizes. Parboiled bran is relatively darker and more oily. The oilyness of parboiled bran causes clogging of screens during milling particularly in rainy days and high humid atmosphere. Deoiled bran is lighter in colour and dusty in nature. The physico thermal properties and particle sizes of rice bran are given in Tables 16.4 through 16.6.

The most important and crucial property of rice bran is the instability of its oil caused by an oil-splitting enzyme, lipase, inherently present in it. The enzyme, lipase acts as a catalyst. The fat and enzyme are spatially distributed in aleurone and

TABLE 16.4. Physico thermal properties of rice bran

Property	m.c. range %, (w.b)	Temp. °C	Raw bran	Parboiled bran
Bulk density kg/m³	8-14 * 6 - 16.5	—	276-291 * 285 -239	267-314 —
Sp. Gravity	8-14	—	1.4-1.48	1.45-
Porosity, %	8-14	—	81.3-79.3	82-76
Angle of repose	8-14	—	59.3-51.8	57-46.2
Static conff. of friction on m.s.	8-14	—	0.593-0.508	0.61-0.563
Thermal conductivity (Steady state) kcal/hr m°c	8-14	43	0.035-0.049	0.028-0.049
Thermal conductivity (unsteady state kcal/hr m°c	8-14 * 6 - 16.5	36 30 - 43	— *0.0 65 - 0.102	0.14-0.26 —
Specific heat Cal/gm°c	10.3-12.0 * 6 - 16.5	—	0.224-0.33 * 0.369-0.496	0.67-.69
Thermal diffusivity, m²/hr	8-14	—	0.0024- 0.0021	0.0024-.0021

(Srivastava, 1976, *Devadattam and Chakaraverty, 1986)

TABLE 16.5 Particle size distribution of raw and stabilized bran

U.S. Sieve No	Size μ	Raw bran (% on sieve)	Stabilized bran by 15 min. steaming at 1.6 kg/cm² (% on sieve)
12	—	0.7	2.3
20	—	7.5	7.7
30	—	9.0	9.4
40	420	8.8	11.8
50	—	9.2	59.0
70	—	16.0	9.8
100	149	21.2	—
200	—	26.2	—
Pan	—	1.5	—

TABLE 16.6 Particle sizes of raw and defatted rice bran

U.S. No.	Size μ	*Raw (Japonica) weight % on sieve	Defatted bran weight, % on sieve
16	—	6	—
20	—	9	14.3
30	—	18	—
40	420	22	27.3
60	250	34	14.0
80	—	10	—
100	149	0 5	9.2
150	—	0.2	—
Through 100 mesh	—	—	11.9

* Yokochi, 1972

testa layers respectively in intact rice grain. So long the bran surface is uninjured and protected by the husk, the enzyme remains dormant and the enzymatic activity is not perceptible. As soon as the bran surface is ruptured and separated from the brown rice in milling operations, the lipase comes in contact with the oil bearing layers and they are intimately mixed with each other causing a very rapid rate of hydrolysis of fats into free fatty acids. As the reaction is hydrolytic in nature it may be called hydrolytic type of rancidification. It is apparent that the rate of hydrolysis will be further enhanced with the increase of moisture in bran. The free fatty acids can then be more readily oxidised than the natural oils by the oxidative agents resulting in oxidative rancidity with the production of unpleasant odours and flavours. The composition of fatty acid esters is given below :

Composition of fatty acids in rice bran oil (OTRI, 1974)

1. *Saturated acids*	—	16—20%
(i) Palmitic acid	—	13—18%
(ii) Myristic acid	—	0.4—1%
(iii) Stearic acid	—	1 —3%
2. *Unsaturated acids*	—	80—84%
(i) Oleic acid	—	40—50%
(ii) Linoleic acid	—	20—42%
(iii) Linolenic acid	—	0 —1%

The hydrolysis of triglycerides of fatty acids (i.e. neutral fats) into free fatty acids (FFA) in presence of lipase enzyme (biocatalyst) is presented below :

$$\begin{array}{l} CH_2COOR_1 \\ | \qquad\qquad +3H_2O \\ CHCOOR_2 \xrightarrow[\text{Lipase}]{} \\ | \\ CH_2COOR_3 \end{array} \quad \begin{array}{l} CH_2OH \\ | \\ CHCOOR_2 \\ | \\ CH_2COOR_3 \end{array} + \begin{array}{l} CH_2COOR_1 \\ | \\ CHCOOR_3 \\ | \\ CH_2OH \end{array} + R_1COOH + R_2COOH$$

$$\begin{array}{l} R_1COOH \\ + \\ R_2COOH \\ + \\ R_3COOH \end{array} + \begin{array}{l} CH_2OH \\ | \\ CHOH \\ | \\ CH_2OH \end{array} \leftarrow \begin{array}{l} CH_2OH \\ | \\ CHCOOR_2 \\ | \\ CH_2OH \end{array} + R_1COOH + R_3COOH \leftarrow$$

Immediately after milling the FFA content of bran is normally below 3%. After milling the rate of increase of FFA in bran may be as high as 1% per hour under favourable conditions. Alkali refining of crude oil for edible grade oil is considered uneconomical if its FFA content goes beyond 10% level.

The problems in processing of rice bran for edible oil and defatted bran for feed, food and other purposes are as follows :

   (i) rapid hydrolysis of oil into FFA and glycerol ;

  (ii) oxidation of fat into fat peroxide in presence of peroxidase enzyme ;

 (iii) the presence of excessive amount of fine particles in the bran ;

 (iv) abnormally high refining losses even in crude oil of low FFA content ;

  (v) excessive colour in the refined and bleached oil.

 (vi) the tendency of the finished oil to undergo flavour reversion ;

(vii) use of traditional hullers leading to the production of bran of low oil content contaminated with high percentage of husk, earth and other impurities ;

(viii) lack of completely modernised rubber roll type rice mills for the production of pure bran free from any silica and other impurities ;

 (ix) scattered location of small and medium size rice mills which makes it difficult to transport fresh bran to the oil extraction plant within a short period ;

  (x) a complex cultural, socio economic problems.

Problems i to vi and ix can be solved to a large extent by the effective stabilization of bran whereas vii and viii can be solved by modernisation of rice mills. But it is difficult to overcome the problem x.

Stabilization of bran extends the storage period of bran without any appreciable change in FFA content. Moreover, stabilization of rice bran offers the following advantages :

(i) it imparts hardening effect to the bran for the better extractibility ;

(ii) it increases the particle sizes and reduces the problem of fines and filtration ;

(iii) it increases the bulk density and reduces the handling problem.

Factors affecting rate of formation of FFA in bran during storage are as follows :

(a) Storage temperature ;

(b) Moisture content of bran ;

(c) Storage relative humidity ;

(d) Variety, type and particle size of bran ; and

(e) Contamination of bran with microflora or insects.

Effect of Storage Temperature

Formation of FFA in raw bran was found to occur at a fairly rapid rate even at a storage temperature of 3° C whereas parboiled rice bran was quite stable when stored at a temperature of 25° C (Loeb, 1949).

Effect of Storage moisture content of bran

The rate of hydrolysis of fats into FFA decreases as the storage moisture content of bran decreases. Even the stabilized bran of low moisture content should be stored in moisture proof polythene lined or polythene bags at room temperature for a long and safe storage.

Effect of Relative humidity

Rate of FFA formation increases with the increase of the relative humidity of storage and the final moisture content of bran as well (Loeb, 1949). The equilibrium moisture content of bran depends on the relative humidity and temperature of the environment.

Particle size

Finer the particle size of the bran higher is the rate of formation of FFA.

Insect infestation

Some of the insects and microflora can contribute lipase to the bran. Therefore, for the control of insect infestation of stabilized bran during storage, fumigation of the stabilized bran and its container is necessary. The bran can also be stored safely in sealed thicker polythene bags without any insect infestation.

CHAPTER 16

Methods of Utilization of Rice Bran

So far, six basic approaches have been tried. They are as follows :

1. Low temperature storage tends to reduce the FFA rise but unacceptable high levels of FFA are reached in a comparatively short time.
2. Storage of bran at low relative humidity retards the rise of FFA in bran but it should be preceded by drying of bran to a low moisture content (by heat treatment) otherwise it is not very effective.
3. Simultaneous milling and extraction with the hexane solvent (X—M process) shows considerable promise, but it is a very costly process and its high technical know how is not available.
4. Various Chemical treatments except HCl treatment and exposure to inert atmosphere have been proved to be ineffective.
5. Treatment of bran with microwaves etc. is effective, but the cost of processing becomes prohibitive.
6. Heat treatment of bran has been found to be most effective, feasible and economic and studied extensively.

The results of the studies on heat treatment of bran are summarised below :

The entire heat treatment process can be divided into two major heads : (i) dry heat treatment and (ii) wet heat treatment.

Dry Heat Treatment

Dry heat treatment can be further divided into : (1) Convection heat treatment ; (2) Conduction heat treatment ; (3) Radiation heat treatment including infrared heating ; (4) Dielectric heat treatment and (5) Frictional heat treatment.

Convection heating

When bran was heated by convection for 1 hr at 110° C, the FFA contents of bran were 4% and 7% after 25 and 50 days of storage at 25° C. Therefore convection heating requires a long time for stabilization.

Conduction heating

If bran in thin layer is dried uniformly by conduction heating for 20 minutes at a bran temperature of 90° C then it is stabilized and can be stored safely for 2 months at 25°-30° C where there is no insect infestation. Therefore, conduction drying is very efficient provided a thorough mixing arrangement for uniform heating of bran is ensured.

Infrared heating

When bran was heated for 10-15 minutes at 110° C by infrared lamps, lipase was inactivated and the treated bran could be stored safely in an air tight container for 2 months keeping FFA level below 7%.

Frictional heating

There is possibility of using some form of frictional heat for developing the required temperature for inactivation of lipase. Particularly Handler type of oil expeller can be used for the above purpose (Viraktamath, 1971).

Wet Heat Treatment

Yokochi (1972) reported that for the stabilization of rice bran, it should be steamed at 95° C and then dried to about 3% moisture content followed by an air cooling. The stabilized bran can be stored for 3 to 4 months.

Srimani (1972) recommended that the bran should be steamed with live steam for 3 to 5 minutes and then dried to the desired low moisture content to bring down the residual enzymatic activity to zero.

Desikashar et al. (1969) reported that steaming of raw bran for about 15 minutes and subsequent drying could inactivate the enzyme. They also reported that steaming of raw paddy or steaming of soaked paddy during parboiling could inactivate the lipase enzyme.

Rice Bran Stabilizers Under Development in India

A. On the basis of wet heat treatment the following rice bran stabilizer of 0.5 tonne/day capacity has been developed by Jadavpur University, Calcutta (Srimani, 1972).

It consisted of a screw conveyor for direct steaming of bran and a penumatic type of bran dryer fitted with an air suction unit and cyclone separator. Bran is exposed to live steam for a period of 5 minutes in a semicircular trough fitted inside with screw conveyor. The speed of the screw conveyor is so adjusted that the retention time of bran is 5 minutes. Then the steamed bran is dried with hot air in a heat insulated 4 m tall vertical column under fluidized condition and the treated bran is separated from the hot air by a cyclone separator and collected in a close container. Though the capacity of the plant was originally designed for 0.5 tonne/day only its capacity can be increased by changing the design of the cyclone separator, increasing the speed of the screw feeder and increasing the suction capacity of the blower.

B. A close conduction heating type rice bran stabilizer has been developed by CFTRI, Mysore. It consists of an electrically heat jacketed revolving drum provided with a tightly fitting lid. The lid is also fitted with a vent valve and temperature cum pressure gauge. The stabilizer is operated as follows :

After charging the bran into the drum and closing the lid with vent valve open, the bran is heated until steam begins to emerge from the valve. After allowing the air to escape for about 2 minutes the valve is closed and heating is continued until dial thermometer records a temperature of 110-115° C. The temperature is maintained for about 5 minutes after which vent valve is opened and the steam is allowed to escape. The material is discharged from the toaster by tilting and is allowed to cool. Bran thus treated could be stored for three months at 37° C and 70% RH with FFA below 10%. This revolving toaster unit has been demonstrated in some rice mills. But its use has been restricted as most of the remote villages are not electrified and the capacity of the unit is also limited.

C. A continuous rice bran stabilizer of 0.5 tonne/day capacity developed and patented by Chakraverty at PHTC, consists of a steam jacketed screw conveyor with mixing device and a

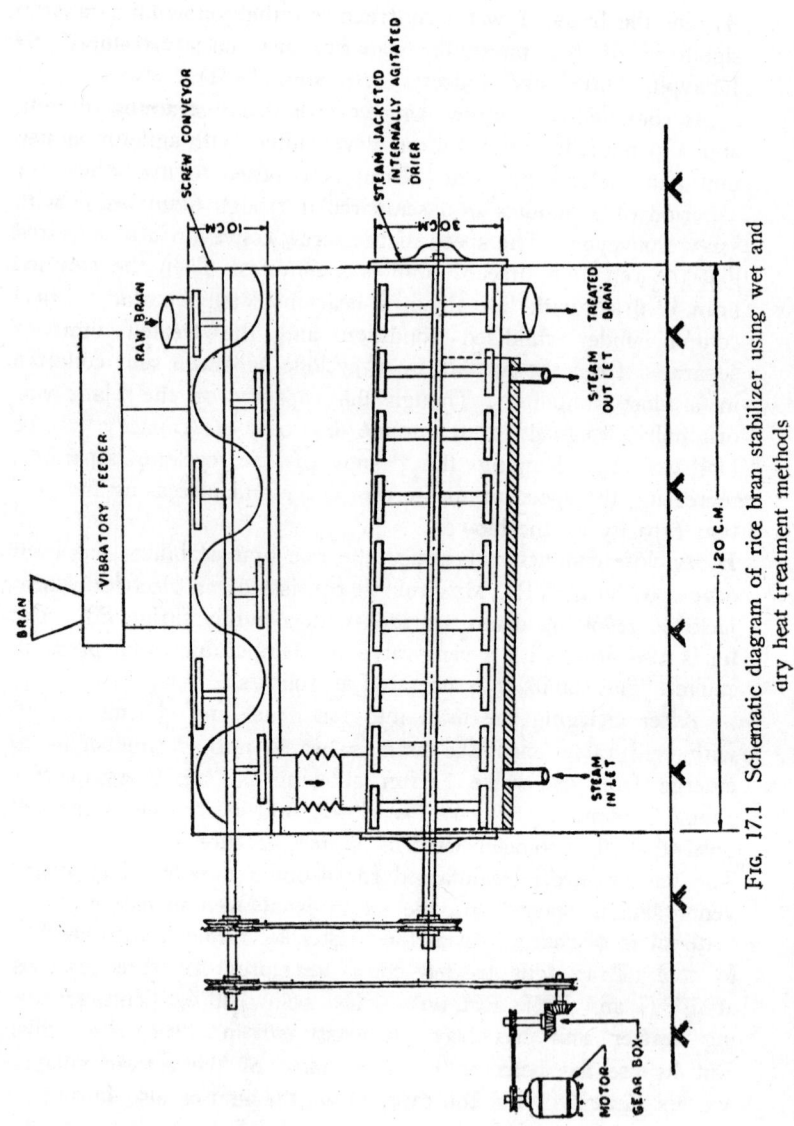

FIG. 17.1 Schematic diagram of rice bran stabilizer using wet and dry heat treatment methods

cylindrical conduction type dryer (Fig. 17.1).
The screw conveyor is placed above the dryer. The outlet of the screw conveyor and the inlet of the dryer are connected by a chute. The screw conveyor connected with a steam pipe is used for direct steaming of bran whereas the steam jacketed cylindrical dryer fitted inside with paddle type agitator is used for conduction heating as well as drying of bran. The dryer with the internal rotary paddle type bran mixing system is inclined at an angle of about 3° with the horizontal. Fresh raw bran (with low FFA content) is fed at the hopper and passed through the screw conveyor where it is steamed at 100° C for about 5 minutes. The steam treated bran is then allowed to pass through the steam jacketed and internal agitated dryer where it is thoroughly mixed and heated to 100°C for 10 minutes by conduction and uniformly dried to 4-5% moisture content. The stabilized bran can then be stored for 2 months at 25°-30° C and 70% RH with FFA content below 5%.

The steam jacketed dryer unit alone can be used for the stabilization of bran by dry conduction heating. The fresh raw bran in thin layer is to be uniformly heated at 90° C for 20 min in the dryer and dried to 4-5% moisture content. Then the bran is to be cooled. The dry heat treated bran can be kept in the sealed polythene bag and stored at 25°-30° C for 45 days with its FFA content below 5%.

Extraction of rice bran oil

Oil extraction methods can be divided into two major groups : mechanical method and solvent extraction method.

In mechanical method either hydraulic press or oil expeller is used to press oil out of the bran which has already been preprocessed by steaming and drying. The high pressure employed is in the range of 70 to 280 kg/cm². But the output of oil is low compared to the solvent extraction method. The mechanical method had been in use in Japan for many years in the past. Now-a-days the mechanical method has been abandoned but it may be popular once again in near future because of the shortage of petroleum products.

In solvent extraction method usually n-hexane (b.p. 66° to 70° C) is used. This method is now universally used mainly due to high oil output.

Solvent extraction method

Three systems of solvent extraction operations are in use, ·
namely, batch, semi continuous and continuous systems. The
continuous system has certain advantages over the batch system,
as it can be used for the production of oil from various oil
seeds and meal and rice bran as well. But the capacity of the
plant is higher and the initial investment is high.

The batch type is believed to be exclusively suitable for rice
bran oil extraction. It is popular due to its simplicity in operation and low cost of installation. The solvent extraction method
is described below :

Pretreatment of bran prior to extraction is an essential step
for either batch or continuous system. Pretreatment consists of
either direct steaming and drying of bran or drying of bran
alone at 90°—100° C to 6—8% moisture content. Pretreatment
of bran reduces amount of fines and moisture content and
thereby increases the particle sizes, aids the release of oil from
bran, imparts hardening effect to bran particles for better
extractibility lower filtration time and it eliminates the problem
of fines. Without pretreatment, the fines would create problems
like resistance to percolation of oil, channeling resulting in
longer steaming time for the desolventization of meal and low
rate of extractibility.

In the continuous system the steam treated bran is pelletized
in the pelletizing equipment to enlarge the particle size of the
bran to 6 to 8 mm pellets. It not only eliminates fines but also
reduces the moisture content to some extent. But it is a very
costly method due to requirement of high electrical power per
unit mass of pellets. Because of the limited scope, only batch
extraction method has been described below.

Batch extraction method

The treated bran containing 6-8 % moisture is charged to
each of the five stationary batch extraction vessels which are
fitted with sugar bag at the false bottom, each holding 0.5 tonnes
of raw bran. Thick sugar bag serves as a filter. Steam at 2 atm
pressure is applied to force out miscella. The miscella from the
extractor passes through a strainer. Hot vapour is effectively
used for heating the miscella in the heat exchanger. Last traces

of solvent in the oil are removed in the stripper. The bottom steam is used to drive the solvent out of the meal. Meal with a residual oil content of 1-3% and moisture content of 8-12% is discharged from the extractor by opening the door of the extraction vessel and by raking it out.

It takes $2\frac{1}{2}$ hour for each cycle of batch. Typical capacity of a plant is 24-25 tonnes per day of 24 hours. A simplified flow diagram of the batch extraction method is shown below.

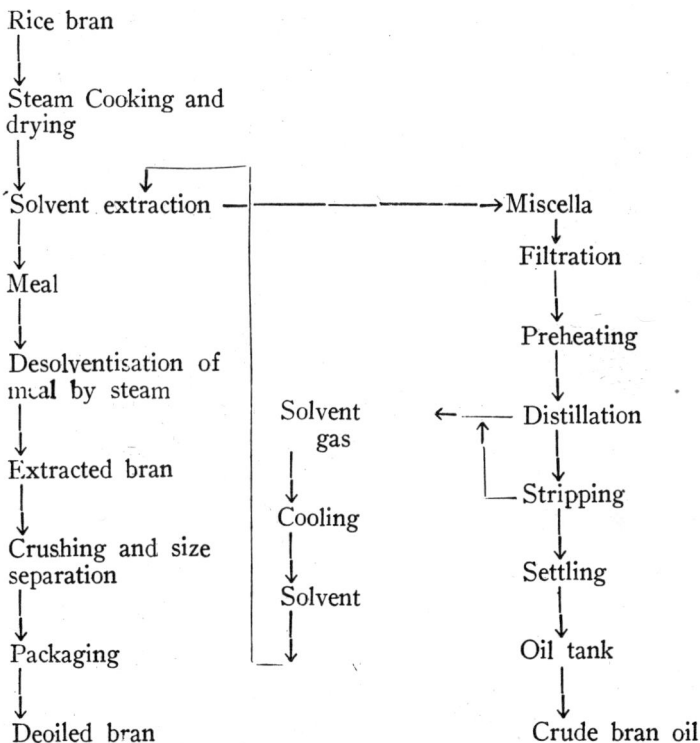

Flow diagram of batch solvent extraction method.

Refining of crude rice bran oil into edible grade oil

Because of the presence of fatty acids, gum, wax, colouring and odouring matters etc., the rice bran oil is the most difficult oil among all vegetable oils to refine.

A simplified flow diagram of the refining process is shown below.

Crude rice bran oil
↓
Preliminary dewaxing and degumming
↓
Separation by Misco type super Centrifuge
(Yield of gums, crude wax 4-6%)
↓
Neutralisation with alkali
↓
Separation of alkali foots by Misco Super Centrifuge
↓
Neutralised Oil
↓
First washing by water
↓
Second washing by water
↓
Third washing by hot water
↓
Separation of warm waste water by settling
↓
Removal of waste water by super centrifuge
↓
Vacuum bleaching (with the use of activated bleaching earth)
↓
Filtration by filter press
↓
Bleached oil
↓

↓
Deodourisation
(High temp. 220° C, vacuum 3-5 mmHg)
↓
Continuous Cooling
↓
Filtration
↓
Refined edible oil
(62-66% yield)
↓
Dewaxing
(by winterisation at 5° C)
↓
Filtration by bag filten
(at 5-8°C)

↓
Filtration by filter press
↓
Winterised Oil
(Yield 54-58%)
↓
High grade edible oil
(Salad oil)

Flow diagram of oil refining process (Yokochi, 1972)

Several patented methods are available for the refining process. Generally the following steps are adopted :

(i) Preliminary dewaxing and degumming process to re-

move hard wax, gums, mucilages and some other impurities.
(ii) Neutralization process for the removal of FFA.
(iii) Decolourization process for the removal of colouring matters.
(iv) Deodourisation process for the removal odorous matters and unsaponifiable matters and
(v) Winterization operation for the removal of soft wax.

Uses of bran, bran oil and various constituents

Edible grade Oil

Because of the very low content of linolenic acid and high content of tocopherol bran oil has distinct advantages over other vegetable oils. Different grades of bran oil such as salad oil, cooking oil and so also shortenings can be produced by refining and suitable hydrogenation of bran oil.

Industrial grade crude oil

Soap manufacture

Rice bran oil with high FFA content is highly suitable for the manufacture of soft soap and liquid soap. In addition to alkali soaps other metallic soaps obtained from bran oil, namely, aluminium, barium and calcium soaps find market as components of lubricants.

Free fatty acid manufacture

The process consists of hydrolysis of the triglycerides of fatty acids into fatty acids and glycerol, separation of glycerol and purification of mixed fatty acids. The use of hydrogenation in combination with fractional distillation enables the manufacture of pure stearic and oleic acid of desired quality.

Protective Coatings

The manufacture of surface coatings like alkyd and resin based paints, enamels, varnishes and lacqueres also represent the usage of rice bran oil.

Plasticisers

Recently fatty acids and fatty oil based plasticisers are being used in the plastic and rubber industries.

Tocoferol

Tocoferol has nutritional and antiacid effects. Crude oil contains 2-4% tocoferol. During deodourising process a significant amount of it is lost. Only 1-2% of tocoferol remains in edible oil.

Rice Bran Wax

Rice bran wax is a proper substitute of carnaubawax due to high milling point (72°-84° C), hardness and non tackyness. It is being used for coatings of candy, fruits and vegetables as it prevents moisture loss and shrinkage of the said products. It can also be used as component in formulations like carbon paper base, stencils, candles etc.

Uses of defatted bran and bran

Feed

Defatted bran can be best utilised as an ingredient of cattle and poultry feed. In regard to this aspect defatted bran is more suitable than raw bran due to its higher protein and fat contents, higher digestibility and more stability towards storage quality.

Food

Defatted bran can be successfully used as an ingredient in the bakery products such as bread, cake, biscuits etc. After finer grinding, it can be added to baking flour upto 20 per cent.

Fertilizer

On account of the presence high fat and wax contents, regular raw bran is not only unsuitable for plants but also harmful for their roots. But defatted bran contains all the three manurial factors (NPK values) in right proportion.

Medicinal Use

As rice bran contains valuable vitamin B-complexes, amino

acids, phosphoric acid compound etc., it is useful in the field of medicine and dietrics. Protein can also be easily extracted from rice bran.

BIBLIOGRAPHY

1. Chakraverty, A. 1989. Biotechnology and other Alternative Technologies for Utilization of Biomass/Agricultural Wastes. Oxford and IBH Pub. Co., New Delhi, 1989.
2. Chakraverty, A. (Princ. Inv.), 1982. Stabilization of rice bran. Report on the ICAR Project, IIT, Kharagpur.
3. Chakraverty, A. (Princ. Inv.), 1988. Report on the Research Project "Amorphous ash (silica) from paddy straw." Min. of Food and Civil Supp. G.O.I., New Delhi, 1988.
4. Chakraverty, A., 1987, Development of a continuous rice bran stabilizer for wet heat treatment. Handbook on Rice Bran, The Solv. Extrn. Asso. of India, Bombay, 373-376.
5. Chakraverty, A. et al., 1988. Stabilization of rice bran by steaming and conduction drying in a continuous rice bran stabilizer The Harvester, (23) 5-10, IIT, Kharagpur.
6. Chakraverty, A. et al., 1987, Stabilization of rice bran by conduction heating in a PHTC-continuous rice oran stabilizer. AMA, Japan 38(1), 41-44.
7. Chakraverty, A. et al., 1988, Investigation on combustion of raw and acid leached rice husk for production of pure amorphous white silica. J. of Mater Sc., 23(1), 1989.
8. Chakraverty, A. et al., 1983. Stabilization of rice bran by conduction and humid heat treatments. AMA, 14(2), 72-76 Japan.
9. Chakraverty, A. et al., 1985 Investigation on thermal decomposition of rice husk, Thermochimica Acta, 94, 267-275, U.S.A.
10. Chakraverty, A. et al., 1987, Studies on thermal decomposition of rice straw. Thermochimica Acta, Amsterdam, 120, 241-255.
11. Chakraverty, A. et al., 1987, Sorption and desorption characteristics of raw and heat treated rice bran. Drying Tech. J., U.S.A., 5(25), 205-212.
12. Chakraverty, A. et al., 1990, Production of amorphous silica from rice husk in a vertical furnace. AMA, Japan.

13. Chakraverty, A. and Devadattam, D.S.K., 1985, conduction drying of raw and steamed rice bran. *Drying Tech. J.,* U.S.A 3(4) 567-583.

14. Chakraverty, A. and Kaleemulla, S., 1991. Conversion of rice husk into amorphous silica and combustible gas. Energy Conv. and Mgmt., U.S.A. 32(6), 565-570.

15. Chakraverty, A. and Kalumulla, S. Production of amorphous silica and combustible gas from rice straw. *J. of Mater. Sc.,* London, U.K. 1991, 26: 4554-4560.

16. Devadattam, D.S.K. and Chakraverty, A., 1986. Some physico-thermal properties of raw bran related to drying technology. *Drying Tech. J.,* U.S.A. 4(1), 145-154.

17. Desikachar, H.S.R. et al., 1969. Steaming of paddy for improved culinary, milling and storage properties. *J. food. Sc. Tech.*

18. Harris, R.V.1971. Rice bran oil and wax. Interregional seminar on the Industrial Processing of Rice, Feb. 25, 1971, UNIDO, pp. 4-7.

19. Loeb, J.R. et al., 1949, Rice bran oil. IV. Storage of bran as it affects hydrolysis of the oil. *J. Am. Oil Chem. Soc.* 26(12): 738-743.

20. Mishra, P., Chakraverty, A. and Banerjee, H.D., 1986. Studies on physical and thermal properties of rice husk related to its industrial application. *J. of Mater. Sc.,* 21: 2129-2132, U.K.

21. Mishra, P., Chakraverty, A and Banerjee, H.D., 1985. Production and Purification of silicon by calcium reduction of rice husk white ash. *J. of Mater. Sc.,* 20 : 4387-4391, U.K.

22. Nanda, S.K., Chakraverty, A. and Maiti, S. 1990. Starch-based plastic films. Part-1. Preparation of the films. *J. of Polymer Sc.,* 7, 331-333.

23. Oil Technological Research Institute 1974. Project Report. Edible Rice Bran Oil.

24. Sastry, B.S. et al., 1977. Histo chemical localization of lipase in rice grain. *J. Food Sc. Tech.* 14(6): 273-274.

25. Srimani, B.N. 1972. Stabilization of rice bran in closed circuit fluidized bed heat transfer system. Final report of CSIR Scheme No. 4 (147)/67 GAu II.

26. Srivastava, P.K., 1976, Some physical and chemical properties of rice bran in relation to its handling, storage and stabilization, M. Tech. Thesis, IIT, Kharagpur.

27. Viraktamath, C.S. and Desikachar, H.S.R., 1971 Inactivation of lipase in rice bran in Indian rice mills. *J. Food. Sc. Tech.* 8(2).

28. Viraktamath, C.S. Large Scale trials for stabilization of rice bran with steam. *J. Food. Sc. Tech.* 11(4): 191-193.

29. Yokochi, K. 1972. Rice bran processing for the production of rice bran oil and rice bran protein meal. UNIDO Publication.

CHAPTER 17

Food Grain Storage

Introduction

The challenge of feeding ever growing human population cannot be met with the increase of food production alone. During the last two decades, production of food has been increased significantly. In order to make further progress, it requires inputs of improved seeds, fertilizers, pesticides and advanced post harvest technologies of preservation and utilization, apart from improved production practices and irrigation. The losses during growing crops and post harvest handling, processing, storage and distribution systems vary between 20 and 60% in some of the countries of the world (Food Ind., 1979). It is estimated that 6 to 11% food grains are lost during post harvest operations (Table 17.1). If these losses are minimised the shortage of food in many countries can probably be eliminated. In this context, the improvement of grain storage system is inevitably the first step towards this direction. It may be mentioned that the food grains are stored for later use as seed, reserved food or buffer stock. Insects, microorganisms and rodents not only consume the edible and inedible parts of the growing crops and stored grains but also lead to the deteriorations in quality. Hence integrated approach for the control of pests is essential for maintaining quality during growth, production as well as at the post harvest handling and storage periods.

Grain storage principles

General

The food grains are living organisms. Hence the grain should be stored as a living seed. A grain is physiologically quite stable after harvesting and this stability as well as its viability should be preserved in a good storage method. Under natural conditions, however, stored grain undergoes chemical changes within itself. Its further deterioration is caused by external living organisms, such as insects, microorganisms, moulds, fungi, mites

TABLE 17.1 Percentage loss of food grains production during the period 1962–1965

Stages where loss is caused	Wheat	Rice	Jawar	Bajra	Maize	Gram	Millet	Pulses	Total
Threshing									
Yard	1.0	2.5	2.0	0.5	0.5	0.5	1.0	0.5	1.68
Transport	0.5	0.5	0.5	0.5	0.5	0.5	0.5	0.5	0.15
Processing	2.0	–	–	–	–	–	–	0.92	–
Storage	–	–	–	–	–	–	–	–	–
Rodents	2.5	2.5	2.5	2.5	2.5	2.5	2.5	2.5	2.50
Birds	0.5	1.0	1.0	1.0	0.5	0.5	2.0	0.5	0.85
Insects	3.0	2.0	2.0	1.0	3.0	5.0	0.5	5.0	2.55
Moisture	0.5	0.5	2.0	0.5	0.5	0.5	0.5	0.5	0.68
Total	8.0	11.0	10.0	6.0	7.5	9.5	7.0	9.5	9.33

(Bulletin of Grain Technology, 8(3) 92–97, 1968 and Rao, 1974)

and rodents. The stored grain in bulk is a system in which deterioration results from interactions among physical, chemical, physiological and biological variables. Some of the variables are: temperature; moisture; oxygen; storage structure; physical, chemical and biological properties of grain bulks; microorganisms; insects, mites, rodents and birds. In fact, they seldom act alone or all at once. They interact with the grain in groups, among themselves. Initially the rate of deterioration is slow; but as the favourable combinations of variables are set and the storage period is prolonged, a very high loss in grain quality and quantity occurs (Fig. 17.1).

The major variables which cause various changes and deteriorations in food grains during storage are given below.

Physical	Temperature and Humidity
Chemical	Moisture and Oxygen (or $O_2 : CO_2$)
Physiological	Respiration and Heating
Biological	Insects, Fungi, Moulds, Mites, Microorganisms and Rodents

The deterioration of food grains may be either qualitative or quantitative or both. Insects, microorganisms, fungi, moulds, mites and rodents may cause both these damages. Of the above variables moisture and temperature are the most crucial ones as far as storage of food grains are concerned. The soundness of grain is also an important factor from the standpoint of viability.

Moisture

The moisture of food grain is the first factor to be paid serious attention as it limits the development of bacteria, fungi, mites and insects that cause spoilage of stored grains. The important points to be kept in mind while planning safe storage are: (i) moisture contents of grains below 13% arrest the growth of most of the microorganisms and mites; (ii) moisture contents below 10% limit development of most of the stored grain insect pests; and (iii) moisture contents within a grain bulk are seldom uniformly distributed and are changeable. The need for regular routine measurement of moisture within a grain bulk cannot be over-emphasised.

The limit of moisture for safe storage of cereal grains, in regard to insect pests and microorganisms infestation, is about 13–14%, which is equilibrated with the atmospheric relative humidity of around 70–75%. If a cereal grain is to be stored for a long period, its moisture should be below 12%.

Equilibrium moisture contents of some cereals, pulses and oil seed are given in Table 17.2.

TABLE 17.2 Equilibrium moisture contents of grains

Commodity	Temperature, °C	Relative humidity			
		30%	50%	70%	90%
1. Rice (polished)	28	9.2	10.6	12.5	23.4
2. Paddy	25	7.9	10.4	13.2	17.6
3. Wheat	28	8.6	10.5	13.4	20.8
4. Corn	22	10.5	12.0	14.4	–
5. Sorghum	28	8.9	11.2	13.6	21.6
6. Greengram	28	6.2	9.3	11.8	26.3
7. Groundnut (kernel)	28	3.2	4.8	6.6	18.2

(Hall, 1957, Food Ind., 1979 and Becker and Sallans, 1956)

FOOD GRAIN STORAGE

Causes of Deteriotion of food grains

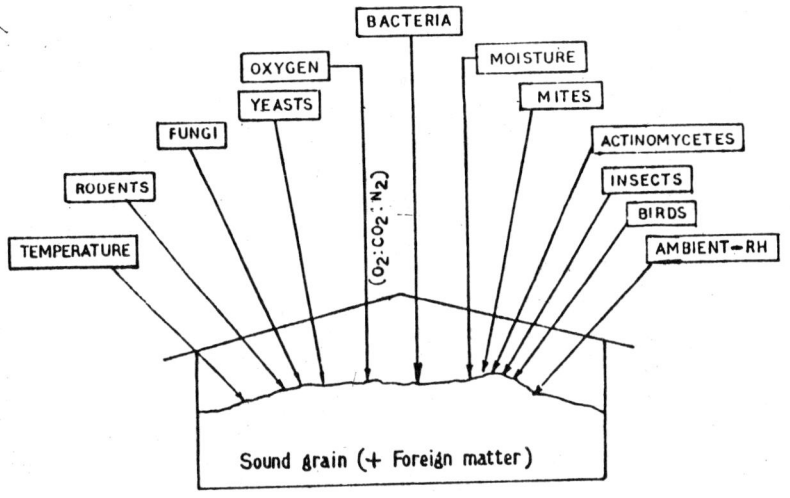

Sound grain (+ Foreign matter)

Changes with time

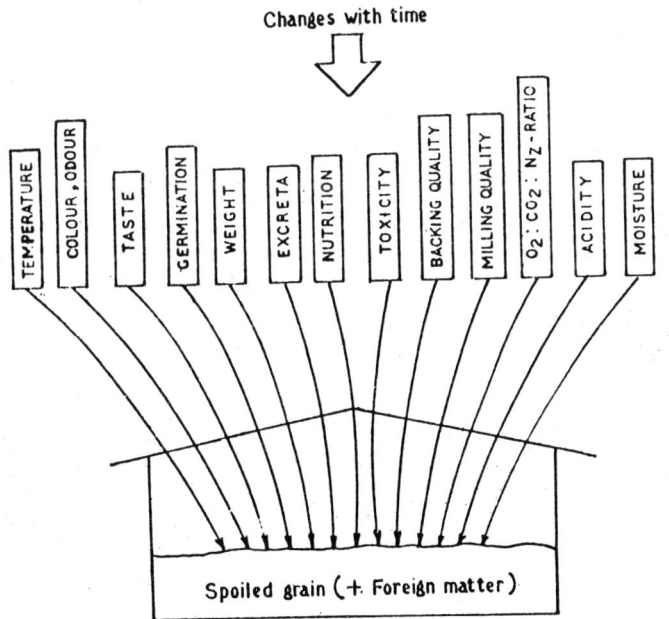

Spoiled grain (+. Foreign matter)

FIG. 17.1 Deteriorations of food grains during storage.

Temperature

The temperature is another important basic factor to be considered along with the grain moisture and equilibrium relative humidity. The relative humidity which is in equilibrium with the grain moisture varies with the temperature. For the storage of brown rice low temperature is generally used in Japan as the rates of chemical and biochemical reactions are always slow at the low temperatures. The metabolic heat produced exclusively by dry grain is about 1×10^{-7} cal/s.cc and by wet grain is approximately 1.3×10^{-5} cal/s.cc. The amount of heat produced by fungi, insects and other organisms infesting the grain is much higher compared to the above values (Sinha, 1973).

In considering temperature for safe grain storage system the following important points are to be kept in mind: (i) generally, mites do not develop below 5°C nor insect below 15°C; (ii) most of the storage fungi do not develop below 0°C; and (iii) the effect of temperature on an organism can be correlated with the amount of grain moisture. The rate of respiration of grain, the growth of microorganisms and the chemical and enzymatic reactions during storage also accelerate upto a certain temperature (Sinha, 1973).

When the grain temperature rises to around 20°C, it starts getting infested easily with insects and microorganisms and at the same time its rate of respiration becomes rapid with the expense of chemical constituents. The grain temperature is always to be considered in conjunction with its moisture content.

Changes occuring in food grains during storage

The changes taking place in a food grain during storage are the chemical changes within itself and the deteriorations caused by various living organisms. However, these changes and deteriorations occur almost simultaneously during the storage.

Chemical changes

Oxidation, enzymatic reactions, and respiration influence the chemical changes in cereal grains during storage. All cereal grains contain certain enzymes that decompose their constituents such as starch, proteins and lipids. These enzymatic activities are enhanced with the rise in grain moisture and temperature. During storage, the lipase which is inherently present in rice bran hydrolyses its fats into free fatty acids and glycerol. Free fatty acids increase rapidly when both grain moisture and temperature are high (Fig. 17.2). Moreover, with the growth of mould, decomposition of fat is further accelerated by the action of its enzymes. It is known that n-capraldehyde, n-valeraldehyde produced by the autooxidation of lipid are related to the generation of stale flavour in old rice. Starch, the main constituent of rice, is converted into dextrins and maltose by the action of amylase in the rice grain. It results in an increase in reducing sugars but this development is not pronounced when the moisture content of rice is around 14% and the temperature is also at a lower level (Chikubu, 1970).

When moisture content of a rice kernel is considerably at higher level the carbohydrates are fermented. As a result alcohol and acetic acid are produced with the formation ot acid odour. During storage of paddy reducing sugars and acidity increase whereas non-reducing sugars decrease. The percentage of germination, non-reducing sugars and acidity are the three most sensitive characteristics of grain storage (Fig. 17.3). The changes in protein during storage are comparatively small and slow.

Besides enzymatic reactions, oxidation by the surrounding air causes changes in colour and flavour. Regarding other constituents of cereal grains vitamins are gradually diminished under ordinary storage condition.

Physiological changes

Respiration
The life of a food grain is manifested by respiration. It should be noted carefully that in aerobic respiration complete oxidation of the hexose yields carbon dioxide, water and energy whereas in anaerobic respiration hexose is incompletely decomposed into carbon dioxide, ethyl alcohol and energy. The direct consequences of the respiration are the loss of mass and gain in moisture content of the grain, rise in the level of carbon dioxide in the intergranular air space and a rise in the temperature of the grain. The respiration rates of freshly harvested grains are different from those of old grains and grains damaged by insects, fungi and moulds. The rate of respiration is high for the old grain and the pest infested grain compared to the fresh grain. The moulds etc. respire at much higher rates compared to the grain itself.

The respiratory rate of stored grain depends largely on its moisture content and temperature. Figure 17.4 shows that at a certain temperature the respiratory rate of brown rice increases as moisture content increases. The moisture content at which the respiratory rate undergoes a sharp change may be called crucial moisture content and it moves towards lower level as rice attains the higher temperature.

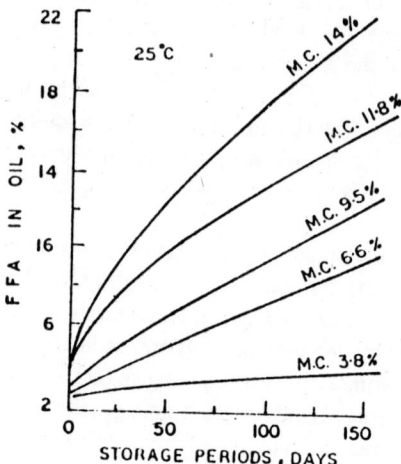

FIG. 17.2 Development of free fatty acid (FFA) in Brown rice at different moisture contents at 25 °C (Chikubu, 1970).

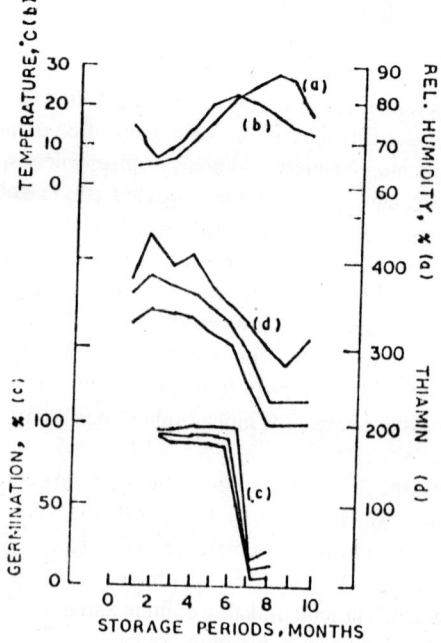

FIG. 17.3 Changes in germination and thiamin content of brown rice during storage (Chikubu, 1970).

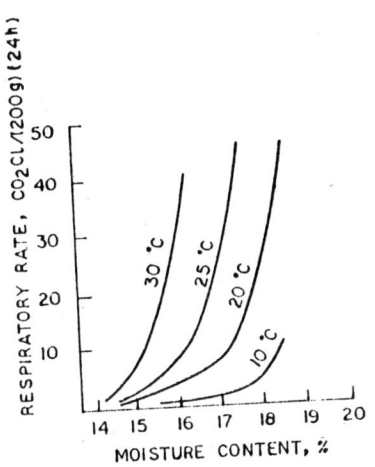

FIG. 17.4 Effect of moisture content and temperature on respiratory rate of brown rice (Chikubu, 1970).

Other factors involved in grain storage are the amounts of O_2 and CO_2 in the air. The respiration of grain under anaerobic condition usually weakens viability and induces quality deterioration. Storing cereal grains under vacuum or air-tight conditions appears to be very effective, but anaerobic respiration of the grain at high moisture content makes it unsuitable. The checked and cracked grains have higher respiratory rates than the whole grains under the same condition.

Longevity
The viability-period of a grain during storage can be short or long. The grain dies owing to the degeneration of protein which, in turn, is influenced by decay of components in the cell nucleus. Generally, the life of a stored grain is regulated by the grain-type, the seed-borne microflora, and by the interaction between temperature and moisture.

Sprouting
Sprouting of the grain during storage occurs mainly owing to generation of heat as a result of infestation. A grain sprouts only when its moisture content exceeds certain limit of moisture content of 30–35%.

Heating
The stored grain is sometimes heated up by itself without any exter-

nal cause. This spontaneous heating can be attributed to the respiration of grain in combination with the respiration of infested pests.

Heating usually occurs when grain is stored in bulk. By respiration alone, however, the temperature may not exceed above 35°C. Under favourable conditions the growth of microorganisms is very rapid and the combined effects of respirations become high, generating more heat. Of the total heating phenomena, 60–70% of heating can be ascribed to the respiration of pests.

Biological changes

The changes and damages of grain during storage brought about by insects, microorganisms and rodents have been discussed earlier. These will be further discussed subsequently.

Moisture migration

Moisture migration in stored food grains occurs owing to the changes in temperature. One of the most important factors which affects storage life of grain is its moisture content. Moisture migration takes place in a bin even if the cereal grain is at a safe storage moisture level of about 12.0% or so. But the moisture content of the top layer may go as high as 25–30%. It results in spoilage of food grains from stored grains in a bin after about one year. Greater losses may occur in stored grains in bins for the following conditions: (1) when grains are stored at a high moisture content; (2) where there is an appreciable difference between ambient and grain temperatures and (3) when a tall or deep bin is used.

Generally, grains are fed to the bins either in warm or in cold condition. The moisture accumulated at the top or bottom of the bin is attributed by the movement of convection-air. Most of the times grains are placed in the bin when the grains are warm. Under this condition the air in the grain near the surface of the storage bin is comparatively cold and moves down along its circumference and then goes up near the centre of the bin, where the air and grain are warm. The air moving through the centre of the bin picks up moisture until it moves across the top of the bin. At this location the grain surface is comparatively cold and the moisture is condensed on the grain, thus raising its moisture content (Fig. 17.5a). In consequence a large quantity of grain is spoiled at the top of the bin.

Sometimes the grains are fed to the bin under cold condition as in the winter. The air currents rise along the circumference of the bin and move down through its centre to the bottom, where moisture condenses on the cold bottom. Under this condition spoilage of grain takes place at the bottom of the bin (Fig. 17.5b) (Hall, 1957).

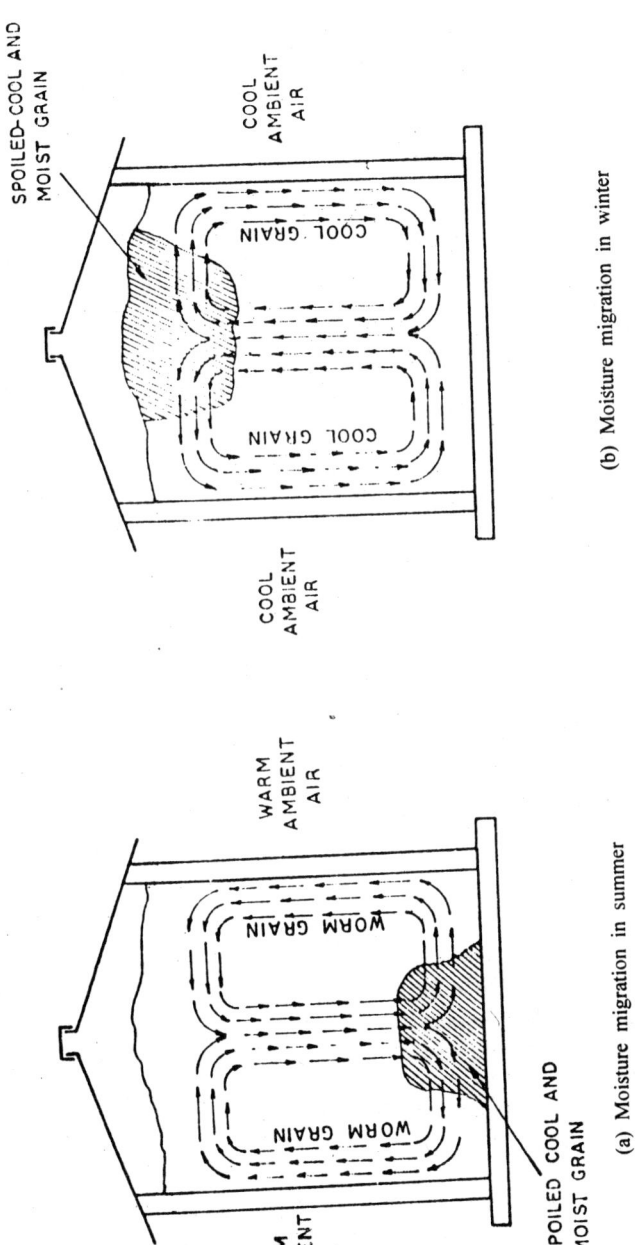

(a) Moisture migration in summer

(b) Moisture migration in winter

FIG. 17.5 Moisture migration in summer and winter

GRAIN STORAGE PESTS AND THEIR CONTROL

Deteriorations caused by insects and microorganisms

There are many causes for the qualitative and quantitative deteriorations of stored cereal grains. However, following are the most important:

(i) Deterioration in the quality of grains, caused by microorganisms;
(ii) alteration in chemical constituents of grain owing to its metabolism
(iii) insects and rodents cause damage by eating and contamination.

Insects produce uric acid, inoculate fungi and bacteria and larvae on the food materials faecal matter, cast skin and foul odour. Quinone and other harmful substances are also being produced on the infested products. Some fungi produce harmful mycotoxins.

Following are the parameters to assess qualitative damage to grain (Food Ind.,1979):

Insects	Moulds	Mites
Moisture	Moisture	Foul odour
Uric acid	Apparent uric acid	Guanine
Exuvae	Discolouration	Allergens
Chitin	Mycotoxins	
Dead insects	Thermogenesis	Pathogen vector
Infested odour	Musty odour	Debris
Frass	Loss of variability	
Killed germ		
Microflora		

Types of grain spoilage

Reduction in mass

About 15 mg of rice kernel can be eaten away by a grain weevil during its growth from egg to adult. A female weevil by breeding through three generations per year has the biotic potential of reproducing 1,500,000 offsprings which are likely to consume 1,500,000 kernels of rice. It is also known that warehouse moth, *Ephestia-elutella*, attack the embryo of wheat kernels making it unfit for germination. These reveal the extent of damage caused by the grain pests and the need of their control (Mitsui, 1970).

Spoilage of grains by heating

Heating of grain sometimes is brought about by insects and pests infestation which ultimately causes serious grain damage.

Reduction in seed germination

A seed grain attacked by a germ eater is not likely to germinate. In consequence germination of seed grains will be seriously affected.

Contamination of grains by insects

Food grains specially the milled products contaminated with dead bodies of insects and their excreta and secretions, often lead to a serious loss of grain quality.

Detection of insect infestation

Determination of infestation can be carried out by the following methods:

(i) Visual examination of surface holes; (ii) Floatation method; (iii) Staining method for detecting egg plugs; (iv) Cracking floatation method; (v) Gelatinization method; (vi) Uric acid method; (vii) Phenol method; (viii) Ninhydrin method; (ix) Aural techniques; (x) Carbon dioxide as an index of infestation; and (xi) X-ray method.

Apart from these methods, milled grain can be analysed for insects and fragments by the standard A.O.A.C. method and grain mites can be detected by any of the two methods, namely, liquid paraffin floatation method and saturated saline floatation method. These methods are not described here in order to keep the volume of the book within limit.

Grain storage pests

Among all the grain storage insects the following 12 species are considered important:

(i) the Khapra beetle; (ii) the borer beetle; (iii) the grain weevil; (iv) the rice moth; (v) the grain moth; (vi) the meal moths; (vii) the pulses beetle; (viii) the flour moths; (ix) the red rust flour beetle; (x) the long headed flour beetle; (xi) the saw-toothed grain beetle; (xii) the flat grain beetle.

Of these twelve insects species the first eight are known as primary pests as these are able to damage all kinds of stored grains. The last four are unable to damage sound grains and these grow on broken grains or infested grains. That is why the last four species are known as secondary pests.

It may be noted that the major orders are coleoptera or beetles, and lepidoptera or moths, which account for about 60% and 9% respectively of the total number of species of stored grain pests.

Some of the major stored grain pests are described below.

Important insect species

Lesser Grain Borer, *Rhyzopertha dominica* (family: Bostrichidae). These insects mainly eat grain kernels. These are also grown on milled grain products.

Khapra Beetle, *Trogoderma granarium* (family: Dermestidae) under tropical climate the Khapra beetles often cause more serious damage to stored grain than the grain weevil or the lesser grain borer.

Grain weevils (family: Curcurionidae). The grain weevils are very destructive to stored rice grains. Of these, rice weevils and small rice weevils are the most important which are distributed all over the world wherever grains are stored.

Saw-toothed grain beetle, *Oryzaphilus surinamensis* (family: Silvanidae). The saw-toothed grain beetle is commonly found in grain and grain products. As it can hardly attack sound grain kernels, it is usually found in grains damaged by primary insects.

Flour Beetle (family: Tenebrionidae). The flour beetles are the most destructive insects for flour bran.

Warehouse moth, Tropical warehouse moth (family: Phycitidae). These are the destructive insects for both stored grains and grain products.

Indian Meal Moth, *Plodia interpunctella* (family: Phycitidae). It generally grows and multiplies on grains and grain products, seeds, nuts, etc. It is especially destructive to wheat and brown rice. But it seldom occurs on milled rice.

Angoumois Moth, *Sitotroga cerealella* (family: Gelechiidae). It is the only moth that develops within the grain kernel. It attacks both stored and field grains. It grows on barley, oat, rye, corn and rice.

Rice Moth, *Corcyra cephalonica* (family: Galleriidae). It attacks rice, wheat, green gram, cocoa, etc. In India it grows well on milled jowar and millets also.

Control of stored food grain pests

Food grain pests can be controlled by preventive and curative methods (Mitsui, 1970).

It is always desirable that preventive measures are taken before occurrence of infestation and subsequently curative measures have to be taken. The preventive measures are undertaken to avoid infestation by the pests while the curative measures are used to wipe out any kind of infestation.

Preventive measures

Preventive measures need consistent and thorough application at frequent intervals. However, preventive methods are divided into the following heads: (1) physical and mechanical measures; (2) chemical measures; and (3) hygienic measures.

Physical and mechanical control methods are: (i) Drying; (ii) Cooling by aeration; (iii) Air-tight storage; (iv) Low temperature storage; and (v) Protective packaging.

Chemical control methods include: (i) Grain protectants; (ii) attractants and (iii) repellants.

Hygienic measures: The entire storage is to be kept under clean and hygienic condition.

Curative measures

Among the curative measures the chemical methods are the most effective which involve the use of insecticides, toxic to the man and require special protective devices to safeguard the lives of the personnel applying these chemicals.

Curative measures are as follows: (i) Physical methods; (ii) Mechanical methods; (iii) Chemical methods; and (iv) Biological methods.

Physical

Heating

All species of stored grain pests at any stage of development will be killed if these are exposed to a temperature of 60°C for more than 10 minutes or to 50°C for 2 h.

Radiation

(a) Direct method

Irradiation of insects by β-rays or γ-rays causes physical disorder such as loss of their reproductive power and lives even. The γ-rays have a strong penetrating power and have the potential to be the most effective method of control of grain storage pests. But any of these methods requires a very costly irradiation plant.

(b) Indirect method (male sterilization)

Adult males can be sterilized by irradiation. A continuous release of sterilized male adults for about one year can completely destroy the entire population of the pests in some specific areas.

In indirect and other chemical methods reinfestation may occur from outside sources of insects brought in contact with the same stored grains. Hence, all other methods are only temporarily effective.

Mechanical methods

Centrifugal force can be effectively utilized for this method. In flour mills, the impact of the flour against the rotating discs, and housing of the entoleter is so great that all stages of insects and mites, including the eggs are killed. The flour thus treated with the centrifugal force comes out of the machine.

Chemical methods

The chemical control methods employ the following: (a) spraying; (b) fogging; (c) dusting; (d) vaporisers and (e) fumigation.

Fumigation has been discussed in detail separately.

Chemo-sterilants: This is a simple method of spraying and dusting chemo-sterilants for sterilization of insects.

Biological methods

Natural enemy: Wherever insects infestation occurs in stored grains, there exists almost invariably parasitoid wasps which are parasitic on them. This method is likely to be applicable for field pests. But its application to stored grain pests had not been successful.

Microbial control method: Various bacteria and fungi are parasitic in nature. Hence these can perhaps successfully be applied to field pests.

Fumigation

Fumigation is an insect controlling method of exposing stored grains to a lethal concentration of highly toxic gas long enough to kill the insects. Fumigants are the effective chemicals for killing stored grain pests. In the gaseous phase, fumigants can penetrate through stored grains anywhere in bags on stacks or in bulk and kill the hiding insects. These do not have any residual effect.

Insecticides

The insecticides for grain storage pests are also divided into preventive and curative insecticides. For control of additional reinfestation from outside sources after fumigation, a contact insecticide (grain protectant) must be applied immediately after the fumigation on the surface of the stored grains.

Principles of fumigation

In any fumigation process, a fumigant acts in accordance with the following flow diagram (Mitsui, 1970).

Application of fumigant → Vaporization→ Diffusion → (Leakage) → Sorption → Penetration → Lethal effect

After application of fumigant, generally it starts vaporising. The rate of vaporization mainly depends upon the kind of fumigant, method of application, temperature, and air flow rate.

Generally, the boiling points of the fumigants are approximately proportional to their molecular weights. Both liquid and gaseous fumigants are common. The low boiling fumigant methyl bromide which is in gaseous form at room temperature, is called gaseous fumigant.

Ethylene bromide having comparatively a high boiling point remains in a liquid state at room temperature is known as liquid fumigant. The methods of application are, certainly, different for the gaseous and liquid fumigants.

There are also solid type of fumigants such as aluminium phosphide tablet. It reacts with the atmospheric moisture to form hydrogen phosphide gas, that has lethal affect on microorganisms.

Diffusion

The vaporised fumigant-gases reach every nook and corner of any storage system by diffusion. The diffusion of gas takes place owing to convection of air. The rate of diffusion depends on: (i) kind of fumigant; (ii) temperature; and (iii) method of application.

Sorption

Reduction in concentration of fumigant-gases in any grain storage system takes place mainly owing to sorption of gases by grain and structural materials of the same storage system. The rate of sorption of fumigant-gases by grains is dependent on: (i) kind of fumigant; (ii) kind of stored grain; (iii) temperature; (iv) gas concentration and (v) exposure time.

Penetration

The penetration of gas in between individual kernels of the stored grain mass is accomplished by diffusion. It is gradually done by molecular diffusion of fumigant-gas due to concentration gradient of gas. Therefore, efficiency of the penetration depends upon (a) kind of fumigant, (b) kind of stored grain, (c) gas concentration, and (d) temperature.

Lethal effect

The fumigant-gas reaches the body of the insect through the aforementioned operations to render the insecticidal effect. The lethal effect mainly depends on: (i) toxicity of chemical agent; (ii) dosage; (iii) exposure period and (iv) temperature.

Properties and applications of fumigants

The common properties, dosage and usage of some of the important fumigants are summarised in Table 17.3.

In India fumigation with ethylene dibromide or aluminium phosphide is adopted for farm storage and methyl bromide or ethylene dibromide or aluminium phosphide is employed in commercial storage of grains. In addition to fumigation surface treatment with malathion or pyrethrum is employed in commercial grain storage. Because of low cost of fumigation and convenience the solid fumigant, namely, aluminium phosphide has become popular. In Food Corporation of India (F.C.I.), during grain storage aluminium phosphide is generally applied at a rate of half a tablet per tonne of grain for fumigation of bulk grain with an exposure period of 5 to 7 days and 7 tablets per 28 cubic metres space with 10 days exposure for shed or godown fumigation. (Rao, 1974).

TABLE 17.3. Necessary information about some common fumigants

Name of the fumigant	Hydrogen Phosphide/ Phosphine/ Phostoxin	Methyl Bromide/ Bromo-Methane	Ethylene Dichloride	Carbon Tetra-chloride	Ethylene Dibromode	Hydrocynic acid/ Hydrogen Cynide	Carbon Disulphide
	(1)	(2)	(3)	(4)	(5)	(6)	(7)
Chemical formula	PH_3	CH_3Br	$C_2H_4Cl_2$	CCl_4	$C_2H_4Br_2$	HCN	CS_2
M. wt.	34.04	94.95	98.97	153.84	187.88	27.03	76.13
Sp. gravity of liquid	0.746	1.732	1.257	1.595	2.180	0.688	1.26
Boiling point (°C, 76 cm Hg)	−87.4	3.6	83.0	77.0	131.0	26.0	46.3
Mode of action	Nerve poison	Nerve poison	Respiratory poison	Respiratory poison	Nerve poison causes blistering	Blood poison destroys haemoglobin	—
Normal state	Solid	Gas	Liquid	Liquid	Liquid	Gas	Liquid
Odour	Garlicky	Odourless	Ether like	Pungent aromatic	Pungent almond like	Bitter	—

contd.

	(1)	(2)	(3)	(4)	(5)	(6)	(7)
Penetration	Excellent	High	Low	Good	Low	High	—
Vapor pressure 76 mm Hg at 250°C	600	161.0	81.0	114.5	14.0	738.8	357.1
Sorption	Very low	Low	High	Low	Very low	High	—
Flammability, % by vol. in air	1–79	Non-flammable	6–16	Non-flammable	Non-flammable	6–41	1.25–44
Solubility in water, g/100 ml.	Very slightly soluble	1.3 at 25°C	0.87 at 20°C	0.8 at 20°C	0.43 at 30°C	Very soluble at 20°C	0.22 at 22°C
Dosage rate	1/2 to 1 tablet	2.46 kg/100 m³	EDCT 32.7	mixture at kg/100 m³	2.46 to 327 kg/100 m³	3.27 to 4.90 kg/100 m³	
Exposure period	5-7 days	24–48 hrs	48–72 hrs	48–72 hrs	7–10 days	24 hrs	—
Remarks	Grain fumigant; gas generated from tablets aluminium phosphide	General fumigant, may be used with caution for growing plants, some fruits and seeds	Seeds and grains, usually mixed with carbon tetra-chloride	Used chiefly in mixture with flammable compounds in grain fumigation to reduce fire hazard	General fumigant, Particularly useful for certain fruits; may injure growing plants	General fumigant, but phytotoxic Safe for seeds but not recommended for fresh fruit and vegetables	Grain fumigant, Usually as ingradient of non flammable mixtures

(Bond, 1973, Monro, 1969 & Mitsui, 1970)

RODENT CONTROL

Exclusion of rodents from a storage system is possible if the storage unit as a whole is kept free from rodents and the rodent population is completely eradicated from the locality. Rat-proof construction is necessary to minimize the damage of food grains by rat. The masonry or metal bins may be tight enough to prevent entry of rodents.

Construction of a rat-proof food grain storage system is the main step in the direction of rodent control. Silos made of either steel or concrete are sufficiently rat-proof. The flat godowns for bag storage are not always rodent-proof. To make these godowns rodent-proof a plinth of about 1 m without steps, with a U-shaped drain at the ground level and concave projection at the top has been incorporated in a standard design. Doors and windows are close fitting and are provided with 30 cm high, 20 gauge

metal plate at the bottom on both sides. About 20% of the total grain storage cost per tonne of grain storage go toward rat-proofing (Rao, 1974).

Rat and mice in stored grain

Rodents are one of the most destructive vertebrate animals on earth.
The rats consume food grain and at the same time spoil it by nibbling it into
brokens, and contaminating it with their droppings of urine. Rats eat about
10% of their weight in food each day and contaminate a great deal, thereby
rendering it unfit for human consumption. The following six species of
rodents are common: (i) *Gerbillus* species (field rat); (ii) *Rattus rattus* (the
black rat); (iii) *Rattus norvegicus* (the brown rat); (iv) *Mus musculus* (the
house mouse); (v) *Bandicoota bandicoota* (the bandicoot); (vi) *Bandicoota
bengalensis* (the bandicoot).

The genus *Rattus* alone has 570 named forms. The Norway rat (*Rattus
norvegicus*), the black rat (*Rattus rattus*), and the house mouse (*Mus
musculus*) cause the most extensive damage. Two or more of these species
are found in most of the countries of the world. In many countries they are
joined by other destructive native rodents such as the bandicoot rat of India
and Ceylon. Jointly, they destroy many million tonnes of food grain each
year.

Rodenticides (for rats and mice)

Hundred per cent effective rat poison that meets all requirements
under all conditions has not yet been developed. Toxicity dosage levels and
relative effectiveness are the most important factors. Less often considered,
but of equal importance, are degrees of acceptance and reacceptance and
the development of tolerances.

Anticoagulants for rat control

Anticoagulants have been proved to be very effective. They are commercially available as concentrations, as well as ready-to-use baits and are
safest for the untrained individual to use. Anticoagulants such as diaphai-
mone, fumarin and warfarin are recommended for general use by the
public. For an effective antirodent measures the following actions are
necessary: (1) Complete eradication of rat population in the locality; (2)
the method should not create bait-shyness; (3) creation of no suspicion in
the rats and (4) it should not be hazardous to human beings.

Warfarin and fumarin belong to the group of chemicals known as
hydroxycoumarins. Hydroxycoumarins or anticoagulant poisons have
been found to meet the above requirements. These chemicals cause
haemorrhage in the circulatory system leading to death. Among others the

two anticoagulants, namely, Ratafin made by Agromore Ltd., and Rodafarin made by Pest Control (India) Pvt. Ltd., are readily available in India (Rao, 1974). The compounds are available in the following three forms: (1) ready-to-use bait; (2) 0.5 per cent dry concentration and (3) 0.5 per cent water soluble compound. Apart from these, other chemicals such as Zinc phosphide, Red squill and Strychnine are also used as rodenticides.

Preparation of baits
    1. Dry baits: Ground granular wheat can be used as bait base. One part of Rodafarin C with 0.5% Warfarin is added to 19 parts of the above bait base. A little quantity of vegetable fat and sugar will improve the taste of the bait. 200 g of freshly prepared bait is placed in a shallow plate for the same purpose.
    2. Liquid baits: About one table spoonful of Rodafarin with sodium salt of Warfarin is dissolved in one litre of water. The solution thus prepared is poured in shallow receptacles at the rate of 25 cc per container and kept at bait stations.
    The dry and liquid baits are placed in alternate bait stations so that the rodents visiting the dry bait stations might have an easy access to a nearby station where they could drink water after having meal. The baits are replenished every day to facilitate maximum possible consumption of poison. It should be continued for 10 days (Rao, 1974).

FOOD GRAINS STORAGE STRUCTURES

    Generally, food grains are being stored in traditional or improved rural storage structures in urban warehouses/godowns and in advanced large silos. The material of construction and the size of the structures vary widely. The farmers usually store their produce in either above-ground or underground storage structures. Mostly local agricultural wastes and minerals are used. Some of these structures are 'patra', 'kothis', 'thekka', 'khattis', 'morai', 'pette', 'pey', etc. for storage of grains in small bulks. These structures are made of bamboo, wood, earthenware, cement-concrete, stones or bricks. In general capacities of these vary from 250 kg to 5,000 kg. However, higher capacities of these are also available. Now-a-days some progressive farmers use plastic and metallic bins also.
    Of the total production of about 120 million tonnes of food grains, 70 per cent is being stored and consumed by the farmers and people in rural areas. Whereas the remaining 30 per cent (marketable surplus), moves through the marketing channel to the urban consumers. Usually the marketable surplus is being handled in jute bags. The godowns are constructed

by the Government and other organized sectors. The different kinds of godowns/warehouses vary in plinth, height, construction of walls and also of the roofs. Their different names are as follows: (1) Tubular truss, (2) Flat roof, (3) Gable type, (4) Nissanhut, (5) Cubicles, (6) Shell type, (7) RCC-circular bin, (8) Ferrocement structures, (9) Rectangular steel bin, (10) Crib type, (11) Air-warehouse etc. ISI specifications of some of these structures are available. The metallic or RCC silos are the most advanced storage structures.

As regards improved storage structures such as improved khattis and kothis of India, plastic lined metal bin of the USA, hemispherical grain silo, silo-cum-elevators, improved flat storage godown of FCI, India, RCC structure of CBRI, and 'Hapurthekka' call for special attention. Recently, (1) Low Density Polyethylene (LDPE), (2) High Density Polyethylene (HDPE), (3) Poly Vinyl Chloride etc. are also used for the manufacture of plastics bins. The ballooning technique of making stacks moisture proof and resistant to insect and rodent attacks is also unique. As a result expensive flexible special lined bags are no more necessary for storage of the hygroscopic material (Food Ind., 1979).

Rural storage structures

The special features of the traditional underground rural storage structures are furnished in the Tables given below.

Some of the common improved storage structures in India are described in the subsequent paragraphs and the special features of these structures are summarized in Tables 17.4 through 17.6, (ISI Hand Book, 1975, IS: 601–604, IS: 631).

TABLE 17.4. Indian traditional underground storage structures

Local name	State	Material of construction	Shape	Dimension	Capacity, tonne	Remarks
'Khani' or 'Patra'	Orrissa A. P.	Dug out with sides plastered with cow dung	rect-angular	depth: 150 cm Sides: 150–200 cm	2–3	Used in some areas
'Khai'	Rajas-than	Similar to a well, lined with stone or sand-cement	Circular or rectan-gular	Depth: 600 cm Dia: 600 cm	Upto 60	Rearly used now

(Source: Maheswari, R.C. and IS: 601, 1955)

TABLE 17.5 Indian traditional above-ground storage structures

Local name	State	Material of construction	Shape	Diameter	Capacity (tonne)
'Khothi'	Bihar, Punjab, U.P.	Unburnt clay mixed with straw and mud-cow dung or brick and masonry (common in rural areas)	Cylind-rical or irregular	Varies in diameter	1 to 50
'Kanagi'	Mysore and M.S.	Bamboo plastered with clay (common)	Cylind-rical	Vary in sizes	1 to 20
'Kotha'	Punjab U.P.	Small shed built with brick and masonry (common)	Cylind-rical	Vary in sizes	5 to 100
'Dholi'	M.P.	Structure built by straw, bamboo, palm leaves and plastered with a mixture of mud and cow dung (common)	Cylind-rical	Vary in sizes	2
'Thekka'	Punjab, U. P.	Gunny or cotton wound around wooden support (common)	Rectan-gular	L = 240 cm B = 390 cm H = 210–330 cm	Upto 30

(Source: Maheswari, R.C.)

'**Anaj kothi**' : It is a circular steel bin for indoor storage having capacity upto 3 tonnes. It has flat top and flat bottom. It is equipped with circular opening at the top for filling and the circular spout for discharge of grains. Walls are made of plane or corrugated M.S. steel. These are usually made of 4 to 6 rings which are bolted together. The bin is airtight and it can be fumigated.

'**Kanak kothi**' (steel bin): It is an outdoor structure of a prefabricated steel bin with a hopper bottom. It is made of 16 gauge curved M.S. sheet. It has also metallic ladder and pully arrangement for filling the grains (Fig. 17.6).

TABLE 17.6 Salient feature of improved storage structures in India

Name	Material of construction	Shape	Dimension (cm)	Capacity (tonne)	Remark
'Anaj kothi'	Corrugated steel sheet airtight, bolted with plates	Circular	Ht = 105 ⫶ Dia = 100 ⫶ and Dia = 150 ⫶ Ht = 210 ⫶	1 ⬚ 3	Indoor structure
'Kanak kothi'	Corrugated steel sheet, provided with an aeration arrangement	Circular	Ht = 182 ⫶ Dia = 218 ⫶ Ht = 244 · Dia = 244 ⫶	6 ⬚ 10	Outdoor structure
Alumi-nium bin	Corrugated alumi-nium sheet	Circular	Ht = 275–430 Dia = 370–430	15–35	Outdoor structure
'Dhan kothi'	Made with RCC rings	Circular	HT = 300 Dia = 125	1.5–6	Indoor and outdoor structure
'Anaj ghar'	Masonry structure built on 60 cm high platform, plastered with cement from inside and outside both	Rectangular	L B Ht 225 225 165 – 8 290 290 250 – 10 825 290 250 – 30		Outdoor structure

L– Length, B = Breadth, Ht = Height   (Source: Maheswari, R.C.)

Size and capacity of 'Anaj kothi', specified by ISI

Capacity, tonne	Height, cm	Dia, cm	M.S. Sheet, gauge
0.5	125	80	28
1	165	100	26
2	210	125	24
3	210	150	24

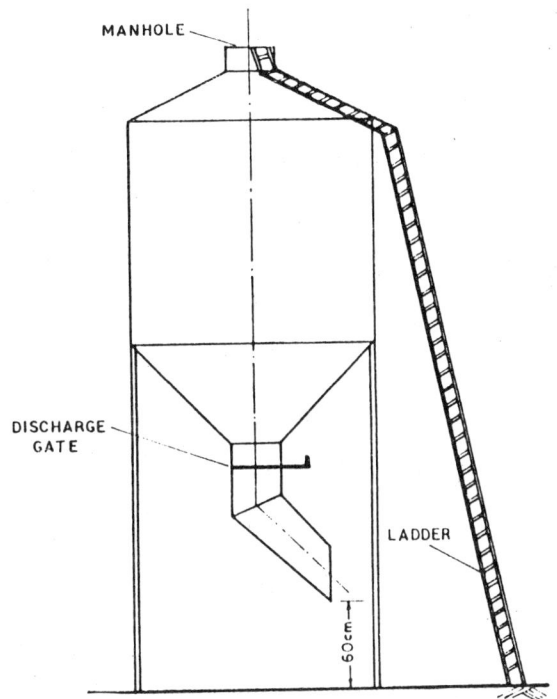

FIG. 17.6 'Kanak Kothi' (Steel Bin)

Specifications of 'kanak kothi'

Capacity, tonne	Height (cm)	Diameter (cm)	Total height (cm)	M.S. sheet, gauge
6	182	218	335	16
10	244	244	427	16

Aluminium bin
It is an outdoor structure, circular in shape.

Specifications of aluminium bin

	15 tonnes	28 tonnes	35 tonnes
1. Body diameter, cm	370	430	430
2. Overall height, cm (excluding plinth)	275	350	430
3. Height of cylindrical portion, cm	190	250	325
4. Platform diameter, cm	395	450	450
5. Height of platform, cm	60	60	60

(IS: 631, 1961)

The bin consists of a cylindrical body of several corrugated aluminium curved sheets and a conical roof made of flat aluminium sheets. Bolts and nuts are used for assembly of the body and the roof. This bin is constructed on a platform or plinth of 60 cm height which provides a permanent system against ground moisture. At the same time the spout which is embedded in the platform allows for easy bagging of the grain. The bin is filled through manhole at the roof. Both the manhole and the spout are provided with locking arrangements (Fig. 17.7).

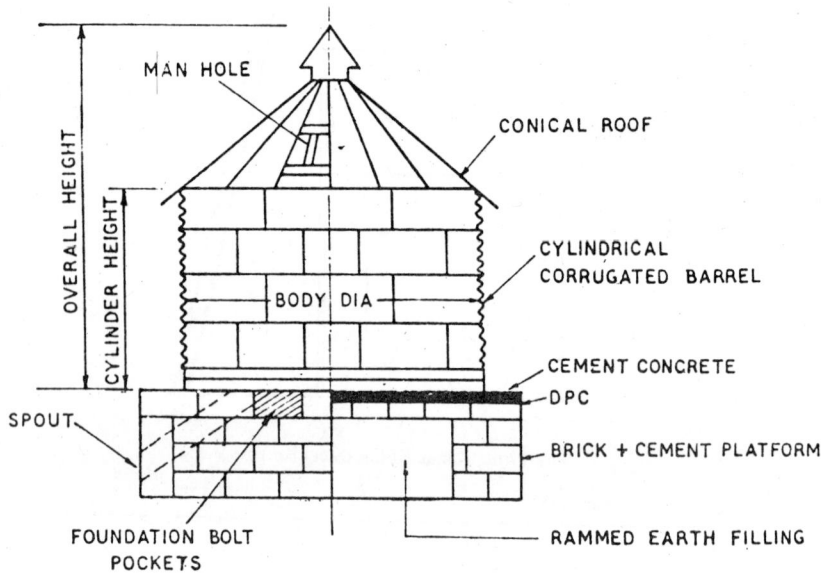

FIG. 17.7 Aluminium bin

R.C.C. bin ('Dhan kothi')

R.C.C. storage structure is circular and water proof. Its capacity varies form 1.5 to 6 tonnes. It can be built at the site. The bins having capacity less than 6 tonnes can be made with 30 cm high R.C.C rings. The joints of the rings are sealed with cement. A manhole of 60 cm dia on the top and sliding door or a spout near the bottom are provided for filling and discharging grains. Slope at the bottom is preferable. Manhole and spout should have locking arrangements. Specifications of the bins are tabulated below (Fig. 17.8).

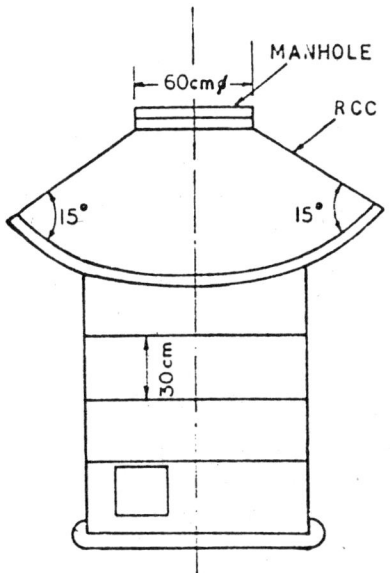

FIG. 17.8 'Dhan Kothi' (R.C.C. bin)

'Anaj Ghar' (Cement-masonry bin)
   These rectangular bins are also meant for outdoor storage structure. These are built on 60 cm high platform. Filling of grain is done through a 60 cm dia manhole on the top. The sides are made of brick wall of 23 cm thickness and are plastered with sand and cement on both sides. The roof is of R.C.C. A spout at the bottom and floor slightly slanting towards the discharge spout makes the discharge of grain easy. There are locking

Specifications of R.C.C. bin

Capacity (tonne)	Height (cm)	Diameter (cm)	Thickness (cm)			Remarks
			Wall	Roof	Platform	
1.5	150	120	7.5	7.5	7.5	5 rings cast on site
2.0	210	134	7.5	7.5	7.5	7 rings cast on site
2.5	180	150	7.5	7.5	7.5	6 rings cast on site
3.0	210	150	7.5	7.5	7.5	7 rings cast on site
6.0	210	210	10.0	7.5	7.5	7 rings cast on site

arrangements with the manhole and spouts. The walls also can be made of R.C.C., instead of brick for 30 and 60 tonnes structures.

Specifications of these bins are given below :

Capacity, tonnes	Dimensions, cm	No. of partitions
6	225 x 225 x 165	Nil
10	290 x 290 x 250	Nil
30	825 x 290 x 250	3
60	825 x 555 x 250	6

Bag and bulk storage

In godowns (Figs. 17.9a and 17.9b), the food grains are stored in bags. Rice, 'dhal' (milled pulses) and other milled products are stored in bags. Bag storage has occupied a dominant place in the country because of comparatively small capital investment for godowns and lack of sufficient bulk storage facilities.

Whether a bulk storage or bag storage to be used is based on the following: (i) type of grain to be stored; (ii) length of storage period required and (iii) whether a particular grain or different kinds of grains to be stored.

The relative advantages and disadvantages of these are summarised in Table 17.7.

Location of godowns

1. The structure shall be located on a land where there is no chance of any flood.
2. Structure shall be at least 0.5 km away from kilns, bone crushing mill, garbage dumping ground and tanneries.
3. The structure shall be at least 30 m away from dairy and poultry farms and at least 150 m away from factories and other possible sources of fire.
4. There shall be no tree near the structure so that its roots can affect the foundation.
5. The structure shall always be kept clean.
6. The structure should be situated near a main road. At the side of structure there shall be sufficient space for parking.
7. If the structure is situated near railway station loading and unloading facilities shall be made available.

8. A small office room of 4.5 m × 3.5 m size and a store room of 3.5 m × 3.5 m size and a room for guard are required.

Capacities and dimensions of some common godowns are tabulated in Table 17.8. The drawings of the common godowns are furnished in Figs. 17.9(a) and 17.9(b).

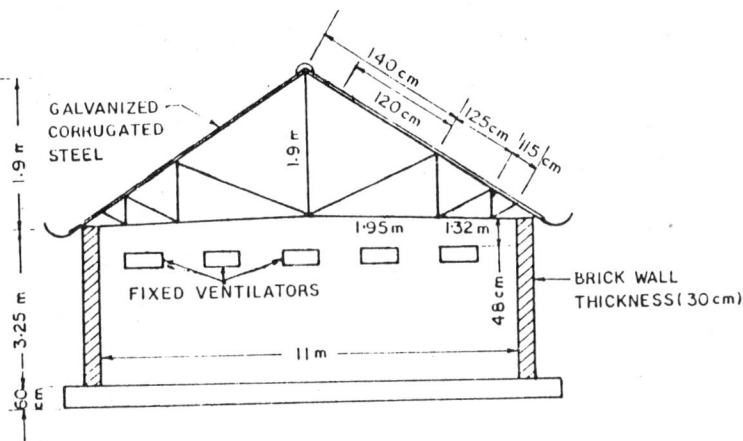

(a) Structure of a typical godown (L–28.5 m, H–3.25 m, Window–(1.5 x 1.2) m (Nos.–10))

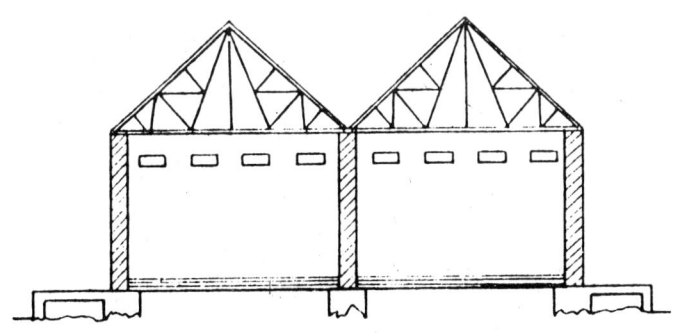

(b) Conventional trusses

FIG. 17.9 A typical godown structure and conventional trusses

TABLE 17.7 Merits and demerits of bag and bulk storage

Item	Bag	Bulk
Land requirement	Double that of bulk storage (2 acres/ 5000 T wheat)	Half of the bag storage (1 acre/5000 T wheat)
Cost of storage facility	Slightly cheaper than bulk storage	Comparatively costlier
Maximum storage period	1–2 years	5–10 years
Feasibility of mechanical operation	Difficult	Mechanically operated
Period of construction	12–18 months	12–18 months
Feasibility of shifting the facility	Nil	Mettalic structure can be shifted
Economics of handling	Cheaper	More costly
Fumigation	More costly	Cheaper
Cost of jute or other bags	Substantial	Nil
Storage loss (weight)	About 1–1.5 per cent in 1 year storage	Upto 0.2 per cent for any storage period
Possible lossess: (a) Rodents	It can be made rodent proof	Rodent proof
(b) Birds	Difficult to avoid	Bird proof
(c) Insect	Fumigated	Fumigated
(d) Effects of humidity and temperature	Can be minimised	Can be controlled by aeration
(e) Drainage	Can be controlled	Nil

Stack plan

The floor space is marked into equal rectangles to ensure uniformity in stacking and in accounting. A minimum space of 1 m is to be left

TABLE 17.8 Capacities and dimensions of godowns

No. of bags	Tonnes	Internal dimensions	
		Length, m	Bredth, m
1050	100	12	7.5
2625	250	20	9
5250	500	27	12
10500	1000	33.5	18
21000	2000	50	27

(IS: 607, 1965)

TABLE 17.9 Stack heights for different food grains

Grain	No. of layers	Stack height, m
Paddy	24	5.64
Wheat, barley, maize, gram jowar and other millets	20	5.04
Rice and milled pulses	16	3.96
Wheat bran	20	5.04
Milled cereals and pulses	12	2.13
Seed grains	10	2.00

around each stack. Stack dimensions are on the basis of bag dimension (0.7 m $\times$ 0.6 m) and floor dimension. Bags are placed in blocks containing one layer lengthwise and other layer widthwise. The common dimensions of stack are: 9.14 m $\times$ 6.09 m, 7.43 m $\times$ 12.2 m etc. Stack heights for different food grains are given in Table 17.9. Various stack plans used for different capacities are shown in Figs. 17.10(a) through 17.10(d).

Dunnage

It comprises wooden planks or polythene sheets. Wooden planks of 1.5 m $\times$ 0.9 m size are convenient to place below and are easy to carry. The height from the ground is 0.2 m. These should be strong to bear a load of about 0.07 tonne/m^2. Polythene sheet of 0.03 mm thickness is used. It should be black in colour. Stacking of bags are generally done in two rows. One is arranged lengthwise and other is set breadthwise which constitute a block. Cross stack is made as follows: lengthwise layer alternates with breadthwise layer in the height.

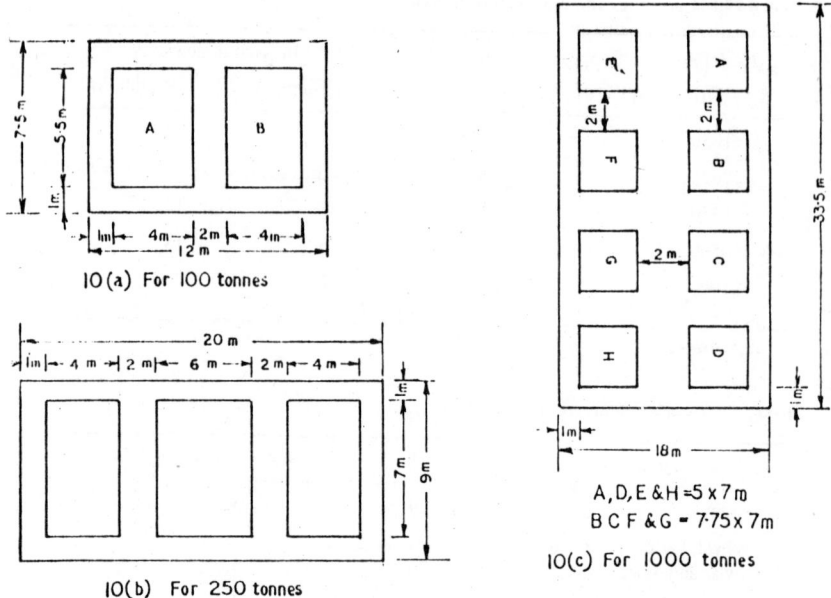

10(a) For 100 tonnes

10(b) For 250 tonnes

A,D,E &H =5 x 7 m
B C F &G = 7·75 x 7m

10(c) For 1000 tonnes

Stacking arrangements of bags in godowns

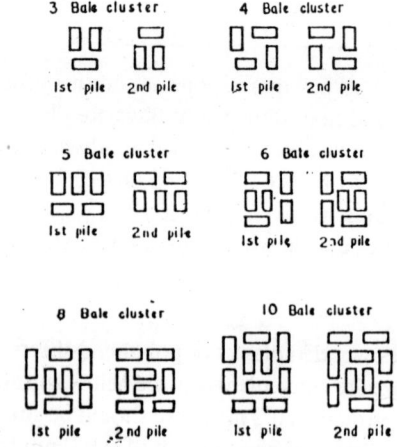

3 Bale cluster   4 Bale cluster

1st pile   2nd pile   1st pile   2nd pile

5 Bale cluster   6 Bale cluster

1st pile   2nd pile   1st pile   2nd pile

8 Bale cluster   10 Bale cluster

1st pile   2nd pile   1st pile   2nd pile

10(d) Stacking arrangement of brown rice in Japan
(Apo Proj / TRC/IV/68,1970)

FIG. 17.10 Stacking arrangement of bags in godowns/Ware houses

Foundation

Depth and width of foundation depends on soil condition of each locality. The practice is to take the column and walls to a depth of 1.22 m and the platform retaining walls to a depth of 0.9 m below the ground level.

Plinth

Where the godown is to be served by the broad gauge railway, plinth height has to be 1.06 m from the ground level whereas 0.76 m height is for the metre gauge. On the roadside, a height of 0.76 m is enough.

Height of walls

A height of 5.64 m from plinth level allows stacking of food grains to a height of 20 bags. The height of walls will be decided by the number of layers of bag to be stored.

Thickness of wall

In general, brick walls of thickness 0.39 m will be needed.

Roofing

Either corrugated galvanized iron sheet or black corrugated sheet may be used for roofing. Galvanized sheet is durable. In coastal areas galvanized sheets deteriorate fast. In such location asbestos sheets are recommended.

Flooring

Floor should be damp proof, rigid and durable.

Finish

Internal walls are to be plastered with cement. Internal surfaces should be white washed and external faces should be colour washed. All steel works should be provided with two coats of paints. The galvanized iron sheets should also be painted.

Doors

Rolling shutters are found to be the most suitable types of doors for godowns. Generally, rolling shutters of the size 2.44 m × 2.44 m are to be used.

Ventilators

Ventilators of the size (0.61 × 0.22) m for both longitudinal walls are satisfactory. A ventilator is needed in each alternate bay at the top. Ventilators of the size (0.3 x 0.3) m are needed at the bottom in addition. The top and the bottom ventilators should not be in the same bay. The ventilator should be provided with wire gauge and shutter so that they can be tightly closed for airtight arrangement for fumigation.

Silos

A silo is a tall storage structure which is nothing but a deep bin. Concrete has been in use widely in the construction of high capacity silos. Concrete is a durable and economical material. But it should be used in prefabricated or precast form, steel is perhaps the most common building material used for the construction of modern grain storage facilities. However, the use of steel silos has been limited in India and many other countries.

The schematic representations of the silos are shown in Figs 17.11(a) and 17.11(b).

The major advantages of concrete silos are as follows:

(i) These structures are moisture proof, vermin proof and insect proof; (ii) These have high strength, durability and workability; (iii) There is maximum space utilisation per tonne of stored material with a reasonable cost of storage; (iv) Practically, no food grain loss takes place in filling; storing and emptying and (v) Silos are completely fire proof and have long life.

Steel silos have the following main advantages: (i) Steel members have high strength and these can be used as prefabricated members; (ii) Steel silos are gas and water tight and have long service life and (iii) Steel can be readily disassembled or replaced.

The main drawback with the steel silos is that these are susceptible to corrosion.

Optimal configurations of silos

The optimal configurations of silos of capacities ranging from 100 T to 2000 T for different H/D_1 ratios (viz. 1 to 12) are furnished in Table 17 (A). A small variation in the H/D_1 ratio affects much on the weight of concrete and steel and the overall cost of silo. The mean of the recommended values should be adopted for the practice. In general, the total cost of silo is the main criterion for the selection of optimal height to diameter ratio (Dubey, 1984).

GRAIN PRESSURE THEORIES

Theoretically, the grain in bulk is considered to be semifluid and the storage structures are classified into shallow bin and deep bin. A shallow bin is one in which the plane of rupture of the material stored emerges from

TABLE 17(A). Optimal configuration of silos

Capacity, tonnes	H/D$_1$ ratio					
	Based on total cost	Based on cost of concrete	Based on cost of steel	Based on area of form work	Based on weight of concrete	Based on weight of steel
(1)	(2)	(3)	(4)	(5)	(6)	(7)
100	9–11	3–5	10–12	7–9	8–10	9–11
500	9–11	5–7	10–12	6–8	7–9	5–7
1000	7–9	5–7	10–12	7–9	7–9	7–9
1500	7–9	5–7	10–12	6–8	5–7	7–9
2000	6–8	4–6	8–10	5–7	4–6	7–9

(Dubey, 1984)

the top of the filling before it strikes the opposite wall. A deep bin is a structure in which the plane of rupture of the material stored meets the opposite wall before meeting the top surface of the filling material (Figs. 17.12(a) through 17.12(c)).

The grains stored in silos (i.e., deep bins) exert pressure on its sides in addition to the vertical forces. The horizontal pressure varies during filling as well as emptying operation (Figs. 17.13a through 17.13c). It also varies with the location of the discharge hole. Janssen studied the pressure in deep bins for the first time in 1878. On the basis of his theory the following equations had been developed.

$$P_L = \left(\frac{WR}{\mu'} \right) \ (1-e^{-(Ku-h)/R});$$

$$P_W = WR \left[\frac{h R}{\mu' K} (1-e^{-(Ku-h)/R}) \right] \text{ and}$$

$$P_V = \frac{P_L}{K} \ .$$

Actually, the value of K lies between

$$\frac{1 - \sin \theta}{1 + \sin \theta} \text{ and } \frac{1 + \sin \theta}{1 - \sin \theta}$$

where, for a consistent system of units:

P_L = Lateral pressure,
P_w = Vertical pressure transferred owing to wall friction,
P_v = Vertical pressure,
W = Specific weight of grain,
K = Ratio of lateral pressure to vertical pressure in the grain,
h = Depth of the grain to a point under consideration,
R = Area of the bin-floor/perimeter and
μ' = Coefficient of friction between grain and bin wall.

There are different theories to predict pressure in deep bins, but Janssen's equation is still most widely used in the design of deep bins.

Airy and Rankine developed grain pressure theories for shallow bins. Airy's equation is as follows:

$$P_L = wh \left[\frac{1}{-\sqrt{\{\mu\,(\mu + \mu')\}} + \sqrt{(1 + \mu^2)}} \right]^2$$

Rankine's equation as given below is still widely used in shallow bin-design:

$$P_L = wh\,[(1 - \operatorname{Sin} \theta) / (1 + \operatorname{Sin} \theta)],$$

where

μ = Coefficient of friction of grain on grain
= $\tan \theta$, where θ is the internal angle of friction
μ' = $\tan \theta'$, where θ' is the angle of wall friction

Both these equations are based on the assumptions that the pressure is caused by a sliding wedge of grain and there is no surcharge. Rankine's equation further assumes that there is no active frictional force between the stored grain and the bin wall.

According to Coulomb, active and passive pressure exists against retaining walls. The active pressure is taken as the pressure exerted on a wall by grain when the maximum internal friction of the grain is being used in helping the grain support itself.

Coulomb's equation is given by:

$$P_L = wh\operatorname{Cos}\phi' \left[\frac{\operatorname{Cosec}\beta\,\operatorname{Sin}(\beta - \phi)}{\sqrt{\operatorname{Sin}(\beta + \phi')} + \sqrt{\{\operatorname{Sin}(\phi + \phi')\,\operatorname{Sin}(\phi - i)\}/\operatorname{Sin}(\beta - i)}} \right]^2$$

Where

β = angle between bin wall and horizontal

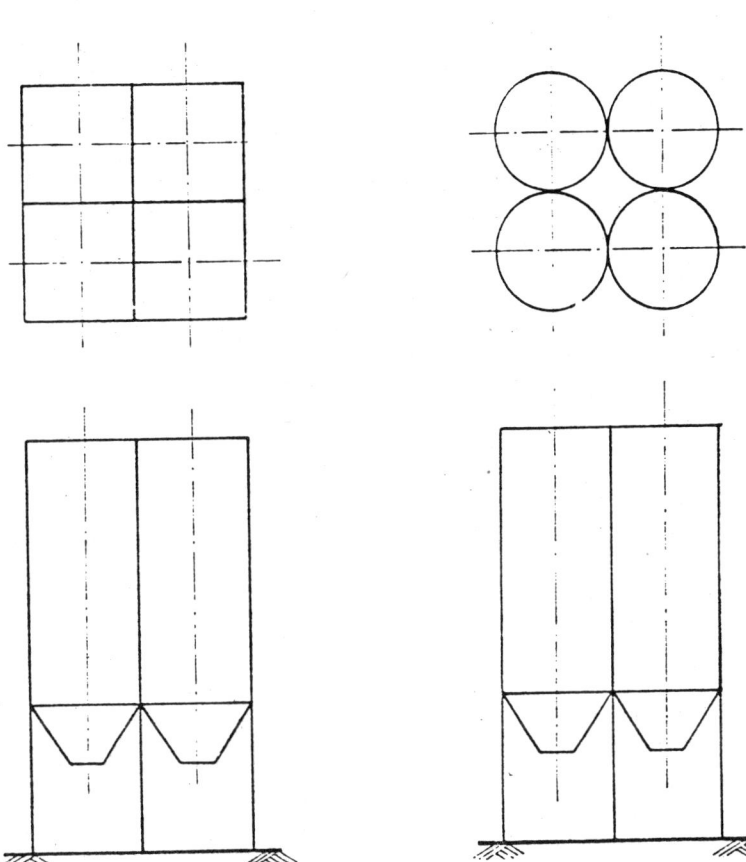

(a) Square cross-section   FIG (b) Circular cross-section

FIG. 17.11 Schematics of the plan and elevation of the Silos

i = angle of surcharge of the grain surface

ϕ, ϕ', P_L, w and h are as given earlier

For most of the bins, $\beta = 90°$. Thus, the above equation reduces to:

$$P_L = whCos\phi' \left[\frac{Cos\phi}{\sqrt{Cos\phi'} + \sqrt{\{Sin(\phi + \phi')\,Sin(\phi - i)\}/Cosi}} \right]^2 .$$

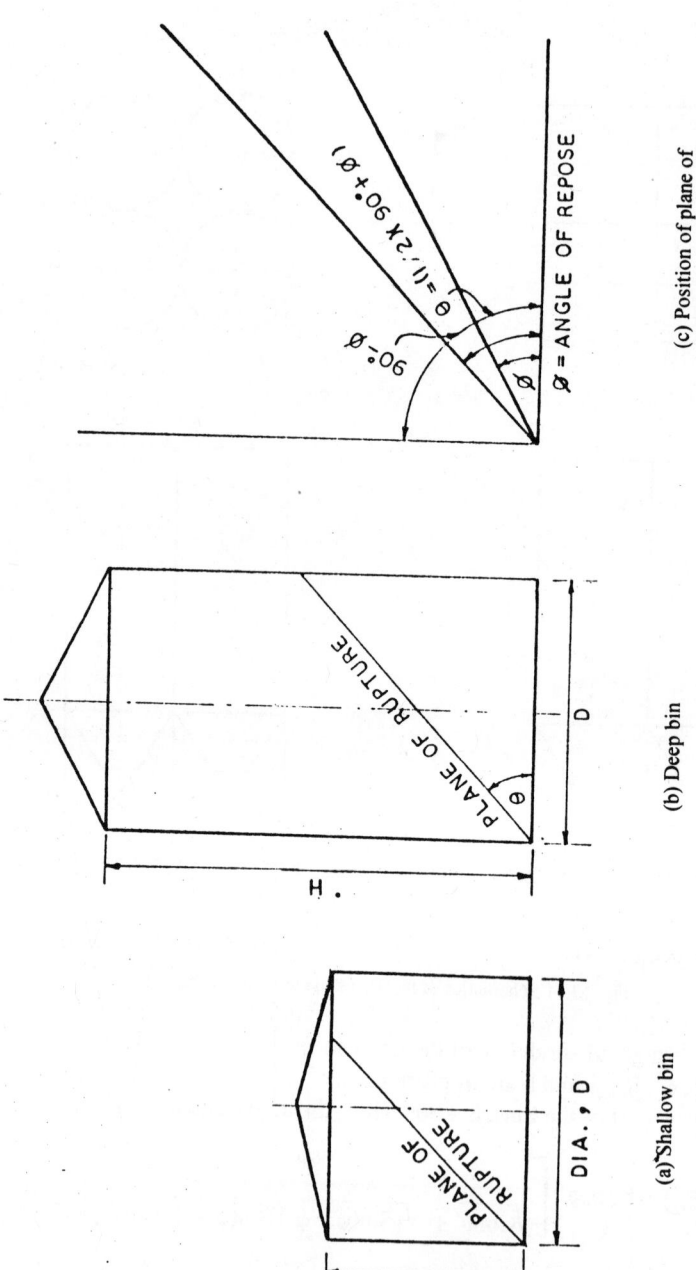

(a) Shallow bin

(b) Deep bin

(c) Position of plane of rupture between vertical wall and angle of repose

Fig. 17.12 Relation among shallow bin, deep bin and plane of rupture

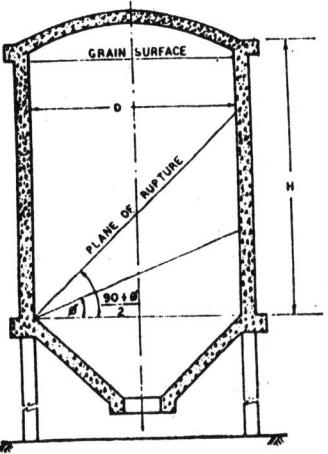

FIG. 17.13(a) Silo (i.e. Deep Bin).

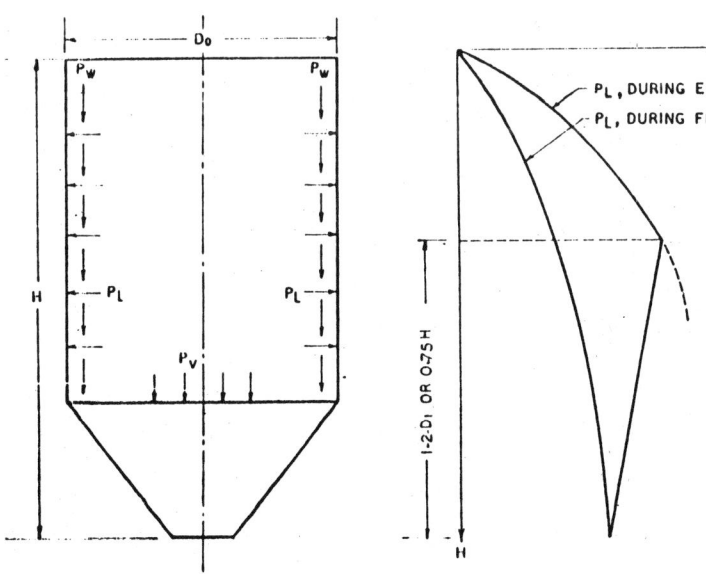

13(b) Stress analysis in silo.

13(c) Pressure distribution in silo during emptying and filling operations.

Lateral pressure owing to surcharge loading will be over-estimated by the Coulomb equation.

Unlike Rankine, Coulomb assumed the existence of wall friction and the vertical component of wall force, F_V Which can be determined by :

$$F_V = P_L \tan\phi'.$$

ECONOMICS OF STORAGE AND PROCESSING OF RICE

Storage in godowns

The three types of storage of cereal grains practised in India are: (i) storage in village bins or godowns; (ii) scientifically built modern godowns and (iii) most advanced silos. Nearly 75 per cent of cereal grains grown in India are still stored in the very old type of unscientific rural godowns and bins occurring very high losses of grain. Generally, in the rural godowns labour charges, maintenance cost and cost of gunny bags are involved. Bagged storage occupies a much larger storage area for a given weight of stock and the deterioration of the grains will be more if the building is not properly constructed or adequately water and moisture proof. However, the cost analysis of paddy-storage in traditional and improved godowns are given in Tables 17.10 A through 17.10 C (Shivanna, 1971).

The economics of paddy storage in both village-godowns and silos reveals that silo-storage is more economical than the traditional bag storage in godowns considering the usual 5 per cent losses that occurs in ill-ventilated godowns. Though capital investment is much higher on silo-storage, the paddy can be kept clean and safe after mechanical cleaning and drying which facilities are not easily available in the conventional godown-storage.

Storage in silos

The modern methods of grain storage in scientifically built godowns and silos are definitely advantageous. The bulk holding of grain is simpler and requires much less floor area in silos. If bulk transportation of grain, either in lorries or railway wagons is resorted to, the transport cost may become considerably cheaper. The paddy storage in silos posed some problems, one of which was the maintenance of quality during storage. Though 14 per cent is the acceptable grain moisture level for safe storage, damage of grains has been noticed due to variation in the atmospheric relative humidity and temperature particularly during rainy seasons. For safe storage of paddy in silos a regular aeration system should be there to counter the effects of high atmospheric temperature and relative humidity.

TABLE 17.10(A) Cost of storage of paddy in the traditional godowns (H.N.R. Rice Mill, Mannargudy, S. Rly.)

Particulars	Construction or instalment cost	Total expenditure per month for	
All data based on storing 2,250 tonne- of paddy in four godowns, 10,000 bags (57 kg/bag) in each godown		2,250 T of paddy	per T of paddy
	Rs.	Rs.	Rs.
1. Construction of godowns, office building, etc. Depreciation on building @ 5%	2,04,000.00	850.00	
2. Three weighing balances Depn. on machinery @ 10%	3,000.00	25.00	
Total non-recurring expenditure	2,07,000.00	875.00	0.39
	Expenditure per month for 2,250 T of paddy, Rs.		
3. Cost of material—paddy @ Rs. 485.00/T Interest @ 7.50%		6,820.31	3.03
4. Supervisory staff	224.00		
Provident fund and bonus (8.4)%	26.90		
Repairs, stationery etc.	50.00		
Municipal tax and insurance premium for the paddy	305.50		
Total recurring expenditure		606.40	0.27
5. Cost of gunnies—40,000 bags @ Rs. 2.50/bag—Rs. 1.00 lakh interest @ 7.50%	625.00		
6. Labour charges to store 40,000 bags @ 6 paise/bag	2,400.00		
Total expenditure on process		3,025.00	1.34
Cost of storage of paddy in the godowns		11,326.71	5.03

(Source : Shrivanna, 1971)

TABLE 17.10(B) Cost of pre-cleaning and mechanical drying of freshly harvested paddy (Modern Rice Mill Project, Tiruvavur, S. Rly)

Particulars	Construction or instalment cost	Total expenditure per month for	
All data based on drying 60 tonnes of paddy from moisture 25 to 14 per cent in two dryers, 12 T of paddy per batch, 1,500 tonnes per month of 25 working days	Rs.	2,250 T of paddy Rs.	per T of paddy Rs.
(1)	(2)	(3)	(4)
1. Machinery —Two enscalpers, two dryers with one bucket elevator and screw conveyer, furnace oil tank	1,06,327.50		
Laboratory equipment—sheller, whitener, sampler and broken separator	35,761.00		
Depreciation on machinery @ 10 per cent	1,42,088.50		
Total non-recurring expenditure		1,184.10	0.79
	Expenditure per month for 1,500 T of paddy		
2. Supervisory staff: Quality control, engineering and storage departments	2,600.00		
Provident fund and bonus (8+4) per cent	312.00		
Mechanical store, spares and repairs to machinery	500.00		
Total recurring expenditure		3,412.00	2.28
Two enscalpers (25 & 25) T/hr, (10 &10) HP work 60 hrs/month			
Total working capacity of both is 25 T/hr	120.00		
3. Bucket elevator—To dry 12 T of paddy in 4 hrs—10 HP	500.00		
Two buffalo blowers—work 3 hrs per batch—24 HP	900.00		

(1)	(2)	(3)	(4)
Two spreaders (1 & 1) HP work 3.5 hrs/batch	87.50		
Furnace oil consumption—to get 85 to 90°C hot air, 3 hrs/batch @ 60 L/Hr for two burners @ 30 paise per litre	6,750.00		
Furnace oil pump works 34 hrs per month 10 HP	34.00		
Constructing brick furnace to burn furnace oil	150.00		
Laboratory Analysis—5 HP—10 samples are analysed in one hour—one sample for 6 tonnes of paddy	12.50		
Total expenditure on process		8,554.00	5.70
Cost of pre-cleaning and mechanical drying of paddy		13,150.10	8.77

(Source: Shivanna, 1971)

TABLE 17.10(C) Cost of conveying and storage of paddy in the silos (Modern Rice Mill Project, Tiruvavur, S. Rly)

All data based on storing 7,200 tonnes of paddy in 12 silos (6 silos of 1,000 tonnes capacity each and another 6 of 200 tonnes each)	Construction or instalment cost	Total expenditure per month for	
		2,250T of paddy	per T of paddy
	Rs.	Rs.	Rs.
(1)	(2)	(3)	(4)
1. Construction of silos and building near the weigh bridge	22,11,670.00		
Depreciation on building @ 5 per cent		9,215.30	
Interest @ 5 per cent for 18.65 lakhs (loan taken)		7,771.00	
2. Machinery : Weigh bridge, conveying equipment, accessories and contingencies	5,64,621.50		

(1)	(2)	(3)	(4)
Depreciation on machinery @ 10 per cent		4,705.20	
	27,76,291.50	21,691.50	3.02
Expenditure for 7200 T of paddy, Rs.			
3. Cost of paddy @ Rs. 485.00/tonne Interest @ 7.50 per cent		21,825.00	3.03
4. Insurance and municipal tax for the silos and insurance premium for paddy	2,028.00		
5. Supervisory staff; stock and storage, engineering and administrative overheads	3,143.00		
Provident fund and bonus (8+4) per cent	376.15		
6. Mechanical stores, spares, repairs, stationery etc.	580.00		
Total recurring expenditure		6,127.15	0.85
7. Bucket elevator and screw conveyer 50 T/hr each	504.00		
Working capacity (W.C.) 25 T/hr, 17.5 H.P, 3-belt conveyers 50 T/hr, 17.5 HP, 35 T/hr. W.C.	566.00		
2-belt conveyors 25 T/hr–10 Hp Remaining HP of the silo machinery –48HP–50 T/hr (loading and unloading)	1,382.40		
Aeration blowers 13.0 HP work 12 hrs/day	390.00		
Total expenditure on process		2,842.40	0.40
Total cost of conveying and storage of paddy in the silos		52,486.05	7.30
2–A Cost of pre-cleaning and mechanical drying (1,500 tonnes) of paddy		13,150.10	8.77
Cost of pre-cleaning, mechanical drying (1,500 tonnes), conveying and storage of paddy (7,200 tonnes) in the silos		65,636.15	16.07

(Source: Shivanna, 1971)

After mechanical drying of paddy, it must be cooled down to ambient temperature and properly tempered before sending into storage to avoid the subsequent development of hot spots and moisture migration, resulting in moisture pockets at the cooler spots of the silos. So also, elimination of foreign matter from paddy before storage is essentially required to avoid spontaneous heating owing to fungal and bacterial activities in the silos. The cost analysis of paddy storage in silos is furnished in Table 17.10(C) (Shivanna, 1971).

Cost of storage in traditional godowns and modern silos

The traditional bag storage has an advantage that there is no apparent heavy capital investment. The overall cost of storage in rural godowns and silos came to Rs. 5.03 and Rs. 7.30/tonne of paddy/month respectively (Tables 17.10(A) and 17.10(C)). If 5 per cent losses occurring in village godown-storage were considered (and assuming no loss was occurring in silo storage), the overall cost came to Rs. 17.15 per tonne of paddy.

By comparing these figures with the cost involved in pre-cleaning, mechanical drying, conveying and storage of paddy in silos which was Rs.16.07/tonne of paddy (with the difference of Rs. 1.08/tonne of paddy), the silo-storage thus appeared to be more economical (Tables 17.10(B) and 17.10(C)).

The major factors augmenting the cost of paddy storage in silos were financial such as interest on loan taken for silo construction and purchase of paddy. The cost of furnace oil consumption for drying was also an important factor. If husks were used as fuel in place of furnace oil, however, the drying cost would have been reduced considerably. Depreciation on building and machineries were comparable with bagged godown storage. But the cost of gunny bags, labour etc. came in.

The silo storage had many advantages in saving manual labour which was difficult to obtain during peak seasons of transplantation and harvesting coinciding with the procurement season. It also minimized the grain losses and the investment on the cost of gunnies, and gave a definite advantages in the form of a long hygienic storage. But proper care had to be taken in the initial stages of pre-cleaning, drying and cooling of paddy before sending into silos (Shivanna, 1971).

BIBLIOGRAPHY

1. Becker, H.A. and Sallans, H.R. 1956. A study of the desorption isotherms of wheat at 25°C and 50°C. Cereal Chem. 33, 79–90.

2 Bond, E.J. and Monro, H.A.U. 1961. The toxicity of various fumigants to the Cadelle Tenebroides mauritanicus. J. Econ. Entomol. 54, 451–454.

3. Bond, E.J. Chemical control of stored grain insects and mites in Grain Storage: Part of a System, 1973, Sinha, R.N. and Muir, W.E. (Eds), (Proc. Symposium of grain storage, Canada, June 6–9, 1971). The AVI Pub. Co. Inc., Connecticut.

4. Boumans, G. 1985. Grain Handling and Storage, Development in Agril. Engg. 4, Elsevier, Tokyo.

5. Brown, A.W.A. 1961. Insect Control by Chemicals, John Wiley, New York.

6. Brown, W.B. 1959. Fumigation with methyl bromide under gasproof sheets. Pest Infest. Res. Bull. 1, 2nd edition, London, D.S.I.R. 44.

7. Chikubu, S. Storage condition and storage method in Training Manual for training in storage and preservation of food grains, 1970, APO Proj., Japan.

8. Christensen, C.M. (Ed.), 1974. Storage of Cereal Grains and Their Products, AACC, St. Paul, 549, U.S.A.

9. Clarke, J.H. 1968. Fungi in stored products. Trop. Stored Prod, Inform. 15, 3–14.

10. Cotton, R.T. 1963. Pests of Stored Grain and Grain Products. Burgess Publishing Co., Minneapolis, 318.

11. Dale, A.C. and Robinson, R.N. 1954. Pressure in deep grain storage structures. Agr. Eng. 35, 570–573.

12. Dubey, O.M. 1984. Optimum design of RCC silos for bulk storage of paddy, M. Tech. Thesis, IIT, Kharagpur, India.

13. Dykstra, W.W. 1968. The economic importance of rodents. Proc. rodents as factors in disease and economic loss. Inst. Tech. Interchange. Honolulu, Hawaii, 47–52.

14. Food Industries, 1979. Infestation Control (Chapter), Chem Engg. Ed. Dev. Centre, IIT, Madras, India.

15. Graves, R.R. et al. 1967. Bacterial and actinomycete flora of Kansas, Nebraska and Pacific Northwest wheat and wheat flour. Cereal Chem. 44, 288–299.

16. Hall, C.W. 1957. Drying Farm Crops. Agricultural Consulting Assoc., Reynoldsburg, Ohio. 336 p.

17. Heseltine, H.K. and Thompson, R.H. 1957. The use of aluminium phosphide tablets for the fumigation of grain milling. 129, 778–783.

18. ISI Hand Book. 1975. Indian Standards Institution, New Delhi, India.

19. IS: 601, 1955. Underground rural food grain storage structure, ISI, New Delhi, India.

20. IS: 602, 1955. Code of practice for constructions of 'Morai' type rural food grain storage structure, ISI, New Delhi, India.

21. IS: 604, 1969. Code of practice for construction of food grain storage structure suitable for trade and Government purpose for the southern region. ISI, New Delhi, India.

22. IS: 607, 1965 (Revised). Bagged grain storage structure, ISI, New Delhi, India.

23. IS: 631, 1961. Specification for Aluminium-food grain storage bins. ISI, New Delhi, India.

24. IS: 6940, 1973. Methods of test for pesticide and their formulations. ISI, New Delhi, India.

25. Karon, M.L. and Hillery, B.E. 1949. Hygroscopic equilibrium of peanuts. J. Am. Oil Chemists Soc. 26, 16–19.

26. Maheswari, R.C. A note on Traditional grain storage structure (unpolished), RPEC, IIT, Kharagpur.

27. Mallik, S.K. and Gupta, A.P. 1983. Plain Reinforced Concrete. Oxford & IBH Pub. Co. Pvt. Ltd., Calcutta.

28. Majumdar, S.K. et al. 1973. Control of microflora on moist grain. Anales de Technologic Agricale, 22(3), 483.

29. Milner, M. and Geddes, W.F. 1954. Respiration and heating. Chap. IV, pp. 152–220, in Storage of Cereal Grains and Their Products.

30. Mitsui, E. Stored product pests and their control in Training Manual for training in storage and preservation of food grains. 1970: APO Proj., Japan.

31. Monro, H.A.U. 1969. Manual of fumigation for insect control. FAO, United Nations, Rome, Manual 79, 381.

32. Parkin, E.A. 1963. The protection of stored seeds from insects and rodents. Proc. Intern. Seed. Test Assoc, 28, pp. 893–909.

33. Rao, Y.P. 1974. A note on Storage and preservation (unpublished), R.P.E.C., IIT, Kharagpur, India.

34. Report on 'Storage Structures'. 1961. Min. of Food & Agriculture, New Delhi, India.

35. Ripp, B.E. 1984, (Editor), Controlled Atmosphere and Fumigation in Grain Storages, Elsevier, New York.

36. Sinha, R.N. 1973. Interrelations of physical, chemical and biological variables in the deterioration of stored grains in Grain

Storage: Part of a System 1973 (Proc. Symposium on grain storage, Canada, June 6–9, 1971). Sinha, R.N. and Muir, W.B. (Eds). The AVI Pub. Co. Inc., Connecticut.

37. Shivanna, C.S. 1971. Traditional and modern methods of storage of paddy. The Food Ind. J. 4(1).

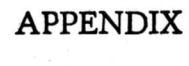

APPENDIX

TABLE 1. Grain equilibrium moisture content, per cent, wet basis. Relative humidity, per cent

Grain	Temperature °C	10	20	30	40	50	60	70	80	90	100
Paddy	23	4.9	7.3	8.7	9.8	10.9	12.4	13.5	15.9	19.0	— [1]
"	30	—	7.1	8.5	10.0	10.9	11.9	13.1	14.7	17.1	— [2]
"	44	—	—	—	—	—	10.3	12.3	14.3	16.5	— [3]
Wheat white	25	5.2	7.5	8.6	9.4	10.5	11.8	13.7	16.0	19.7	26.3 [4]
Wheat	32	—	5.3	7.0	8.6	10.3	11.5	12.9	14.3	—	— [5]
"	49	—	—	6.2	7.4	9.6	10.4	11.9	13.6	—	
Shelled corn (WD)	25	5.1	7.2	8.5	9.8	11.2	12.3	13.9	15.5	18.9	24.6 [4]
Shelled corn (YD)	32	—	—	5.3	6.6	8.3	10.2	12.1	13.9	—	— [5]
"	49	—	—	—	5.3	6.5	7.8	9.3	10.7	—	— [5]
"	70	3.9	6.2	7.6	9.1	10.4	11.9	13.9	15.2	17.9	— [5]
Sorghum	25	4.4	7.3	8.6	9.8	11.0	12.0	13.8	15.8	18.8	21.9 [4]
"	32	—	7.0	8.7	10.2	11.8	12.2	13.1	14.8	—	— [5]
"	70	—	6.6	8.0	9.4	10.7	11.6	12.7	14.3	—	— [5]
Oats	25	4.1	6.6	8.1	9.1	10.3	11.8	13.0	14.9	18.5	24.1 [4]
Barley	25	4.4	7.0	8.5	9.7	10.8	12.1	13.5	15.8	19.5	26.8 [4]
Rye	25	5.2	7.6	8.7	9.9	10.9	12.2	13.5	15.7	20.6	— [4]

Sources: (4) Coleman et al. (1955), (3) Hogan and Karu (1955), (2) Bakharev (1960), (5) Haynes (1961) (1) Henderson (1970).

TABLE 2. Constants in Henderson's Equation

Material	c $1/o_k$	n
Paddy	1.22×10^{-5}	1.35
Shelled corn	1.98×10^{-5}	1.90
Wheat	10.6×10^{-7}	3.03
Sorghum[1]	6.1×10^{-6}	2.31

TABLE 3. Bulk densities of grain at different moisture contents

Grain	Moisture content % (w.b.)	Density Kg/m^3	Ref.
Paddy	14.0	587.9	(2)
	18.0	615.2	
Wheat	11.0	789.8	(1)
	14.i	756.1	
Corn (shelled)	13.0	736.9	(1)
	16.2	720.9	
Barley	16.8	592.7	(1)
	10.8	576.7	
Sorghum	12.0	752.9	
	14.3	752.9	(1)

Sources : (1) Lorenzen (1958), (2) Wratten et al. (1968).

TABLE 4. Specific gravity of cereal grains

Grain	Moisture content % (w.b.)	Specific gravity of kernel
Rice	8.6	1.36
Wheat	8.5	1.41
Corn	6.7	1.29
Barley	7.5	1.42
Millets	9.4	1.11
Oats	10.33	0.99

TABLE 5. Heat of vaporization of grain moisture

Grain	Moisture content % (w.b.)	Temperature °C	Heat of vaporization kcal/kg
Wheat	13	38	629.4
	13	65	611.6
	17	38	589.9
	17	65	573.8
Corn	13	38	698.8
	13	65	679.4
	17	38	644.4
	17	65	626.1
Sorghum	13	38	624.4
	13	65	606.2
	17	38	593.3
	17	65	576.6
Water	—	38	576.1
	—	65	560.0

Source : Haynes, B. C. (1961).

TABLE 6. Thermal properties of cereal grains

Grain	Moisture content % (w.b.)	Temperature range °C	Specific heat kcal/kg °C	Thermal conductivity kcal/m hr °C	Thermal diffusivity m²/hr	Reference
Paddy	12	—	0.3934	—	—	(1)
	15	—	0.4255	—	—	
	17	—	0.4469	—	—	
Wheat	9.2	—	0.370	0.1198	—	(2)
	11.7	26.50 to 31.0	—	0.128	0.000414	(3)
Wheat, hard white	12	—	0.367	—	—	(2)
Wheat, soft white	15	—	0.391	—	—	(4)
	14.4	9.0 to 23.0	0.5	0.116	0.000295	
Corn, yellow dent	9.8	8.3—23.2	0.438	0.1308	0.000338	(4)
Oats	13.2	26.6—31.1	—	0.102	—	(3)
	12	—	0.380	—	—	(1)
	15	—	0.415	—	—	
	17	—	0.439	—	—	

Sources : (1) Hasewell, G. A. A Note on the specific heat of rice, oats and their properties, Cereal Chem., 1954.
(2) Babbit, E. A. The thermal properties of grain bulk, Can. J. Res. F-23, 1945.
(3) Oxley, T. A. The properties of grain in bulk, Soc. Chem. Indus. J. Trans. 63, 1944.
(4) Kazarian, E. A. and Hall, C. W. Thermal properties of grains, Trans. ASAE 8, (1), 1965.

TABLE 7. Average composition of cereals and legumes

	Raw brown rice	Whole wheat	Whole Maize	Sorghum	Millets	Legume Lentils	Broad beans (kernels)
Moisture (per cent)	12.0	12.5	13.8	11.0	11.8	12.2	10.6
Calories/ 100 gm	360	330	348	332	327	351	354
Protein, (per cent)	7.5	12.3	8.9	11.0	9.9	23.7	25.0
Fat, (per cent)	1.9	1.8	3.9	3.3	2.9	1.3	1.8
N-free extract, (per cent)	77.4	71.7	72.2	73.0	72.9	57.4	53.7
Fibre, (per cent)	0.9	2.3	2.0	1.7	3.2	3.2	5.9
Ash, (per ctnt)	1.2	1.7	1.2	1.7	2.5	2.2	3.0
Thiamine, mg/100 gm	0.34	0.52	0.37	0.38	0.73	—	—
Riboflavin, mg/100 gm	0.05	0.12	0.12	0.15	0.38	—	—
Niacin, mg/100 gm	4.7	4.3	2.2	3.9	2.3	—	—

TABLE 8. Recommendations of grain drying conditions

	Raw Paddy	Wheat	Ear Corn	Shelled Corn	Barley	Sorghum	Oats
1. Maximum harvest moisture content of grain for drying							
(a) With natural air, %	25	20	30	25	20	20	20
(b) With heated air, %	25	25	35	35	25	25	25
2. Maximum moisture content of grain for safe storage in a leak proof structure, for 1 year, per cent	12	13 (12)s	13	13	13	12	13 (12)s
3. Maximum safe temperature of drying air for heated air drying for dried grain to be used for							
(a) Seed, °C	43	43	43	43	40	43	43
(b) Food, °C	43	60	54	54	40	60	60
(c) Feed, °C	—	82	82	82	82	82	82
4. Depth of grain bed preferable for static drying with heated air, cm	23-45	40-50	152-610	40-60	40-60	40-60	40-60
5. Maximum depth of grain at various moisture levels for drying in bin with blower capacities as listed in (6) below							
Moisture content, %	25 20 18 16	30 25 20 18 16	30 25 20	30 25 20	25 20 18 16	25 20 18	25 20 18 16
Depth of grain, m	1.2 1.8 2.4	4.6 6.1 1.2 1.8 2.4	4.6 6.1	1.2 1.5 1.8	1.2 1.8 2.4	1.2 1.8 2.4	1.2 1.8 2.4
6. Minimum air flow required at different moisture contents and depths as listed in (5), $m^3/min/m^3$							
Natural air	3.2 2.4 1.6 2.4 1.6 0.8	4.0 1.6 0.8 2.4	4.0 4.0 2.4	4.0 2.4 2.4	3.2 2.4 1.6 0.8	3.2 2.4 3.2 1.6 1.2	3.2 2.4 3.2 1.6 1.2
With supplemental heat (max. 9° C rise)	3.2 2.4 3.2 2.4 1.6 0.8	4.0 1.6 0.8 2.4	4.0 4.0 2.4	4.8 4.0 2.4 2.4	4.0 3.2 2.4 1.6 0.8	4.0 3.2 2.4 3.2 1.6 1.2	4.0 3.2 2.4 3.2 1.6 1.2

S : For seed.

Source : Crop Dryer Manufacturers Assn. Rev. Feb. 9, 1956.

TABLE 9 Cost of processing per tonne of paddy (all data based on cleaned paddy)

Item	Particulars	(1) Huller rice mill				(2) Emery cone sheller-polisher rice mill				(3) Modern rice mill			
		Fixed (Rs.)	Recurring (Rs.)	Processing (Rs.)	Total (Rs.)	Fixed (Rs.)	Recurring (Rs.)	Processing (Rs.)	Total (Rs.)	Fixed (Rs.)	Recurring (Rs.)	Processing (Rs.)	Total (Rs.)
	Expenditure												
1.	Precleaning and drying storage	0.39	8.24	1.07	9.70	0.39	8.24	1.07	9.70	0.79	2.28	5.70	8.77
2.	Parboiling and drying	1.58	1.87	5.25	8.70	1.58	1.87	5.25	8.70	1.94	5.16	0.40	7.50
3.	Milling	0.39	2.80	4.37	7.56	2.08	2.54	1.12	5.74	4.26	8.89	11.76	24.91
										4.58	12.45	4.68	21.71
	Total cost of processing	2.36	12.91	10.69	25.96	4.05	12.65	7.44	24.14	11.57	28.78	22.54	62.89
	Cost of paddy				485.00				485.00				485.00
	Net Expenditure				510.96				509.14				547.89
4.	(a) Value of raw byproducts				10.80				27.00				39.50
	(b) Value after processing of byproducts												
	(c) Realisation by sale of				10.63				36.36				55.22

(Contd.)

polished rice	516.80	524.40	532.00
Net Realisation			
5. (a) By sale of rice and by-products	527.60	541.40	571.50
(b) By sale of rice and by-products after processing	533.43	560.76	587.22
Net profit			
(a) By sale of rice and by-products	16.64	42.26	23.61
(b) By sale of rice and by-products after processing	22.47	51.62	39.33

Yield of polished rice from 1, 2 and 3 types of mills are 68, 69 and 70 per cent respectively valued at Rs. 760 per tonne (average Government price). If the polished rice is sold in the open market @ Rs. 1,050 per tonne an extra net profit of Rs. 197.20, 200.10 and 209.00 is recoverable from huller, disc sheller-polisher and modern rice mill respectively.

Source : Shivanna, C.S. 1971, J. of Food Sc. and Tech., Vol. 9, No. 1, p. 8.

INDEX